Where's the best place on earth—for *you*?

If you're not sure, start taking Barbara's quiz and discover what you really want:

When buying a house, which is most important to you?

a) Good vibes
b) The community
c) Local services
d) Privacy

You're moving to the boondocks and there is no high-speed Internet access. What do you do?

a) Rent an expensive satellite dish
b) Use a local internet café when the need arises
c) Get by with dial-up
d) Do without altogether

How would you prefer to travel?

a) Low-emission public transportation
b) Bicycle
c) SUV
d) On foot

more . . .

You're in the mood for music. What do you do?

a) Go to a rock concert
b) Go to a bagpipe festival
c) Listen to some of your old favorite records
d) Go to a folk music benefit

Having fun? Then go to page 25, take the full quiz, and learn about the real estate and lifestyle choices compatible with your values and goals. With NEXTVILLE as your guide, you'll soon be making your dreams come true!

Praise for NEXTVILLE

"Thorough and thoughtful . . . This well-researched guide goes beyond a 'real estate' focus to a more comprehensive exploration . . . It offers practical information and insights based on national surveys and numerous interviews, citing real people and real places as examples . . . It could prove useful for younger readers looking for a place to settle down."
—*Los Angeles Times*

"Corcoran shares her interesting predictions of 'the next big things' in real estate."
—*Library Journal*

"A witty, readable guide to *amazing places*. A must-read for people seriously shopping for real estate as well as for armchair dreamers."
—DANA BUCHMAN, designer

"Barbara Corcoran dishes out inspiring advice on where and how to fabulously live."
—BONNIE FULLER,
author of *The Joys of Much Too Much*

"Whether you're just toying with the idea of moving, considering a second home, or seriously ready to relocate, don't make a final decision without first reading this book."
—BARBARA STANNY,
author of *Secrets of Six-Figure Women*

"An incredible how-to guide . . . to find that next dream home in that perfect-for-you community, and it shows you don't have to be wealthy to do so!"
—DAVID CAPLAN, entertainment journalist

"Barbara's book is essential! You won't want to put it down and when you do, you will run to the Realtor's office."
—GUY "DOC" HOLLIDAY,
CEO, USA Elite Technology

NEXTVILLE

Amazing Places to Live
Your Life

BARBARA CORCORAN

with WARREN BERGER

SPRINGBOARD PRESS

NEW YORK   BOSTON

Springboard Press
Hachette Book Group
237 Park Avenue, New York, NY 10017

Visit our Web site at www.HachetteBookGroup.com

Springboard Press is an imprint of Grand Central Publishing.
The Springboard Press name and logo are trademarks of Hachette Book Group, Inc.

Originally published in hardcover by Springboard Press.

First Trade Edition: June 2009

The Library of Congress has cataloged the hardcover edition as follows:
Corcoran, Barbara.
    Nextville : amazing places to live the rest of your life / Barbara Corcoran with Warren Berger.
        p. cm.
    Summary: "The leading real estate guru in the U.S. gives Boomers the inside scoop on the best places to retire—and offers the retirement rules they can't afford to miss."—Provided by the publisher.
    ISBN: 978-0-446-17827-3
    1. Retirement—United States. 2. Retirement—United States—Planning. 3. Retirees—United States—Life skills guides. 4. Quality of life. I. Berger, Warren. II. Title.

HQ1063.2.U6C67 2008
646.7'9—dc22
                                        2007039663

10 9 8 7 6 5 4 3 2 1

ISBN 978-0-446-17828-0 (pbk.)

Book design and text composition by L&G McRee

PRINTED IN THE UNITED STATES OF AMERICA

This book is dedicated to the three best men in my life:

My dad, who taught me the joy of living in the moment.

My husband, Bill, who brought me the joy of unconditional love.

My son, Tom, who gave me the joy of being his mother.

Contents

Introduction

It's not easy buying a smart piece of real estate in a down market. It takes a sharp eye, the cunning of a fox, and guts. After all, why buy the place now if you think you might get it cheaper later? Add to this the additional challenge of trying to get top dollar for the house you've lived in and cared for for the last twenty years. Not easy. Well, here's my short guide on how to sell your house for the most money and snatch a steal of a deal on a new dream home you'll be enjoying for the next many years.

You will need:

1. A Sharp Eye

- **The real trick to buying today is identifying a neighborhood where prices have already hit bottom** and may even be on their way up. These are the towns filled with happy people who are enjoying the benefits of a proactive government and a strong local job market. While you're looking at houses, it's smart to keep an eye out for inexpensive new cars. New cars always mean there are new jobs to be had and lots of young families are moving in. Both are good for real estate values.

- **Before you settle on a particular town, take a ride around the neighborhood and count the FOR SALE signs.** If you see more than one sign for every three blocks, real estate prices will still fall more before they hit bottom. Get back in your car and move on to the next town.

- **If you're thinking of moving into an active adult community, don't be afraid to ask the management for detailed financial information.** You'll want to see how often they've raised fees on homeowners, what the average age of residents is, and exactly what percentage of the units have been sold.

- **No matter how much you want to spend on your new house, you should know what the typical home sells for in the town before you begin to shop.** The best home to buy is one priced firmly in the middle of what most homes in the town sell for. If you buy a $600,000 home in a town where most homes sell between $450,000 and $500,000, it will prove a bad investment. You'll have the prettiest house with the most big bedrooms and swanky baths, but you'll have to find another oddball buyer like yourself when it comes time to sell. Unlikely.

- **Some of the best places today** with low unemployment, affordable homes, and prices already on their way up are Binghamton, New York; Amarillo, Texas; Charleston, West Virginia; Corpus Christi, Texas; and Des Moines, Iowa.

- **Don't buy in an area filled with old people.** No matter how prestigious it is to brag about the mansion you own in Sarasota, house prices in fancy places filled with wealthier, older folks never keep pace with the more youthful communities that surround them. You should scout out a younger, more hip town nearby. Besides, you'll have more fun, and you'll automatically start feeling younger.

- **Buy next door to like-minded souls,** whether you're looking for the boomerang life, looking to live green, pursue your passion, find your purpose, or form a new community, you'll live a more fulfilled life in a community of like-minded souls. The best way to find out who really lives there is to go to a morning drop-off or afternoon pickup at the local grammar school. It's here you'll see the fancily clad ladies or the soccer moms in sneakers. You'll see firsthand the whole kaleidoscope of people who will soon be your new neighbors.

- **Buy in a town with high SAT scores.** Nerds are always good for real estate because good schools are on the top of every family's list when shopping for a home. You can easily get a free school report online at homefair.com.

- **Even if you're not planning on taking a new job when you're seventy-five, you should buy in a town that's creating lots of local jobs** for younger people. Without young families moving in, house prices won't move up much and the inheritance you'll leave for the grandchildren you love will be a lot less when your house gets sold by your attorney.

2. Cunning of a Fox

- **You can find the best bargains in today's market only if you dig below the surface.** Everyone knows bank-owned properties are good deals and there are plenty to choose from in almost every community. But when you jump into those dark waters, you'll be swimming with the sharks and you'd better know how to compete. If you're a smart shopper, you'll go with a shrewd broker on your right flank to tell you what the house is *really* worth and an experienced contractor on your left to tell you which improvements are needed and what they'll really cost.

- **Today's best deals aren't only foreclosed properties.** Lots of individual homeowners are under stress and willing to short-sell long before the bank grows worried. All you need to do is locate the local broker who specializes in short sales to get the early scoop on who needs to sell fast and cheap. And if you really want to get in early, spend a Sunday afternoon riding around your own neighborhood. It's easy to spot the worst house on the best block because the lawn's unkempt, the house needs painting, and there's too much stuff in the backyard. Behind the chipped door is a homeowner who's having a hard time meeting the mortgage payment. You can leave a note telling the owner how much you love the house and that you're interested in buying it.

- **You'd be crazy to buy today without taking advantage of all the inside information available online.** You can find any town's job statistics and you won't get caught unawares by an unexpected property-tax hike. And if you go to rottenneighbors.com, you can even get the inside scoop on the loser next door long before you sign the wrong contract.

3. Guts

- If you're a risk taker and are comfortable putting your money down where you have a shot at getting the biggest return, **buy a home in an up-and-coming neighborhood.** Nighttime is the best time to snoop around and check it out, because most young people work during the day. Keep an eye out for the young, creative community, a sure sign that the neighborhood is about to emerge.

- **It takes real guts and a lot of chutzpah to buy in today's real estate climate** because every buyer is afraid of being played the fool. Just the thought of paying too much today for a place we might get cheaper tomorrow is enough to make us lose sleep in our new home. Most of us feel more comfortable overbidding the next guy in a frenzied seller's market because we know the high price we just paid is less than what the next guy will likely pay the next day. Although buying something when prices are still going through the roof feels smarter, the fact is it's really the worst time to buy. There are fewer homes to choose from, low bids are flatly refused, and the high price we're willing to pay is the result of overheated emotions. Most of us would not have paid that same high price if we'd had more time to think about it.

I believe today's troubled real estate market presents the single best buying opportunity of the last century. In past downturns, when prices were low, interest rates were high, sometimes to the tune of 14 to 18 percent! And when interest rates were low, as they are today, house prices were going straight through the roof. I believe today's buying opportunity is nothing short of a real estate miracle! And I believe these times will never come again, so for those of us searching for our own "Nextville," there's no better time to find it than now.

BARBARA CORCORAN
November 2008

The Power of Place

I believe it's out there. Somewhere in this world, there's a place where you're meant to be. This book is about helping you find that very special place—where you can do what you've longed to do and become the person you've always wanted to be. Where you can begin the glorious next act of your life.

The urge to seek out the place where you belong is nothing new. Restless souls have been on this journey forever. It has made us explore, settle in new countries, build whole new worlds, and then try to find our way back to the old country again. It has led people out West to California and down South to Florida. It happens on a smaller scale, too. Within the city of New York, people are constantly moving. They move from Brooklyn to Manhattan, go uptown, then downtown, east, west, and then back to Brooklyn again. I've spent most of my life in the wacky world of real estate, and it's been downright mind-boggling to watch so much movement and so many territorial shifts. At first glance you might think that they're dictated by how much money people have and how much houses cost. But there's more to it than that. People can always find a bigger place in the town where they already live. They move to that "next place" because they're searching for something more—a place where they can do a better job of living.

The quest to find the perfect place takes on even more importance as you reach a certain stage in life. For some of us that stage is age fifty; for others it's forty; and today for many of us it's even younger. But I've found that the exact number makes no difference, because it's defined by your mind-set more than by a figure. It's the age when we each start to think, *seriously* think, about something more than today or tomorrow or even next year. It's the age when we start to think about the rest of our lives.

Many more people are thinking about this right now than ever simply because so many baby boomers are rapidly approaching the time in life we used to call retirement. Just think: every eight seconds, one more lively boomer turns sixty.

But our generation is approaching the next stage in life differently. As it turns out, we're just not the retiring types—never have been and never will be. We don't even like to use the word. "Retirement" suggests that you're on your way out, that your usefulness is over. But unlike our parents before us, we believe we're just getting started at this age. It's almost as though all of life before this was just a means to get us ready to go on to the next great thing. So instead of retiring, it's more like graduating.

But graduating to *what*? And *where*? These are the two big questions for all of us, and as we answer them in the coming years, there'll be another mass movement of people. Different people, different ages, different circumstances—but all with one thing in common: we need to find our next great place.

Where Do We Go?

Thirty years ago I arrived in New York City, a twenty-something Jersey girl hoping to find myself in the big metropolis. New York looked to me like a city that loved change, and it transformed me the moment I set foot there. New York would prove to be where I would discover my potential—the place I was truly meant to be. This was my first lesson in the power of place: by finding the right place, I could start to build the person I really wanted to be. This same lesson was reinforced many times in the years that followed because in my new job as a real estate broker I would help thousands of other people find the place where *they* truly belonged.

A dozen years later my little start-up company would become one of the most successful brokerages in the country, bringing me a ton of money and a lot of fun. But for me, the real measure of my success—the one thing I would always take the most pride in—was my innate ability to match up the right person with the right place based on his or her unique needs and personality. This, I learned, is the guts of the real estate business. I had to really listen as people told me where they'd been and where they hoped to go, and over time I came to see the clear connection between our dreams and the places we choose to live. I began to understand that places and dreams are always joined at the hip.

And so I truly believe in the transforming power of place. I believe that when you go to a new place—when it's the *right* place—you have permission to start over, to do things you couldn't or wouldn't do before. In short, you have an opportunity to meet the better you. It's never a cure-all, of course, because we often bring our emotional baggage with us when we move. But the new place at least lets you make a clean break with your old patterns of day-in, day-out living. It gives you a chance to shake your life up and reopen your eyes to see the world afresh.

I'm totally defined by where I am. When I'm in a place with energy and lots of color, surrounded by people I love, I feel I can accomplish anything! I also feel comfortable enough to do nothing at all. Place is always at the center of my life. Every one of my happy memories is tied to a specific place, and if I try to separate the experience from the place where I lived it, the memory simply dissolves when the context is gone. The same is true when I dream about tomorrow—my vision needs a frame in the form of a place, and without it, I can't picture my dream. So I believe that if you want to make a dream come true, you first need to find the right place.

Finding Yourself First

Landing the perfect place isn't easy. It's a process that calls for some honest thought and heartfelt emotion. Over the years in my real estate business, I saw that whenever people approached a real estate decision from a purely logical viewpoint, the decision was never a good one. The happiest people were always those who had an immediate, visceral reaction to a place and trusted it. They'd arrive, look around, smell the air, and say, "This is for me." And the funny thing is, when I'd asked them earlier to describe their ideal place, they'd described something totally different from the place they ended up falling in love with. That's why smart real estate brokers often say, "Buyers are liars." It's not that buyers intend to mislead, but they're often dead wrong when they try to predict where they'll live or what they'll choose. I feel that if you want to find the place that really gets your juices going, you need to discover what inspires you. You need to get in touch with what makes you comfortable and uncomfortable. In short, you need to know yourself before you can find the right place.

This book aims to help you get in touch with your true feelings about where you really want to live. To do this, I developed a few tools, including my own "Where to Live Happily Ever After" quiz. I tried to keep the assessment simple because I, for one, was never able to pass a long test in school. I think my little quiz will help you begin to discover where you really belong.

We searched high and low and found lots of real-life people happily living their dreams in their dream spots. I listened carefully to how each of them got there and soon discovered that all these happy people could be divided into eight different groups, each group motivated by something different. That's how I landed on the organization of the book—chapters built around eight different types of people. Each chapter addresses a particular passion or way of living, and within that chapter I've chosen the surprisingly best places to pursue that dream. The places span all regions of the country and also include some overseas options. It's a different way of looking at the world—instead of picking places by region or weather, I picked the places that match up with what's in a person's soul. It's not that I don't like palm trees as much as the next guy, but I think if you're looking for someplace to live the rest of your life, there are more important things to consider. Like, *What am I going to do with my time when I get there?*

Thinking Outside the Hammock

Past generations didn't really examine this question too much when they thought about retirement. When my dad suggested to my mom, "Let's move down to Palm Bay where Marion and Gregg are," my mother began packing and that was that. My father was focused on escaping after years of hard work to a haven in Florida where they could both relax and play a little golf, and that was as far as their thinking went. But our generation is living longer and we also want to live larger. When it comes to retirement, we're thinking way outside the hammock.

Florida's a Great Place to Hang...
If You're Your Parents!

Florida can be a wonderful place—my parents live there and love it, in fact. But it's *their* dream place, for their generation. Our generation has new dreams and needs new places to bring those dreams to life.

To me, Florida is as much a symbol as a real, live place. It symbolizes the conventional—a predictable approach to retirement. For so long, it was *the* place to retire, and its popularity has taken its toll on the state through the years. These days, Florida has too much traffic and not enough water (the drinkable kind, that is). Many areas grew too quickly, with buyers overpaying for real estate. Now take a drive through onetime Florida hot spots and you'll see a FOR SALE sign on too many blocks. People are leaving for a number of reasons, one of them being their concern about the next big storm and the exorbitant cost of home-owners' insurance that protects against hurricane damage. Some older retirees leave because Florida doesn't provide for some basic needs, like easy transportation; the state has actually been losing a growing number of people over seventy-five of late, some of whom are returning to northern states that provide better senior services. Meanwhile, younger boomer retirees tend to steer clear of Florida simply because it's seen as "too old" or—as my parents affectionately call it—"Heaven's waiting room."

The biggest problem of all is that retiring to Florida seems too predictable. "Boomers tend to want to make a distinctive personal statement in terms of where they choose to live," says William Strauss, whose book *Generations* studies the differences between age groups. "For the most part, they have no interest in following the same path as their parents."

As we researched this book in partnership with boomer Web sites such as What's Next (whatsnext.com) and real estate sites such as Trulia (trulia.com), surveying countless boomers along the way, we discovered interesting patterns in what people want today as they move toward the next stage of their lives.

And we hit on a major rule for many of them: *Retirement today is about doing, not resting.* Consider the fact that two-thirds of boomers say they intend to keep working, at least part-time, throughout their so-called retirement. With these people in mind, I devoted chapter 3 to great places to live and start a new business or career. For boomers who don't plan on working, there still needs to be something to focus on, something to soak up all that energy. So in this same chapter I also picked some amazing places to pursue a variety of passions.

We also found that many of our new generation of retirees want to stay connected as they enter the next phase of life. Numerous people we surveyed stated that when it comes to choosing the right place, the most critical factor is the people who would be surrounding them. They're looking for a lifelong support group they can count on. Personally, I've always been afraid of ending up in a place with people who don't know or care about one another—it would be my idea of a miserable life. Lots of people seem to share my fear, and this explains the growing trend of people creating their own small retirement communities with a circle of friends or even something larger. In chapter 4, I explore this new trend and show you all kinds of fascinating modern retirement communities now forming around the country. They run the gamut from four ordinary boomer women sharing a house to new twenty-first-century communes where you don't have to be a hippie to join. I've even thrown in America's best nudist colony just for the fun of it.

The desire to be connected is leading lots of boomers back to the city, creating the new species called the "ruppie." I know it sounds silly, but it's short for "retired urban person." And the movement does make sense. Many of us spent our youngest and most exciting years (so far, that is) in a city environment; it's the site of our happiest memories. Now we have the money to go back and enjoy the city in ways we never could before. I call this "living young," and chapter 5 profiles some of the hottest up-and-coming cities and exciting neighborhoods. I also take a look at the new booming popularity of college towns as retirement destinations. College towns have every amenity you could want, but their most precious resource is youth—and youth, it turns out, is highly contagious.

Another pattern in boomer retirees is the growing hunger to feel useful and live a life that has a larger purpose. Many people who were successful in business and have loads of money expressed a need to contribute to something bigger, something with social meaning. They're boomers coming into full bloom as caring, responsible, and engaged members of society. Two chapters are dedicated to these powerful souls—one with places to "live green," in an eco-conscious way (chapter 6), and the other focusing on the perfect places to help other human beings or endangered animals (chapter 8).

Yet others dream of disconnecting. This, too, is characteristic of our generation, which has learned to live with too much media noise and far too much daily pressure. With our busy, plugged-in lives, we've not had enough time to get away from it all. And so for every person who longs to connect, there are two who dream of disconnecting.

Some of the places I've picked for this book are pretty farflung—spots in Africa, in Alaska, in New Zealand. They might have been out of reach for past generations, but today more than a few of us are willing, able, and unafraid to travel far afield in pursuit of our dreams, no matter how far out. The whole idea of pursuing some kind of exotic retirement was once an indulgence of the rich, but that has slowly changed. Today lots of us can afford to retire in a distinctive way and in a far-off locale—and often it actually costs a lot less than where we are living now. For these romantics among us, I've dedicated chapter 7 to the notion of escape, with a touch of adventure. This is for the brave souls willing to trade comfort for the challenge of getting lost in something completely different and totally exotic.

Zoomers, Ruppies, Huddlers, and Boomerangs: They're Not Rock Groups, They're New Types of Retirees

In the not-too-distant past, most retirees tended to go with the flow and their migration to the sun belt followed a predictable pattern. But all of that is changing, according to demographers and retirement experts studying the movements of the boomers. Our new generation of retirees is moving in several directions, not just one. In particular, there are four types of new retirees really shaking things up.

The "Zoomers." They are so dubbed because they zoom to far-off places that would've been way off the radar of yesterday's retirees. According to Bob Adams of the Web site Retirement Wave (retirementwave.com), a growing number of retirees are now opting for countries such as Panama and Nicaragua, where two hundred thousand dollars can buy a beautiful home with an ocean view. Having traveled throughout their lives, many boomers are more comfortable living abroad than their parents would've been. And with airport transportation so accessible and the Internet helping to make the world a smaller place, "people now feel as if any place on the globe is within reach," says boomer expert Mark Gleason of the What's Next Web site. Hence, it's no longer so far-fetched to dream of retiring to Panama City—not only can you get there fairly easily, but your family and friends can and will come visit. Add in affordable amenities (such as movie tickets that cost two dollars!) and the fact that many countries are bending over backward to attract American retirees by offering perks and discounts on everything from medical costs to taxes, and you begin to see the allure of the zoomer retirement option. But perhaps above all else, retiring abroad is a bold lifestyle statement—a way to ensure that your "second act" in life is completely different from the first.

The "Ruppies." "I've been in cities all across the country and in all of them, there's a growing movement back downtown that's being fueled, in part, by empty-nesters and retirees," says John McIlwain, a housing expert with the Urban Land Institute. These back-to-the-city retirees have been dubbed "ruppies" (retired urban people) by the urban planner Kyle Ezell. So what's driving people downtown? Not their cars, that's for sure. One of the big attractions is that in a city you can walk anywhere and do anything. And the fast-paced lifestyle is a way to stay young even as you age (see chapter 5 for more details).

The "Huddlers." According to gerontologist Maria Dwight, many of today's retirees are hungry for human contact and a sense of community. "It's something that many of them have missed out on, living in the suburbs," she says. As they seek out some way to gather and bond with like-minded souls, boomers are either joining prebuilt communities (such as the "active adult communities" that are springing up from coast to coast) or creating their own communities from the ground up.

The "Boomerangs." When it comes to retirement, many are of two minds—they want to go chase the dream, but they also want to stay close to family and roots. One solution is the "boomerang" lifestyle, wherein people opt for just a part-time slice of retirement paradise—second homes, time-shares, house swaps, fractional ownership of villas or ship cabins—allowing them to go away and then come back. If that brings added complexity to life because there's more than one place to look after or multiple mortgages to pay off, that's nothing for the boomers. "They're used to juggling complicated lives," says Gleason. "Why should their retirement be any different?"

Not all of us need to venture far and wide to find the place of our retirement dreams. Many of us, in fact, feel that the best place we can ever be is the place where we already are. This is part of a new trend that is running parallel to that of people venturing farther away for retirement; it's called "aging in place." And there are lots of compelling reasons why people decide to stay put in retirement. Wanting to be near family is usually first, but there are other factors having to do with friends, work, or just the fact that we're already living in a place we absolutely love and can't imagine leaving. And so chapters 9 and 10 of this book offer ideas on how we can stay close to our roots yet still get a juicy slice of another world on a part-time basis. This is the "boomerang" lifestyle, where we venture out to find our far-off dreams but always come home to our base. And if we're determined never to leave our house, there are ways to turn the house itself into the ideal place for our retirement—by retrofitting and adapting it to suit our evolving needs throughout the next stage of life.

So, everyone belongs somewhere. Each of the chapters in my book speaks to the soul of a different individual. You'll find yourself within these chapters, and I expect you'll find yourself in a few of them. I'm convinced the right place must fulfill our deepest desires—a sense of purpose, a need to feel connected, and so on—while also satisfying our practical needs, such as good medical services, safety, and walkability. In other words, each place must be highly livable. After all, this is not another vacation—it's your life. I kept this firmly in mind as I gathered and picked my favorite places around the country and the world. In all, one hundred places made it into the book, in brief mentions, mini profiles, or longer profiles. Each has something unique to offer.

How We Discovered Such Surprising Places

Smart real estate brokers and agents from around the world proved to be our best resources. Some are old friends, but many emerged from the in-depth surveying we did both online and in person. I asked them to part with their own best-kept secrets, and real gems emerged. The most valuable suggestions always came from Realtors—like me—because real estate people just can't visit a place without thinking about buying there. And when we discover a true gem, we're too generous and not smart enough to keep it for ourselves. It's just not our nature. Our Realtors were the perfect scouts for this kind of project because it's at the heart of what they do. We relied on a global network of them, in cities and small towns across the United States as well as in foreign remote or exotic spots such as Nova Scotia or Dubai. They shared tips about little undiscovered oases. They guided us to enclaves that few people know about. They were able to point us to destinations you don't see in every travel guide. They proved slightly ahead of the curve in terms of figuring out the next great places to live, the ones that are still emerging.

Their expert input was critical for me because I didn't want to round up the usual suspects when it came to choosing the best retirement spots. I wanted places that would surprise you—even if I picked a well-known city, you might never have thought of it as a great place to retire. But if many of the places seem slightly off the beaten path, that's not just because I wanted to be different. The truth is, I feel places that are *on* the beaten path have already lost their magic because they've been overrun.

People's dreams and passions come in so many different colors, and I wanted this book to be a big Crayola box with enough crayons for everyone. You might find some of the places undeniably offbeat and quirky: Retiring to a funky trailer park in Austin? Living on a narrow boat in the English canals? Well, people are doing it and having the time of their lives. And there's no reason you shouldn't know about the full range of possibilities and at least consider them. Some places in the book are more demanding and are intended for the brave of heart. I know, for instance, that not everyone is prepared to bear the hardships of living in no-frills Malawi. But for a few of us, that is precisely the place where we belong.

Because there are so many near and far options available today, I've really tried to narrow them down to the very best. I hope the places in this book give you some answers. But more important, I hope the book succeeds in sending you on a quest to find the perfect place, intended just for you. In the pages that follow, I've created some tools to help you start that journey. So turn the page to chapter 2—and maybe it will be the beginning of the best chapter of your life.

Chapter 2

What If I Don't Know Where I Belong?

oo many options always confuse me. I like to think there's only one real answer to every question. But there's more, and that's what's so damn troubling about retiring. Think about it: Retirement is a blank slate. You can do anything. Go anywhere. It's a world of endless possibilities. Sure, it's exciting—but it can also be paralyzing. When I sold my business for a truckload of cash, I was confident I'd have no trouble filling in the blanks of how I'd use my time. After all, I thought, I'd made a small fortune and would have no limits on how I'd spend it. My life had been a rags-to-riches example of how to create something out of nothing. I thought I was perfectly suited to take a short ride into the sunset and then create a whole new and exciting world for myself. Instead, I almost went crazy.

The fact is, it's a huge personal challenge to navigate the uncharted waters of a big second act, especially without a map to guide you. I soon learned that the trusted old blueprints that had worked for me in life so far were pretty much obsolete the moment I decided to move on, shift gears, and start fresh. Maybe if I had made a bigger effort to think things through ahead of time and create a new road map, I would have transitioned with more grace, but I didn't. And according to the experts, most people don't.

"People just don't think about a lot of the important issues before they retire," says Dr. Cynthia Barnett, a life coach who specializes in counseling retirees. "They may work out the financial details, but usually it stops there. There's not much thought given to big questions like 'How will I stay busy, and productive, and engaged with life?'"

And when you don't think through those questions ahead of time, you can get blindsided, as I and another optimist named Jim Strawn did. When Jim retired from a hugely successful career as a radio executive in Atlanta, he plotted out the money aspects of retirement, but not the rest. "I was not ready, mentally, for what was coming," Jim says. "I thought it would be fun to sleep late each day and play a little golf. I figured I'd find things to do as I went along." But he ended up bored, frustrated, and scared. "To be honest," he says, "I lost my confidence for a while, because I started to wonder if there was any place for me, anywhere I could use my skills and be productive. I started to feel like everything was passing me by."

Fortunately, Jim regained his bearings as he rediscovered a lifelong passion for books and managed to turn it into a new business (more of Jim's story is in the next chapter, about pursuing your passions). Although it worked out in the end, Jim regrets that he wasted a few good years struggling with retirement—all because he "just had never taken the time to figure out, 'What's going to make me happy for the next twenty years?'"

Most of us assume that how much money we have is the big card that determines whether our next phase in life will measure up to our dreams. But there's a lot more to it than that. The real challenge is answering the more complicated question, *Now that I can do what I want, what do I really want to do?* It requires working out the logistics of where, when, and with whom. And then figuring out if you can afford it. For most of us, the financial part is pretty straightforward compared to the tougher lifestyle questions. But because money tends to be top of mind when people think about retirement, let's start there.

The Elusive "Magic Number"

I find that all of us—rich, poor, or in between—are afraid of the same damn thing: running out of money. Along with that comes the fear of losing control of our lives, of not being able to pay our bills or remain self-sufficient. It's enough to make you lose sleep at night when you think about it, and so most of us don't.

But that's a mistake, because time ticks away and our worry has nowhere to go but home. It's a much better idea to address your financial questions head-on and move forward. So here's a simple formula. Start by asking yourself the typical questions I hear batted about: *How much money do I need to retire comfortably? What's the magic number?* My answer is, there *is* no magic number! For each of us, many variables can change the number based on the decisions we make—decisions such as where we choose to live, how we choose to live, and whether we'll continue working full- or part-time in our so-called retirement years. And then there are the wild cards we're each dealt. These are the things we don't have any control over, such as how long we might live, our health, our kids, and the whole grab bag of life's other circumstances that can change overnight. I think it's stupid to worry about variables we can't change anyway, so why not just take stock of what we know we have now and start to dream about the rest of our life?

We generally have a rough idea of our financial assets. What we need, though, is a definitive number put down on paper. This way you'll at least begin with a clear picture of what you have to work with. Start with the equity in your home (if you own). For the great majority of Americans, our home is our real social security, and the equity we have in our home is almost always more than we think. So first make a short list of everything you own of value, starting with your home. Call your local broker for a value estimate, comparison shop by attending neighborhood open houses, or get a quick estimate on a Web site such as Zillow (zillow.com) or Trulia (trulia.com). You simply punch in your address, and chances are good you'll like the number you get.

I know a lot of people have gotten spooked by what's been happening in the housing market recently. There's so much bad news out there about what's wrong with today's housing market that most people don't realize that two out of three of all major markets in America are still appreciating. Still, some of us may be reluctant to sell or buy because of all the scary headlines. But the truth is I've learned that a difficult market can be the best time to move because confusion creates bargains. And even if you get less for your house than you originally hoped, you can make up that difference in the new place you acquire. On top of that, when it comes time to retire, almost everybody moves from a more expensive house to a less expensive one, for two simple reasons. First, we typically downsize because we don't need as much house anymore. Second, most of us move from a more expensive to a less expensive community. We have more flexibility— we're no longer tied to certain school districts, business centers, or commuter lines—and because of that, it's totally doable to move to a new place that's twice as lovely and a fraction of the price.

Paradise can be a bargain. According to current trends, your new home will cost about half to two-thirds of what you'll get for your old one. That leaves some wiggle room and leftover money. Here's an example: Let's say you live in Chicago and want to move to the popular retirement city of Tucson. In Tucson, a median-priced house is around two hundred thousand dollars. That's less than half of what you'd get for your median-priced house in Chicago—$425,000.

And it's not only housing costs that are less. The everyday cost of living also is less. In the Chicago to Tucson example, your daily cost of living would get cut by about one-third. You can compare the cost of living between any two cities online at Sperling's Best Places (bestplaces.net) and Retirement Living Information Center (retirementliving.com), two of the best sites for such statistics.

Some of the best places to retire are also low-tax states—for example, Tennessee, Alabama, Arkansas, Wyoming, and Alaska are all on our list of dream places, in part because they offer such good tax deals. Tax Foundation (taxfoundation.org) is a good resource for getting the tax lowdown on different areas in the United States. And if you decide to move overseas, you can really stretch your bucks big-time. In Panama, for example, everything from real estate to restaurants costs about half of what it does here. That's one reason why Panama is among the places featured in chapter 5.

So, bottom line: your nest egg can go pretty far when it comes time to buy your next home. Even with the recent turbulence in the real estate market, a home remains a great place to park your money. If you do the needed prep work and use common sense when choosing your next property, you'll be able to make the next chapter of your life a lot more affordable.

But for many of us, the bigger question is not *what* we will be able to invest in for our retirement, but *where*. And all the number crunching in the world can't answer this for you. The figures can tell you what you can afford, but they won't tell you if you belong there or whether you'll be happy.

How to Protect Your Nest Egg by Spending It

Putting your money into property is one of the best ways to protect it. Here's why:

1. You can't spend it. The money is locked up unless you sell the property, and that doesn't happen easily or overnight. Even if your kids start putting the squeeze on you, this is money you can't simply hand over and won't spend unnecessarily. Paying the mortgage is forced savings, and that makes it one of the most reliable retirement funds.

2. You can borrow against it. If you're a brave soul, it's smart to borrow against the equity in your current home to buy your retirement home early.

3. You can rent it out. Even if you're not ready to move there yet, buying your retirement home early and renting it out is a way to earn back some of your investment. And if you end up changing your mind in the next five years and decide it's not the place for you, you'll still have a second pot of equity bubbling on the back burner.

It may sound scary, but it's true: one great way to hold on to your nest egg is to spend it.

Finding Fulfillment

So how do we begin to unravel this question of *where*? For some of us, it's a matter of doing side-by-side comparisons of places with an eye on universal characteristics such as weather, crime rate, and cost of housing.

When we surveyed people on the Trulia real estate Web site, asking baby boomers what they were looking for in their ideal retirement spot, these were their top priorities:

- Safety
- Affordable housing
- Good weather
- Nice scenery
- Friendly people
- Good health care
- A nearby airport

It's easy to hop online and compare places based on these basic qualities. There are magazines and books out there that make it even easier by doing the comparisons for you, and there are lots of "ten best" lists based on the same characteristics. The box on page 21 lists some "insider" tips that can also help with your priorities.

But I think these generic features of a place are only a starting point, not the answer. Although qualities such as nice weather, safety, and good health care are the basics we all want or need, they don't distinguish a place. They're not the things that make it special. And though a magazine may tell you that a town is a pretty good place to live for people in general, it doesn't tell you if it's a good place for *you* to live. After all, you're not "people in general," you're you. And in your heart of hearts, you probably desire something much more than good weather.

Determined to dig out some of those deeper desires in our research, we did another study, this time on the boomer Web site What's Next (whatsnext.com), where we tried to get beyond weather, safety, and other generics. We asked what people really *dreamed* about. We asked what mattered most to them on a level that was more soulful and less superficial. And we discovered

Is That Town a Good Investment? Barb's Insider Tips

Despite its ups and downs, real estate remains a good solid place to park your retirement money—*if* you invest wisely. There are lots of ways to tell if a community represents a good investment, but here are a few lesser-known ways I think are most important:

Check out the local job market. Even if you're not getting any younger, the community you buy in should be. A good job market means there's an influx of young people, and that's a must for increasing real estate values. You can see how many jobs a town is gaining or losing by checking with the local chamber of commerce. And here's my shortcut: notice how many new cars there are on the streets. Young people buy lots of new cars.

Look for a charming downtown. It's the heart of any town, and a town without one lacks the necessary curb appeal. It's a town without a heart.

Buy in a town that has a stock of older homes. If every house is new, one house looks like the next and the town can't develop the character that drives up real estate values.

Count the FOR SALE signs. If too many people are moving out, you don't want to be moving in. One sign every three blocks means real estate prices will soon take a dive.

that most respondents—a whopping 80 percent, in fact—dreamed of pursuing a passion, engaging in something they loved to do. A majority of people also expressed an interest in being part of a community of like-minded people. And many were drawn to the idea of living out retirement in a way that allowed them to make a meaningful contribution to the world around them.

TYPICAL VERSUS MAGICAL		
Typical Qualities	vs.	Magical Qualities
Safety		Particular type of community
Affordable housing		Opportunity to pursue a specific passion
Good weather		Chance to learn/reinvent yourself
Quality health care		Opportunity to contribute to something larger

Our findings echo trends that are already coming to the surface with the new generation of retirees. Today, beyond the basics of sun and safety, we have a growing hunger for meaning, for social connection, for passionate living, productive work, and personal fulfillment. This changes the equation entirely as we look at possible places to retire. Now the question becomes "Is this a place where I can find fulfillment?"

Before you can answer that, you need to understand what fulfillment means to you. What do you, and only you, really want? If it has something to do with pursuing a passion, then *which* passion? And if you're talking about getting involved in a cause, then *which* cause? The answers have to come from within—but you can get there with a little help from the outside.

In the past couple of years, a whole new industry has been springing up, dedicated to helping people figure out where their passions lie and what they ought to do next. There's a new breed of life coaches—considered "retirement coaches"—and new coaching companies such as New Directions and My Next Phase have been launched as well.

If you're not ready to sign up for coaching (and it's not cheap, costing anywhere from $100 to $250 an hour), then it can be helpful to look at what the coaches do when guiding their clients toward a better understanding of what to do next. I'll start your thinking by sharing some key questions with you.

For the most part, coaches try to get people to answer four basic questions:

- ▸ Looking back over your life, what are the things you've felt most passionate about?
- ▸ What jobs have you had that made you eager to get up in the morning?
- ▸ If you knew you had only a limited amount of time on this planet, what would you want to do first?
- ▸ Without mentioning your old career, how would you describe yourself to new people you meet?

That last question is an important one, insists Dr. Cynthia Barnett. In her retirement coaching program, she asks clients to introduce themselves to her as if they were meeting her at a party. What retirees often discover is that they have a hard time describing themselves divorced from their jobs. For many, their job *is* their identity. Without that crutch to fall back on, "you have to start digging deeper into yourself in terms of describing who you are," Barnett says. "Suddenly it's a case of 'I'm no longer a CEO—so who am I?'" One exercise is to practice what you might like to say as an answer to the classic cocktail-party question, "What do you do for a living?" According to Barnett, when you come up with an answer you don't mind saying out loud, that can be a good first step in figuring out what you want to do next.

As you try to answer these various coaching questions, "it's a good idea to get away from your everyday life because it can help you think in fresh ways," says Ron Manheimer, director of the North Carolina Center for Creative Retirement. His group runs weekend retreats where retirees can explore possibilities and bounce ideas off one another.

While you're figuring out what you want to do next, Manheimer suggests you focus on "creating a balance between your various interests and passions." One way to do this is to create a pie chart for your new life, with one slice devoted to work, another to family, and still another dedicated to particular passions you'd like to have more time for. Life coach David Corbett of the firm New Directions has coined the term "life portfolio," arguing that your life should be as balanced as your stock portfolio—with an even mix of paid work, leisure, family time, learning, and giving back. Corbett suggests we keep watch over our life portfolio throughout retirement, constantly diversifying and rebalancing it for as long as we live. I personally like this idea because the happiest people I know always seem to have their lives in balance. Why should it be any different when we retire?

My World-Famous Real Estate Quiz

If retirement coaches can give batteries of tests to help us figure out what we want to do next in life, why not have a test that can help us figure out where we should live next? As far as I know, there is no such test, so I developed one just for you. After all, we can spend all the time in the world figuring out what we want to do, but at some point we've got to do it and we've got to do it *somewhere.*

With this in mind, here is what I believe to be the world's first "Where to Live Happily Ever After" quiz. It's based on my premise that if you're looking for something outside yourself, such as a great place to live, it's best to begin with what's inside. What makes you happy and what makes you sad? Where do you feel most comfortable or most threatened? I've tried to tap into these feelings and then connect them to certain types of life-styles and environments that will satisfy most of your needs—that is, places that will allow you to become your best self.

My quiz uses the principles of the famous Myers-Briggs Type Indicator personality test. It's divided into two parts: the first addresses your individual preferences and is fairly straightforward, and the second digs deeper into the nuances of your personality.

You may notice some quirky Britishisms in my test. That's because a bloke named Simon Weaver from my company wrote it. Don't read too much into that—it's merely the way Simon talks. Just pick up your pencil and have some fun.

Barb's "Where to Live Happily Ever After" Quiz

Part One: Preferences

1. It's Friday night and you have nothing planned. What are you going to do?

a) Hit the city and check out a new bar you heard about
b) Invite friends over
c) Go out for a quiet meal with someone you love
d) Surf the Internet

2. You're in New York City and you're hungry. What's going to do it for you?

a) Sushi: it's cheap, it's healthy, it's cool
b) Ethiopian food: you've heard it's great and you've always wanted to try it
c) Familiar chain restaurant: you're hungry and not in the mood to take chances

d) Anywhere: you're not particular and the closest place will do

3. You're going to rent a movie. What do you choose?

a) *Star Wars*
b) *The Big Chill*
c) *It's a Wonderful Life*
d) *Gandhi*

4. Where would you most like to visit?

a) Prague, Czech Republic
b) Australian outback
c) Mexico
d) India

5. You're in the mood for music. What do you do?

a) Go to a rock concert
b) Go to a bagpipe festival
c) Listen to some of your old favorite records
d) Go to a folk music benefit

6. You're in a deli and the staff doesn't speak English. How do you react?

a) Try to speak to them in their own language
b) Patiently point to everything with a smile on your face
c) Become irritable and wish the store hired English-speaking staff
d) Wish you'd ordered online

7. You've been on the beach for a couple of hours. What's your mind-set?

a) Ready for a swim
b) Looking for something else to do

c) Thinking about the dog at home
d) Thinking about skin cancer

8. You are best man/maid of honor and the groom/bride wants to go mountain climbing as a bachelor/bachelorette party activity. How do you feel?

a) Excited and up for it
b) Want to know who else is going
c) Want to know how far away the mountain is
d) Want to know why you should risk your neck in the first place!

9. You're moving to the boondocks and there is no high-speed Internet access. So what do you do?

a) Rent an expensive satellite dish
b) Use a local Internet café when the need arises
c) Get by with dial-up
d) Do without altogether

10. You're offered early retirement with a full pension. How do you feel?

a) Shocked that you are already considered over-the-hill
b) Pleasantly surprised and a little humbled
c) Ecstatic as you leap up and down, clapping your hands with joy
d) Eager to really start accomplishing something

11. You've sprained your ankle and you're in some discomfort. What do you do?

a) Soak it in an herbal bath
b) Call your doctor and ask about an appointment
c) Head for the emergency room
d) Wrap it yourself and move on

12. How would you prefer to travel?

a) Low-emission public transportation
b) Bicycle
c) SUV
d) On foot

13. When buying a house, which is most important to you?

a) Good vibes
b) The community
c) Local services
d) Privacy

14. Which would you rather lose?

a) Your hearing
b) Your sight
c) Your marbles
d) Your friends

15. What MUST you be close to?

a) Airport
b) Medical facility
c) Restaurants
d) The beach

Part Two: Strictly Personal

1. Two friends call and ask you out on the same night. How do you handle it?

a) Choose the one who is more exciting and stall the other
b) Try to arrange it so you can all go out together
c) Decide you'd rather go out with your partner instead
d) Stay home and play chess

2. If a friend were to mispronounce a word, what would you do?

a) Correct him or her directly but politely

b) Correct him or her in a roundabout "Are you sure you're saying that right . . . ?" kind of way

c) Either not notice or not care

d) Become agitated and splutter out the correct pronunciation in a showstoppingly awkward manner

3. You're in your front yard tending to your shrubs when a stranger walks by and allows his dog to do its business in your bushes. What do you do?

a) Demand the stranger curb his dog immediately and call all your friends to tell them about the dreadful incident

b) Patiently explain to the man that it isn't right for him to let his dog go just anywhere and ask him how he would feel if you let your dog go in his bushes

c) Forgive and forget—you have a big yard, and the waste will probably rot away before you get to it anyway

d) Think about the moral implications of what you've seen, wonder if the offending article might actually be good for the garden, and, when you finally decide to be annoyed, notice the stranger has gone

4. Two friends offer to organize your closet for you. How do you respond?

a) Say thanks very much and order pizza for them while they work

b) Tell them they can if it will make them feel better

c) Laugh and tell them they should organize themselves first

d) Decline, explaining that the closet may not look tidy to them, but you know where everything is and that's the way you like it

5. It's a freezing winter day and due to a bizarre set of circumstances not worth getting into, you're dressed only in bright Bermuda shorts and a T-shirt. You have no money and you're lost. What do you do?

a) Burst into tears, then go to the nearest house you see and demand assistance
b) Use your winning smile to persuade a nearby clothes store to give you some free items
c) Curse the day you were born and demand assistance from on high
d) Figure out how long it will be before hypothermia sets in, decide you can make it, and run as fast as you can to shelter

6. You recognize an old acquaintance coming toward you on the sidewalk; it's someone you were never particularly keen on. How do you handle it?

a) Focus your eyes on everything and nothing and let fate decide if you'll meet
b) Smile politely and ask what the person is doing nowadays
c) Pretend something very special is happening on the face of your watch and stare at it intently
d) Veer off into the street, risking death in order to avoid this potentially horrendous situation

7. It's free pizza time in the office and everyone is angling for the prize slices. What do you do?

a) Dive right into the maelstrom and fight the good fight for the best piece
b) Take charge of the situation, bringing over plates and volunteering to dole out the slices yourself (all the while making sure there's some pepperoni left for you)
c) Let the gannets have their fun—there's enough to go around, after all, and you'll snaffle the last three pieces when the others are gone

d) Stay in your office, wondering what everyone is up to and what that rather enticing aroma might be

8. Your computer has just exploded. Literally. How do you react?

a) Call tech support immediately and demand a new computer, threatening to sue

b) Call friends and maybe even the media so everyone is warned of this potential hazard

c) Call your partner and tell him/her what just happened

d) Pick up a smoldering transistor and have a sniff, seeing if you can make some kind of diagnosis

9. Your tyrannical aunt has decreed that this year's Thanksgiving dinner will be held at her house, no debate allowed. How do you respond?

a) Say NO—you will not countenance such a thing, so you gather your troops and veto the dictatorial dame

b) Call your aunt and tell her how sad you are that she won't be able to make it to your house this year; she is, after all, your favorite auntie and it won't be the same without her

c) Reluctantly agree—you don't want to hurt anyone's feelings

d) Happily say yes; after all, it's cheaper than going to a restaurant

10. A friend gives you an ultimatum: you can play tennis with him, or he'll no longer be your friend. You have been promising to play for thirty years, but you hate it and keep putting it off. What do you do?

a) Give in—how bad can it be?

b) Plead for mercy—your knees are stricken with polymyalgia and no good can possibly come of this

c) Reluctantly agree—you did promise, after all, even if you were only twenty at the time

d) Tell your friend that if his continued friendship comes down to something as silly as this, then he can stick his tennis racket where the sun don't shine

Finished? Okay, pencils down, and let's tally the results. Count the number of A, B, C, and D answers. If you had a majority of A responses, pay special attention to chapters 3 (about pursuing passions), 5 (focusing on living young), and 6 (on living green). If you're a B type, chapters 4 (on community) and 7 (about losing yourself) are calling out to you. A lot of C answers should direct you to chapters 9 (about the boomerang lifestyle) and 10 (on staying close to home). If Ds were in the majority, you should turn to chapter 8 (on finding your purpose). Or then again, you can just read all the chapters—it's entirely possible that you fall into more than one category and that several different lifestyles and locations may be right for you.

The truth is, we all have overlapping needs and desires, and each of us probably has three, four, or five places that would be ideal. In fact, I'm convinced that there's no single answer to the question of where you might best enjoy the second act of your life. If you come across multiple possibilities that appeal to you in this book, you'll have no choice but to travel around vacationing and sampling each delightful spot. Justify it by telling yourself you're doing the necessary homework to get ready for the best part of your life.

It's smart to start your search early. Once you gather options from this book and plan your next half-dozen vacations in carefully chosen spots, you'll begin to put some flesh on the bones of what was once only a vague picture of your retirement. That's when you'll start to turn some of your fear and apprehension about this next phase of your life into the adventure and quest it's meant to be.

Chapter 3

Pursuing Your Passion

*A*s Diane and Ed Lane's careers in advertising were winding down, they didn't know exactly what they wanted to do next. But they had a good idea of what they didn't want to do. "Living in Arizona, I used to watch a lot of people move to the golf retirement communities and just sort of disappear there," Diane says. "To me, that just seemed deadly." Diane was more interested in finding a new life that would keep her creative juices flowing. She didn't have anything specific in mind, but her husband did.

"Art was always my passion when I was growing up and going to school," Ed explains. "But I sort of allowed myself to be talked into doing something more serious with my life, like making a living." He'd done a nice job of that through the years, building the successful local ad firm in Phoenix that he co-managed with Diane. But in the back of his mind, Ed always thought about becoming an artist again someday. Ed and Diane began to vacation in Hawaii, and something about that place stirred the painter in Ed. "The colors were so vibrant in Hawaii," he says. "It's really a painter's paradise. I guess I wasn't the first to discover this, because I found that there were so many artists in Maui. On our trips there, I gradually started to get to *know them. And then I went to the local art center—it's called Hui No'eau, which means 'gathering of friends'—and I was really taken with it. It's housed in an old mansion and filled with all these talented painters, just working away."*

And so the couple made a plan: they'd sell the agency, retire from advertising, and move to Maui, where Ed would at last become the full-time artist he had always wanted to be.

As for Diane, she saw her role mainly as being supportive of Ed's dream. "I didn't really have a dream of my own, other than to help Ed and maybe just take it easy," she says. But shortly after they settled in Maui and set up Ed in his new painting studio at home, Diane took a class in silk painting at the Hui art center. She fell in love right away. As she puts it, "I felt that tap on my shoulder saying, 'This is your new life.'" It wasn't easy. "Having no art training, I had to do a lot of hard work to get my skills up. I worked at it every day, and I'd fall asleep at night with art instruction books on my chest."

Today there are two art studios in the Lanes' Maui home—Ed works in one and Diane in the other. Ed's catalog of paintings is now up to seven hundred artworks and growing; Diane, meanwhile, has created a painted-silk clothing line, Leilani Silks. They each put in full days because, as Ed says, "This is not a hobby. This is serious work, for both of us." But what a way to work: up early each day with a cup of coffee while basking in the Hawaiian morning sunshine, a quick dip in the pool, then off to their separate studios to work.

For Ed it's an old dream come true; for Diane it's a new one, freshly discovered. "I never expected to have this whole new life as an artist," she says. "I think the lesson is that you have to be really open to new experiences, because if you are, the universe just might hand you a wonderful opportunity."

I've always found that my best decisions were made from my heart and the worst were the ones I arrived at logically. Those were the ones that wasted my time and sapped my energy. When I sold my real estate business, everyone agreed that I should learn to relax and take some time to be good to myself. But my idea of being good to myself was to find the next mountain to climb—a new passion to throw myself into. This chapter, about finding your passion and where to make a new life of it, is for people like me.

And there are lots of people like me out there. Everywhere I look, I see others packing up their old lives and old identities to pursue a new passion. A couple like Ed and Diane Lane retire from advertising and become artists, almost overnight, or a long-time office worker named Pam Von Rhee (whom you'll meet later in this chapter) chucks the cubicle life to become a farmer in rural Oklahoma. Then there's the retired small-town veterinarian, Wayne Lubin, starting a second life now as a blackjack dealer at one of the country's glitziest casinos.

These people can't slow to a crawl just because they've reached the next stage of life. Their all-or-nothing personalities make 180-degree turns based on their gut. You know the type, and you may be one yourself. Someone who dips a toe into the water of art or charity and ends up 150 percent into it, maybe even running the show.

Maybe you've always wanted to do something and just never had the chance to dive in because all of life's practical reasons got in the way. You were busy either making a living, taking care of others, or moving along the road to becoming successful in business. But somewhere along the way you missed out on finding deep personal fulfillment and now you want to take a shot at it. Cozy and comfortable is not on your list, and you want to find the place where you can spread your wings, redefine yourself, and follow your heart.

A passion is not a hobby—a hobby is something you dabble in occasionally, but a passion is so much more. When you truly throw yourself into a passion, it becomes the essence of who you are, the source of a new identity and a whole new life. Many boomers arriving at life's turning point are simply deciding, *From now on, I want to do what I want to do.* After years of focusing on external goals and rewards, we're looking for answers inside.

Brian Kurth is the founder of VocationVacations, a company that helps people test-drive their dream jobs to see if they want to make a new career out of them. This is a business that didn't exist a generation ago—our parents weren't that fortunate. "If you look at the previous generation, they didn't work out of passion, but out of pure need," says Kurth. He points out that the whole concept of pursuing your passion would have seemed frivolous in the past because people were too busy making a living to get caught up in chasing dreams. "To my parents' generation, work was a four-letter word that got you to the weekend, and eventually to retirement," Kurth adds. "I believe that generation paid the price so that ours could have the prosperity and the flexibility we have now. We have more of an opportunity to pursue our passions, and it's something we shouldn't waste."

I believe it's more than just a matter of prosperity—we also have more energy to burn. We arrive at our fifties and sixties itching for action and challenges. And because we're expected to live longer, we may have a lot more time to fill in the second half of life. The activities and hobbies once thought sufficient to fill the short window of retirement are not nearly enough. And hobbies get old fast, whereas burning passions can sustain us forever.

Pursuing Your Passion and Getting Paid

In past times, people tended to separate hobbies and all the other things they really enjoyed doing from their actual work. But for many of us now, our true passion *is* our work. Work has become a bigger part of how we define ourselves and derive satisfaction. So what we're seeing now is a blending of work and play, much the way Ed and Diane Lane have done. A lot of us are seeking out passions that not only fill our time, but also fill our tremendous need to be productive—and fill our pockets, too.

Even though most boomers expect to shift gears in their sixties, we're not planning to retire in the classic sense. As mentioned, surveys show that two-thirds of us plan to continue to do some form of work, either full- or part-time, long after we officially retire.

Our drive to keep working is partly tied to financial pressures. Whereas the GI generation could rely on pensions and rock-solid Social Security, our generation has to deal with volatile 401(k)s and a Social Security system that could go bust before it pays us back.

But our reticence to retire isn't all about the money. Most of us want to keep working in our later years purely for the stimulation, according to a recent study by Merrill Lynch. That same study reveals a very interesting way that boomers are beginning to look at work: we reject the idea of either full-time leisure or full-time work. Our goal instead is to find a way to cycle between periods of work and play.

Our play, it turns out, is just as important as our work. Among the boomers we surveyed for this book, 80 percent said they had a particular passion they'd like to devote more time to in their retirement years. And more than 70 percent expressed an interest in starting a business of their own, based on something they now enjoy doing.

The bottom line is, we want to keep working, but on our terms. We want to be doing what we want, when we want, where we want. And how do you find a boss who'll let you do all that? By becoming your own boss.

Right now boomers already account for nearly half of the country's self-employed workers, and that trend will grow in the coming years. To all those young Silicon Valley whiz kids, watch out—the new stars of the start-up business world could likely be your mom and dad.

Of course, it's not easy to turn your passion into a paying job or a thriving new business. Just ask someone who's tried it. "It's more work than I ever could have imagined," says Judy Finch, fifty-nine, a onetime engineer who decided to leave the office life and open a campground in the misty mountains of Pennsylvania. Judy is one of many who spoke to us about the thrills and the challenges of following a lifelong passion for a new second career. (Judy's story is included in the box "Meet the Dream Chasers," starting on page 41.) The common threads for all of them are long hours and some shaky moments at the beginning, but overall lots of satisfaction.

There are risks involved. Statistics show that half of new business start-ups go belly-up inside of four years, and if a retiree pours his or her whole life savings into that failed venture, it's particularly devastating. Older entrepreneurs have to be even savvier than their younger counterparts.

I think it's a smart idea to try your hand at your dream business before you commit to it—because sometimes the reality of it doesn't live up to your dreams. That's the point of Vocation-Vacations, launched a few years ago by Kurth. The company sells one to three-day "immersions" in more than one hundred occupations, everything from wine-making to running a B&B or graphic-design shop.

The Best Place for Your Passion

By test-driving your passion on a short-term basis, you can get a real-world sense of whether a particular activity is as fun as it seems and if it's something you really want to do full-time. If you do decide to dive in all the way, this is when place becomes important. There's no law that says you can't pursue your lifelong passion right in your hometown—people do it all the time. But the simple fact is, the place where you live may not be the best place to do what you've always wanted to do. It's pretty basic, really: If you want to do farming, you've got to go where the farmland is. If you want to open a bookstore, you want to be where the readers are. And if you long to be an artist, you need to go somewhere that inspires you.

Opening a Shop? Here's How to Keep It Open

So you've always wanted to sell books, or buttons, or bangles. How do you do it without losing your shirt? Here are a few quick real estate tips to keep in mind:

1. Rent the corner store with the bigger window. Pay careful attention to the facade and position of your store. Make your canopy a bright or warm color to attract customers and bring them inside.

2. Always pick a sunny space. People spend more money when they're in a happy mood, and a sunny space makes people feel happy.

3. Choose the "right" side of the street. There's always a right and wrong side of every street in any town, and the right side gets 30–40 percent more foot traffic than the other side. Don't hire a fancy pedestrian-analysis company to find out which side's better—just stand on the corner during rush hour and do a head count.

4. Pick your neighbors. If there's empty space next door, find out what tenants will be moving in. Neighbors either attract or chase away customers.

I believe that when it comes to pursuing your passion, context really matters. The whole experience of doing something and doing it well can be greatly enhanced by being in the right place. And there is definitely a best place for almost anything you might be passionate about, from bird watching to wine-making.

Ten Places to Do What You Like to Do Best

No matter what you love to do, there's an ideal place to do it. Find your passion below to see where to take it.

Riding a bike. Pedal on over to bike-crazy Davis, California (profiled in chapter 4).

Taking your dog for a walk. Seattle is one of the dog-friendliest cities. In Marymoor Park—the ultimate off-leash dog haven, according to *Bark* magazine—the dogs run free next to a gorgeous river as salmon leap into the air.

Taking yourself for a walk. Madison, Wisconsin, is deemed the most walkable city in America. I'll explain why when you get to the profile of Madison in chapter 6.

Looking for love. Denver is ranked as the best place to be single by Forbes.com because of its rich nightlife and heavy dating activity.

Looking for sushi. Vancouver has four hundred sushi bars. People from Japan actually come here for their sushi.

Becoming an entrepreneur. St. George, Utah, is one of the fastest-growing entrepreneurial towns. (See the profile of St. George in chapter 5.)

Sleeping. Take your pillow to Minneapolis. According to Bert Sperling of the Best Places Web site, it's the easiest place to get a good night's sleep, mostly because local residents are less stressed.

Meeting people. Charleston is cited by *Travel & Leisure* as the friendliest city around.

If you like piña coladas. Milwaukee is the city for folks who love to drink.

Or getting caught in the rain. Mobile, Alabama, usually has more rainfall than any other city, Seattle included. (However, there has been a severe drought in the South this past year.)

There's another reason why pursuing a passion can be closely linked to moving to a new place. As you do that special thing you've dreamed of doing, it's necessary to reinvent yourself—as an entrepreneur, an artist, or someone else who's different from who you were before. And for many of us, it's hard to re-create ourselves in the midst of our old familiar world. Sometimes it takes a fresh place to make a fresh start. "I don't think we could have done what we did if we'd stayed in Phoenix," says Diane Lane. "Back there, everyone knew us as our old selves—as people who worked in advertising. But in Maui, we could create a whole new identity as artists. In this place, we've become different people."

Meet the Dream Chasers

These seven people followed their dreams to create a bold new second act for themselves.

Wayne Lubin, blackjack dealer. Only fifty-four when he retired from his thirty-year career as a veterinarian, Wayne initially decided to take it easy; his biggest stress was driving the occasional one-hundred-mile trip from his Danbury, Connecticut, home to the Foxwoods Casino in Ledyard. Wayne, you see, has always loved a good game of cards. He'd even dreamed, in younger days, of being a blackjack dealer. Then, two months into his retirement, he decided it was time to reshuffle the deck. He picked up the phone, dialed up the casino, and asked, "How do I become a blackjack dealer?"

A brief training course later, he found himself in the dealer's seat at Foxwoods. "I was surprised at how easy it was," Wayne says. "The training was quick, and from my years as a vet, I had a lot of good experience dealing with the public." He likes to joke that he sometimes encounters wilder breeds at the blackjack table than he ever did at the vet's office. Wayne is part of a growing trend of retirees who are taking jobs at casinos, as the *New York Times* recently reported. For many it's a chance to live out a dream, and that's certainly the case for Wayne. "This is something I always wanted to do and I plan to keep doing it as long as I can. How can you beat it?" He smiles. "I'm being paid to play games!"

Pam Von Rhee, blackberry grower. Pam, fifty-three, grew up in the suburbs of Long Island, but her family would occasionally drive over to a local potato farm, where seeing the simple farming life struck a chord in her. Four years ago—after two decades of toiling in an office—she decided it was time to get back to the land. "I always wanted to grow something," she says. "And I always liked blackberries." Pam and her husband began a search for the perfect spot to put down new roots and found it in tiny Coweta, Oklahoma, where they came upon a twenty-nine-acre spread—just a big field with a little barn. But to Pam it looked like heaven. "I grew up in tract homes in Long Island and I always wanted more open space, and this place sure had it."

They bought the property and set to work. When Pam got her first bushel of blackberry plants, the stalks were "smaller than pencils," she says. "I looked at them and thought, 'No way!' Now they're five feet high." She processes the berries into jams and pie fillings sold at farmers' markets throughout Oklahoma. On that once-vacant property, she and her husband also built their little dream house, with a pool, five horses, and four head of cattle. Lavender grows in abundance and the berries are everywhere. Out there in the middle of it all, Pam rides her tractor, tilling the soil, fertilizing, watering, and picking the fruits of her labor—all skills she's had to teach herself from scratch. By day's end, she says, she is "bone tired. But it's a great kind of tired, do you know what I mean?"

Judy Finch, campground owner. Judy was looking for an escape hatch. She'd gone through a divorce as well as a forced relocation by her job to Georgia, where she never quite settled in ("too hot for me," she says). She'd reached her mid-fifties and was ready to go her own way—but needed a destination. One weekend some friends invited her to go camping in the Pennsylvania mountains. At the time Judy had never gone camping before in her life, but she came away from the trip thinking, "That's a pretty neat lifestyle." A while later her friends told her about a run-down campground site for sale in Tremont Township, Pennsylvania. Nestled among the mountains with panoramic views all around, it had a gorgeous creek, a little lighthouse, and a boathouse. "I fell in love with it at first sight," Judy says.

She bought the campground, moved into the boathouse, and discovered that she was now "the owner, the manager, the mayor, the sheriff—basically, the person who does everything around here." The grounds needed a lot of work after years of neglect. "I had no idea how mammoth the job would be," she says. But most of the renovations are done now, and the Echo Valley Campground is packed with campers. "I may even make a profit this year," she says with a wry chuckle, though she adds that the real reward is just the experience of doing something she enjoys in a place that she treasures. "It's demanding, but I'm convinced that pursuing your passion is the best thing you can do. If you're lucky enough to be in a position to do it, you must!"

Suzanne Greene, ski instructor. In her mid-fifties, Sue was a successful manager at IBM in suburban New York. She went out to Keystone, Colorado, for a week of skiing and, while there, received word from her office that the company was offering a buyout opportunity. Her ski instructor made a half-serious suggestion to her: "Why don't you take the offer and come out here and become a ski teacher?" That's just what Sue did, and today she's one of the top ski instructors in Summit County and also organizes special ski programs for women. "I left a high-paying career to take a job at seven dollars an hour," she says, "and I couldn't be happier about it." It wasn't easy; she had to train hard to get her ski skills up to the professional level. But it helped that she had strong management and people skills from her "first life"; "that made me a better teacher," she says. Sue believes the secret to pursuing your passion is to "approach it as a professional. If you treat something as a hobby, you can get bored with it, but when you dedicate yourself to it full-time, that's a whole different experience."

She also believes that being in the right place is absolutely critical. "I couldn't be living this lifestyle if I stayed in New York, and it's not just because of the ski conditions. The people are different here, and the lifestyle is different. This place allows me to be more active than I was before." Sue, who is now seventy, not only skis, she also bikes and kayaks. "Around here, age isn't even a relevant concept. People will say, 'We're going on a bike ride—wanna come?' They don't care about your age, they just want to know if you can keep up." Needless to say, she can.

Jim Strawn, bookstore owner. Jim, whom I mentioned briefly in chapter 2, had a rough beginning to his retirement. Having worked hard to rise to the level of chief financial officer in his radio career, he figured he'd kick back and take it easy once he left the job. But he quickly grew bored, restless, and depressed. What got him back into the saddle was the chance to help out at a local church organization, which he did for a few years. He helped with the book-keeping, picked up some new computer skills, and was soon practically running the place. That job provided just the bridge Jim needed. "That convinced me that I still had the ability and the desire to be productive," he says.

After a few years with the church group, Jim decided it was time to turn his attention to his lifelong passion—books. He'd been a collector of rare titles for many years, just as a weekend hobby. Then last year Jim took the plunge as he and his wife, Judy, opened Smythe Books in the Atlanta area. "We had to do everything ourselves, from finding the location for the store to designing and laying out the whole place," he says. "It's been a constant learning experience." And does he like that? "It's as good as it gets," Jim says. "I think everybody wants to have their own little niche, and this is mine. And there's no better feeling than when you help someone track down that special book they've been looking for and thought they'd never find."

Bill Sweat & Donna Morris, winemakers. Bill and Donna came up with a plan back when they were still in their thirties. "We decided that by age forty-five, we wanted to be able to leave our corporate environment and go do something on our own," says Donna. They spent the next ten years continuing their successful careers at Fidelity Investments in Boston. As the moment of truth approached (it coincided with their twentieth wedding anniversary), they were still trying to figure out what to do and where. "One thing we knew was that after all those years in financial services, we wanted to make something you could touch and feel," Donna says. In their discussions, they kept coming back to the subject of wine. "We're the kind of people who choose to eat in a restaurant based more on the wine list than the food menu," says Bill. And they both had a particular passion for pinot noir.

But drinking wine is one thing—making it is another. Bill and Donna decided they should get a little hands-on experience to see if they'd actually like being winemakers. Through Vocation-

Vacations, they spent a few days working at a winery. "It was a way to test out our assumptions and see if the reality matched the dream," says Bill. In this case it did; they both loved the experience. The next challenge was to find the place where they could live out the dream. Although some people seek out beautiful sunsets or magical views, Bill and Donna were checking out dirt—specifically, the rare soil where pinot grapes might flourish. They found it in the Willamette Valley of Oregon. So far they've crushed their first grapes but have yet to put anything into a bottle. Bill and Donna have no idea if their wine will be a hit, but they're thrilled with their new life. "When you're running your own business, and actually making something yourself, there's an incredible pride of ownership," Bill says. "I love walking into wine stores and telling them what we do." Donna adds: "That's probably a good way to know if something's worth doing—it should be something that you actually enjoy talking about."

BEST PLACES TO PURSUE YOUR PASSIONS

GALVESTON — Texas

A Bird-Watcher's Paradise

If you love watching birds in flight, Galveston will make your heart flutter. Every fall migrant birds journey south via the Gulf of Mexico and choose one last rest stop before they start the long grueling flight across the ocean. Their final pit stop is always the lovely coastal town of Galveston. And when the birds return in the spring, real bird magic happens because Galveston is the first stretch of land they see after thousands of miles of vast ocean. Ted Lee Eubanks is a Galveston bird-watcher, and he says when the conditions are right on a spring day, it seems as if it's raining birds—you'll see "warblers, orioles, buntings, and tanagers, all in these amazingly bright colors, coming down from the sky by the thousands." They perch on tree branches, on statues, in bushes in backyards, until the whole town is covered with birds.

It's no wonder Galveston, a small city that doubles as an island, draws birders from all over the country and the world. Like the birds, the people arrive in flocks, gathering together at the town's annual "FeatherFest" each spring—a festival dedicated to oohing and aahing the island's five hundred species of birds. But the passion for birds is not just a spring fling. The Galveston Ornithological Society schedules field trips all year long. You pay around thirty dollars, everybody piles into a van, and off you go to the various wildlife refuges and parks that can be found throughout the island.

The birds may come and go, but the people often end up staying here. The locals have taken to calling this island "Galvatraz" because, as they say, "you come but you never leave!" Galveston has the easygoing lifestyle and attitude of a Caribbean island, mixed with just a dash of Hamptons snobbery. It's only fifty miles southeast of Houston, which means oil-rich tycoons and their trophy wives use it as their getaway spot. Mix in the "winter Texans" who come down from the Midwest, add the ethnic blend of hardworking locals, and top it off with hip local college kids (there's a state university based here), and you have what resident Ted Lee Eubanks calls "a very authentic and slightly funky coastal community." In fact, people watching here is as interesting as bird watching.

Galveston also has one of the country's most impressive concentrations of late nineteenth- and early twentieth-century architecture. The stately mansions stand alongside pastel-colored bungalows and shotgun shacks. All of it's affordable, partly because fear of hurricanes has scared off some cautious buyers.

Galveston had a doozy back in 1900 that nearly wiped out the city. But it hasn't had a major hurricane in a couple of decades, and buyers and prices are just getting over the jitters.

If you're a free bird who's not afraid of a little wind, this is a great place to make a nest. Don't wait, though—Galveston is sure to appreciate as the Texas boomers begin to retire here. You might buy now and rent till you're ready to move—it has a great rental market in the summer. Then when the renters pack up to leave, you can show up in the fall and spring—just like the birds.

> **What It'll Cost You:** Galveston real estate is a steal, with the average home price at just over $108,000.
>
> **Inside Tip:** You can pick up a beachfront condo on the less-populated east end of the island for as low as $100,000, says Jason Keeling of Ryson Real Estate in Galveston. And in the downtown historic district, there are hundred-year-old Victorian homes that still cost in the low $200,000s. They are in need of updating, but that's an incredible value for an impressive house that's both downtown and on a beautiful island!
>
> **Sunny Days:** 203/year.
>
> **Median Age:** 35.

GREAT BIRD-WATCHING TOWNS, BY REGION

Northeast/Mid-Atlantic: Essex, Connecticut. Eagles are coming back from near extinction, and one of the best places to see them is in the gorgeous Connecticut River Valley. The state Audubon Society holds its Eagle Festival in the town of Essex every year. When you're not watching the birds, Essex is a quaint eighteenth-century New England town ranked as one of the best small towns in America. It's a place where you can ride the river on an old-fashioned steamboat named the *Becky Thatcher* or march in a Groundhog Day parade that stars a giant papier-mâché hog called "Essex Ed."

Midwest: St. Joseph, Missouri. The Squaw Creek National Wildlife Refuge, thirty miles north of St. Joseph, is a seven-thousand-acre feeding and resting place for birds and migratory waterfowl. More than three hundred species of birds have been spotted at the refuge, and the ones you're most likely to encounter are blue herons, pelicans, and, believe it or not, more than two hundred thousand Canadian snow geese. Boating and fishing have made nearby Big Lake State Park one of the state's most popular outdoor recreation areas. St. Joseph—also known as "St. JoMo"—is a great place to put down roots. It's a lively, authentic Old West town, still proud of the fact that it's the place where the Pony Express started and Jesse James met his demise.

South: Dauphin Island, Alabama. Dauphin Island is one of the best birding spots in the Southeast, with nearly 350 species spotted here. This cigar-shaped fourteen-mile-long island on the Gulf of Mexico serves as a prime viewing spot during migration season in the fall, but it's also amazing in the spring and winter, when the waterfowl and seabirds arrive. A short ride away is Dauphin's twin island, Fort Morgan. Both islands are just a few miles off the mainland, but Dauphin Island in particular feels as though it's a world unto itself. It has no traffic lights and only a handful of shops. Bird-watchers come over on the ferry, congregate on the shores, and share their love of nature.

SAUGATUCK   Michigan

A Great Spot to Open a Bed-and-Breakfast (But They Won't Let You Open a McDonald's)

If you're one of those friendly souls with dreams of opening a cozy bed-and-breakfast somewhere in leafy New England, think again. Maybe you should consider hanging your ROOMS FOR RENT sign instead along the beautiful sand dunes of Saugatuck.

Sauga-where, you ask? If you're not from the Midwest, you may not know about this little gem of a place, which is tucked away on the east side of Lake Michigan. Saugatuck has super-clean beaches with giant sand dunes big enough to gallop on. It's known locally as "the art coast of Michigan," with galleries galore, a funky art school in the woods, and artists setting up easels in the middle of the sidewalks downtown. On top of that, Saugatuck has great shops, world-class golf close by, and its own movie festival that's much like a mini Sundance. All of that means there's money to be made here because there's a growing demand for B&Bs.

Great towns often have a colorful history, and Saugatuck is one of them. For a while it was known as a wild little "sin city," as it was the only place in this part of Michigan where you could buy booze. This attracted bands of motorcycle riders who rumbled into Saugatuck to party, giving the town an even rowdier reputation.

But that was then and this is now. These days Saugatuck is laid-back and mellow. It's often compared to Martha's Vineyard and Key West but feels more undiscovered and has more small-town innocence. Everyone eats fudge in Saugatuck, and the local pizza shop is what passes for a "hot" restaurant. Paddleboat rides are all the rage, and the ferry that takes you across the river is hand cranked, bumping slowly along on a chain that extends from one shore to the other. There's no Starbucks or McDonald's—they've tried to come in, but the locals banded together and said, "No thanks." Those same citizens began a wonderful dial-a-ride bus service as an alternative to driving. Seniors call in and a bus picks them up at their door, taking them anywhere in the area for a whopping fifty cents!

The people of Saugatuck are a motley crew, coming from all over the country and mixing young writers, artists, a large gay community, and lots of retired professionals. There's a fair number of millionaires with yachts and also some lovably eccentric characters, such as eighty-year-old Jane Van Dis, who plays the Statue of Liberty every year in the town's doo-dah Fourth of July parade. Jane also sleeps outdoors in a box once a year to raise awareness for homelessness.

One reason Saugatuck attracts so many creative types is a quirky little place called Ox-Bow. I guess you could call it an art school, but it doesn't have classes, per se. Ox-Bow is more like a collective of artists, with studios set out amid the trees by a lagoon. It was designed as a haven that art students could escape to, without any distractions from the real world. But lots of people who attend Ox-Bow never leave Saugatuck. They stay and become local artists. That's why there are so many art galleries in town, and it's also why the B&Bs all adorn their walls with works by local artists.

There are about forty B&Bs in Saugatuck, ranging from grand old mansions to little cottages. Although the town has been dubbed "the B&B capital of the Midwest," it doesn't mean the B&B market is tapped out, by any means. Fred Schmidt, who oversees the local business chamber, says, "They all do pretty well because we have so many visitors, and at the same time there's a lot of turnover so you'll often find a B&B up for sale." My advice: spend a week in Saugatuck, stop in at the B&Bs, and talk to the friendly owners to scope out the market and see what's available. But be prepared to discover you don't want to leave. Fred, a onetime New Yorker who retired here eight years ago, says: "You won't get me out of here except in a box."

What It'll Cost You: The average home goes for $252,400, but a nice B&B starts at $500,000 and they can run way up. Keep in mind you're buying a home and a business, and a well-run B&B should pay all the expenses, including your financing.
Inside Tip: Jeff Wilcox of Coldwell Banker Woodland Schmidt says, "You can get a very comfortable retirement home in the middle two hundreds" in the underappreciated Sennville neighborhood.
Bonus Fact: If you're a retiree here, you'll save on taxes because

Michigan has homesteading rules. That means retirees don't pay
taxes to run the schools because they don't have kids using them.
Sunny Days: 159/year.
Median Age: 46.

CAMBRIDGE   Massachusetts

A Prime Spot for Book Lovers

For a true bibliophile, opening a bookstore is a way to take your
lifelong passion and share it with the world—all while making a
living. But dreams can be difficult to turn into a reality, unless
you find the perfect spot. To my thinking, Harvard Square in
Cambridge is a book lover's best bet.

Cambridge is the brainiest four square miles in all of America.
Higher education was born here, as Harvard University was
founded not too long after the arrival of the *Mayflower*. By the late
1700s, Cambridge had become known as "the home of the lite-
rati," and today that label still fits. Most important, the Harvard
Square area has the country's highest density of bookstores per
square mile, more than two dozen in all. They all happily stay in
business, so why not consider making one of them yours?

Cambridge welcomes independent booksellers with open
arms. Just as some places brag about their Italian restaurants,
Cambridge brags about its bookstores. And the more specialized
and offbeat, the better. Shops focusing on foreign books, poetry,
occult, or science fiction—all the best specialty bookstores are
found here. There's even Revolution Books, which specializes in
books promoting the Revolutionary Communist Party. To make
it as a bookseller here, you just gotta have a gimmick—or at least
a distinctive niche.

One reason bookstores do so well here is that there's plenty of
foot traffic. The streets tend to have a lively, fast-paced buzz
going pretty much all the time. They're jammed with health-

food stores and music shops next to one-of-a-kind little clothing boutiques offering everything from haute couture to Goth. On every corner there's somebody juggling or riding a unicycle—or both. There are high-stakes chess matches, and everywhere you look, people spill out onto the old brick sidewalks from the cafés and jazz bars, looking for the next diversion. If your bookstore stays open late, you'll get all sorts of wandering souls, including the panicked students desperate to find something for next week's term paper, the date-night couples trying to impress each other with how smart they are, and of course the tourists who feel the pressure to actually learn something while they're visiting Harvard.

People in Cambridge don't like big retail chains. A few years back, the square was invaded by giants such as Abercrombie & Fitch, but there's been a backlash against the chains and a renewed emphasis on keeping small local stores alive and well. There's even a program that lets passersby know if a store is locally owned by placing a CAMBRIDGE LOCAL FIRST decal in the shop window.

You won't need a prime spot with high rent and a lot of space to run a bookstore here. You don't even need a ground-level window. In fact, a number of the square's existing bookstores operate successfully out of basements or second-floor spaces. In Harvard Square, book lovers have a way of finding you.

What It'll Cost You: To set up shop, expect to pay annual rent of anywhere from $50 to $150 a foot in Harvard Square, which might sound high, but it's a lot lower than it was a few years ago. The average home price in Cambridge is a whopping $552,600, and lots of home owners offset their expenses by renting expensive rooms to hardly starving students.

Inside Tip: You can get a nice condo or a modest house for less than $300,000 if you venture just outside Cambridge proper into the adjoining area of Somerville.

Sunny Days: 201/year.

Median Age: 33.

AUBURN-OPELIKA   Alabama

All Golf, All the Time

Millions of us say we plan to retire someday and "play a little golf." It's not my thing, but I understand the allure. I appreciate the dedicated souls such as my husband, who stands in front of mirrors perfecting his backswing, has nightmares about sand traps, and wakes up in the morning having dreamed of birdies. For these addicts, there's a place in eastern Alabama that should be called Nirvana, though its proper name is Auburn-Opelika.

These twin university towns have been named the best golf spot in America by *Golf Digest*. To understand why, you have to start by appreciating that Alabama is the number-one golf state in the country right now. In the late 1980s, the state decided to invest big bucks to create a spectacular "golf trail" running through the entire state. The legendary golf architect Robert Trent Jones was hired for the job. If Jones is the Michelangelo of golf-course makers, this trail is his Sistine Chapel: 432 holes of golf, all in natural settings. The layouts are designed with the Jones rationale that nobody remembers easy golf courses, but you never forget the ones that push you to raise your game to a higher level. The courses are demanding enough for pros, but Jones designed them so that players of all levels could enjoy them, too—he created tee markers pegged to ability level rather than gender or age.

Jones loved all the courses on his groundbreaking Alabama golf trail, but he had a special place in his heart for the Grand National in Opelika—he said it was the single greatest site for a golf course that he'd ever seen. Thirty-two of the fifty-four holes can be found on Lake Saugahatchee's finely sculpted shores. Because the holes don't border one another, "you feel like you're by yourself when you're playing," says Grand National golf director Scott Gomberg, adding, "though you might see deer or a wild turkey running around not far away." Gomberg says that this is a course you can grow old with. It has an eighteen-hole par-3 that's great for retirees, with short holes that still manage to be challenging. And all of it is extremely affordable. At Grand National you pay only $1,300 a year for unlimited green fees—at a private club you'd pay twenty times as much in initiation fees and monthly charges. And if you need a break from Grand National, Auburn-Opelika has two other top-rated courses in Auburn Links and Indian Pines.

When you're not golfing, there's plenty more to do. You can savor the old-fashioned feeling of these classic southern towns, which have some of our country's best historic Greek revivalist and Victorian buildings. Each spring Auburn-Opelika is awash in brightly colored azaleas and magnolias, and the folks down here love to celebrate their heritage with events such as the Victorian Front Porch Tour, when homes are decked out with life-size Victorian figures, live costume characters, and flowers beyond your imagination.

> **What It'll Cost You:** You can snatch up a nice three-bedroom, two-bath house of about 1,600 square feet for an average of $150,000 in Opelika. Auburn is a little pricier, with houses and condos in the low 200s.
> **Bonus Fact:** Alabama is one of the lowest tax states in the country.
> **Sunny Days:** 217/year.
> **Median Age:** 25.

GREAT PLACES FOR GOLF ADDICTS, BY REGION

Northeast/Mid-Atlantic: Perth Amboy, New Jersey. So how does a town without a single decent golf course end up being named by the golf press as "the unofficial golf capital of the U.S."? By being in exactly the right place. Perth Amboy happens to be in a spot that has easy access to twenty-five of the top hundred golf courses in the country, all of them within 150 miles.

This oceanfront town went through hard times in past years, which left many of its old Victorian homes languishing on the market, but it's on the comeback and now's a great time to get in cheaply. The newly refurbished waterfront features new condos, and shops are being built alongside the reclaimed Victorian homes that have always been the heart of the town. There's also a new high-speed ferry that zips you into Manhattan, sure to make home prices jump in the next few years. But the real attraction is the dozens of great golf courses, all within driving range.

Midwest: Sheboygan County, Wisconsin. Golfers fantasize about playing in Scotland, where soft natural beauty abounds and you can lose yourself in the purity of the game. But if you close your eyes and open them in rural Sheboygan County, about halfway between Milwaukee and Green Bay, a similar oasis exists. This modest working-class area has five great courses—one, known as Whistling Straits, is even deemed world-class, considered by many to be one of the top five courses in the world. Because this is a walkers-only course, there are no distractions from carts as golfers enjoy the towering dunes and views of Lake Michigan from all eighteen holes. And when you're done golfing, you can munch on bratwurst, the local delicacy, at Sheboygan's beautiful marina.

Northwest: Bandon, Oregon. Bandon is a place for people who love golf and other fine pleasures, such as a walk on a beautiful secluded beach or a stroll through a charming old fishing village. But let's start with the golf: Bandon Dunes has three distinctly different courses built on a beautiful stretch of sand dunes perched one hundred feet above the Pacific Ocean. A dozen holes run along a cliff that provides a view of the pristine shore below. Next, the beaches around here have some of the most beautiful seashells you'll find anywhere. And Bandon's Old Town is a half-dozen blocks of shops and galleries running right alongside the harbor, where local fishermen pull in their catches right on the docks. Bandon is one of the last unspoiled and undiscovered coastal towns out West.

LAKE CHELAN   Washington

Plant Your Grape Seeds Here Before Everyone Else Does

True wine lovers often share the dream of one day running their own winery. If that's your passion, don't just follow the herd to Napa. These days there are wine regions spread out around the country where the land is cheaper and no less fertile. The great state of Washington has emerged as the second-largest wine producer behind California, and there's a little spot nestled in the North Cascades National Forest called Lake Chelan (pronounced "shell-ON"), where you can still get in early and plant your grape seeds before everyone else does.

Lake Chelan has long been an attraction to vacationers and retirees because it's a pristine, glacier-fed lake. In years past, the shores along the fifty-mile-long lake were lined with apple trees. But today the apple trees are giving way to vineyards. Lake Chelan now has more than fifteen wineries, and many of them have spectacular lake views that make their tasting rooms a delight for all the senses. The lake helps to moderate temperatures and acts as a natural conduit between the rugged mountain peaks above and the fertile valley below. The resulting growing conditions are particularly good for pinot noir grapes, which thrive in the warmth and moisture.

So far only two hundred acres have been planted in this new wine region, but plans are under way to plant hundreds more. "In five years, it'll probably be too late to get anything there, because already we're seeing speculators start to come in and buy up the property from local farmers," says Deborah Daoust of the Washington Wine Commission.

Though it's growing fast, the area around Lake Chelan still has a feeling of remote wilderness. A thirty-mile stretch of the lake remains completely undeveloped, and there are campgrounds along the lake accessible only by boat. In the lakeside region known as Stehekin, where miners and trappers once lived, current residents survive without telephone lines or roads and do everything via the lake. In fact, the whole area is a boater's paradise. The region also draws wilderness buffs who hike the mountain trails in search of wildflowers and the endangered local mountain goats. But more and more these days, people are coming to Chelan in search of affordable vineyards surrounded by some of the most beautiful country in the great Northwest.

What It'll Cost You: The median home price in Lake Chelan is $230,500. If you're looking for land to develop for a vineyard, farmland here goes for as low as $1,000 an acre, but you'll have to put in your own irrigation.

Inside Tip: The lake is big enough that you don't have to be right on it to get great water views. You can get a lake-view house for under $300,000, whereas a waterfront house will cost you twice as much or more.

Sunny Days: 196/year.

Median Age: 42.

GREAT PLACES FOR WINEMAKERS, BY REGION

Northeast/Mid-Atlantic: Charlottesville, Virginia. There are lots of reasons Charlottesville is a great place to live: it's rich in history, it's got parks galore, it's a booming college town, and it's surrounded by the Blue Ridge Mountains. But what most people don't know is that this area is also in the heart of a growing wine region. Virginia's local wine business has tripled in size since the early '90s, and the state now has more than 120 wineries. Charlottesville has proved particularly attractive to newcomers, including musician Dave Matthews, who recently opened a winery in the area. The weather here is similar to European vineyards, and merlots and cabernets do particularly well.

Midwest: Grand Traverse Bay, Michigan. The area around Traverse City, site of the National Cherry Festival, is known for cherries, not grapes. But the region is blossoming as a wine country and has recently been producing a nice variety of pinot noirs, chardonnays, Rieslings, and, not surprisingly, some cherry wines, too. Traverse City is a hopping waterfront town with streets lined with great little shops, including eateries that specialize in "pasties," a kind of meat-and-potato turnover. It also has its own airport, which makes it convenient for a variety of people who come here to vacation. As you move north from the town, there are a couple of lovely peninsulas, Old Mission and Leelanau. There you'll find beaches, a couple of cute little artists' havens, and vineyards that produce half of Michigan's grapes. The lake effect protects the vines and extends the growing season while the recreational fun on the lake keeps the local residents happy.

South: Texas Hill Country. Wine and wildflowers—you'll find plenty of both in the Hill Country of Central Texas. This rugged limestone hill terrain, which borders on two highly livable cities, San Antonio and Austin, has helped to make Texas the fifth-leading wine-producing state in the country. Locals have started wondering if it will be "the next Napa." There are now more than eighty wineries in place, but there's still plenty of wide-open space to put down roots. And the state is aggressively promoting wine as a major growth industry and offering lots of marketing support to local vintners.

More Regional Spots for Five Random Passions

Northeast: Cook in Providence, Rhode Island. If you long to master the culinary arts, you could go to Italy or France. But Providence is a lot closer and cheaper, and it just happens to have one of the best cooking schools in the country. The Johnson & Wales College of Culinary Arts has intensive full-time programs credited with producing some of our country's top chefs, but it's also geared to those who want a taste of cooking greatness without going for a full degree. And living in Providence, with its rich ethnic diversity, great restaurant scene, and street fairs galore, will provide ample tasting and sampling opportunities. Providence has always been known as the Renaissance City be-cause of its uncanny ability to reinvent itself. It's really living up to that name again, now that the waterfront area has been truly revitalized. There's an abundance of life and vitality there. If you want to be inspired, just go down to the river during the weekly summer event known as "WaterFire." The whole town gathers for an evening stroll as music plays, gondolas sail along, and mood lighting is provided by one hundred bonfires set on bra-ziers floating on the water. Median home cost here is $381,000.

South: Hot-tub in Hot Springs, Arkansas. When I retire, my personal idea of heaven on earth will be a room filled with hunky men all smiling at me and waiting to take me out to have some fun. But as I'm very married at the moment, I guess I'll wait a few years before moving out to Hot Springs, Arkansas. There are more venues to meet and collect friends in Hot Springs than anywhere else on earth. They have jazz, blues, and film festivals every season, and on Friday nights everyone turns out for the gallery walks. My favorite thing in Hot Springs is the "Running of the Tubs," when locals deck out their tubs, put them on wheels, and push them down the middle of the main street. How could you not fall in love with a town so ridiculous? But this place is really about indulging. You can bubble away in the natural thermal waters of Vapor Valley and get the famous forty-dollar two-hour massage at the Buckstaff Bath House every week. You'll have more than enough money because home prices (typically under two hundred thousand dollars) and property taxes are both surprisingly low here.

Mountain: Ski in Loveland, Colorado. If you want to live the next stage of your life as a ski bum, think about moving to Loveland. Whereas house prices in Vail, Aspen, Telluride, Sun Valley, and other ski towns have gone through the roof, you can be a bum on a budget in this town. Only forty-five minutes from Denver, Loveland's slopes are breathtaking, and you can ride to the summit on one of the highest chairlifts in the world—13,000 feet up! Some fancier ski towns are all about snow and show, but Loveland is a down-to-earth community that cares about more meaningful things, such as art. The town has a thriving community of working sculptors, and you'll see their work displayed all over town, out on the streets and in the parks, in the form of larger-than-life bronze re-creations of people and animals. The Corn Roast Festival each fall has free corn-eating and corn-shucking contests, plus a fancy parade. Best of all, a condo here costs just under $200,000 and the average three-bedroom house costs between $230,000 and $250,000. You'll have plenty of money left to pay for your lift tickets.

West: Surf in, of course, Surf City, California. Technically this town is called Huntington Beach, but it's had the alter-ego name of Surf City ever since it was immortalized in the Jan & Dean song four decades ago. Back then it was a mecca for surfers and anyone else yearning for the laid-back California lifestyle. And that's still true today, thanks to its eight miles of gorgeous uninterrupted beachfront with monster waves that just keep crashing. Huntington Beach is host to more than thirty national and international surfing championships each year. But it's not just the waves that draw people here—it's the culture. The sunglasses, the souped-up hot rods, the quirky lingo, the funky fashions, and the obsession with surfboard design—all part of a phenomenon and a lifestyle well documented in the town's International Surfing Museum—make Surf City a world all its own. Median home price is a very steep seven hundred thousand dollars, but nearly half the people living here rent, and you can get a nice two-bedroom apartment not far from the beach for under $1,500 per month.

Northwest: Garden on Whidbey Island, Washington. Just set foot on Whidbey Island and you'll find you have a green thumb. The island, located in Puget Sound off the coast of Washington, is just thirty miles from Seattle and is known for its lush gardens where everything blooms and grows. The island has one of the finest rhododendron collections in the world. In addition to the lavish plants, artists and creative types easily take root here. They've created their own little art colony on the island with lots of galleries, a 1930s movie house, and even a Tibetan Buddhist monastery. A three-bedroom house in the Oak Harbor neighborhood runs in the middle three-hundred-thousand-dollar range. Whidbey is, for the most part, a quiet, peaceful place, but the islanders like to play games for fun. Each year they have a giant mystery game with everyone in town vying to solve a fictitious crime. It gets very competitive as neighbors try to outsleuth one another by gathering clues from the local paper, but it all adds up to one of the friendliest (and prettiest) cities in America.

Chapter 4

Forming a New Community

*Y*ou've got to come see this—I think I've found the perfect place for us," Dick Roth said over the phone to his wife, Karen. This struck Karen as a little odd. "At the time," she says, "I thought we'd supposedly already found *the perfect place."*

Just a few months earlier, the Roths—recent empty nesters—had packed up and left their suburban Michigan home to go to New Mexico. Dick, a physics professor in his mid-fifties, opted for early retirement, though he and Karen, a nurse, had no intention of slowing down much. They moved to New Mexico because of the vibrant culture, the local arts scene, and great weather that allowed for year-round running and cycling. They found themselves a nice little house in Albuquerque and they were all set.

But something important was missing. "Dick and I both grew up surrounded by big extended families," says Karen. "We like to be around people." What they encountered in their first few months living in Albuquerque was a typical suburban lifestyle in which unseen neighbors pull their cars into attached garages and lower the doors behind them. "You're lucky if you get a wave," says Karen.

Meanwhile, Dick stumbled across something unusual going on

nearby in Santa Fe. He heard that a group of people had staked out a nice little seven-acre parcel of land with great views and were planning to build their own neighborhood from the ground up. Dick went out to visit the spot and talked to some of the people involved, and that's when he phoned Karen.

Over the next few years, the Roths and twenty-seven other households built the neighborhood from scratch and called it "Commons on the Alameda." All the residents designed their houses differently but with a common theme and style. They wanted to create the look of a southwestern hacienda village. The houses are broken into four clusters, with a small plaza or placita in the middle. A large main courtyard with a burbling fountain sits at the heart of the village, and the neighbors also built a common house.

Cars are banished from view and you have to park in back of your house. The idea here is that whenever you come out your front door, you have no choice but to stroll through the common area, where you'll find your neighbors digging and planting together in the cooperative gardens. The whole community was created with an emphasis on sharing, including a couple of group meals per week in the common house with neighbors taking turns as the cook. Once a month everyone gets together and spends the day doing odd jobs, clearing the grounds, or fixing the fence that runs along the perimeter of the community.

But amid the togetherness, there were early squabbles. "We had to learn how to get along as a group," says Karen, adding, "We've all learned to respect one another and appreciate each other's differences." And there are differences: the community includes people from all walks of life. "We've got lawyers, doctors, artists—we've even got an eighty-year-old sex therapist," says Karen. There are other retirees like the Roths, but there are also families with young children. "I couldn't live around just older people," says Karen. "The young people keep things fresh and new around here." Six babies have been born to the community, and the Roths say they feel a deep connection to the children. "It's like the extended family that we were used to, growing up," says Dick. "That was something we felt like we'd lost a little bit, and here we've gotten it back."

Take a moment to imagine yourself in the place of your dreams. When you picture it, who's there with you? Are you laughing with people who enjoy your sense of humor, sharing a story with a kindred spirit, or listening to someone you find absolutely fascinating? It's nice to be surrounded by sunshine and palm trees, but the people around you will impact your happiness more than anything else.

For many of us in the boomer generation, a sense of community is missing from our lives. The last time we felt like part of a strong community may have been college. Ours is a generation of proud, independent types, not eager-beaver joiners. Many of us have moved to different neighborhoods to suit our changing finances and shifting family needs. Sometimes we've hyper-focused on individual achievement in our fast-paced careers, and that, along with raising kids, left too little room for everyday friends and neighbors.

The solution for many boomers today is to seek out a community of like-minded souls. By surrounding ourselves with people who share our priorities and interests, it's much easier to build friendships. Whether the shared interest happens to be boating, getting back to nature, or saving the world, we have a center pole to dance around. Shared interests create instant rapport. They enable us to make deeper connections with others simply because we start the friendship in a more meaningful place. They're a shortcut to intimacy.

If you're a team player, this chapter's for you. Maybe you're someone who thoroughly enjoys the camaraderie of the office culture and some of your best friends are the people you work with. That's certainly true of me. When I sold my business, I missed most of all the people I worked with and the joy, struggles, and friendships we'd shared.

The loss of community in American life is a phenomenon that's been tracked in recent years by experts such as Robert Putnam, a

Harvard professor and author of *Bowling Alone*. He points out that it can be seen in everything from declining memberships in PTAs to fewer group card games, civic meetings, and bowling leagues. Add to this the increasing demise of fraternal organizations such as the Elks club and Freemasonry, and the bottom line is, aside from working, we don't do many things together anymore. Just the sound of that makes me feel sad. Many of us today have fewer people we can confide in or just shoot the breeze with. And given the fact that staying socially connected is key to being happier and healthier, the loss of community today is a very big deal.

For many of us, staying connected becomes an even bigger challenge in our fifties and sixties. Once our kids are out of the house, we often feel a growing hunger to socialize, mingle, laugh, and talk about what lies ahead. We long to get back to something we experienced while growing up in large extended families or going to school with our pals. We look to reclaim the vibrant, supportive group of people we knew and enjoyed— people who shared our interests, who might notice and even miss us when we're not there.

There's also the fear of ending up alone. Some of us in our fifties, and a few as young as forty, are already wondering who the heck will help care for us in our later years. We're dreading the prospect of finding ourselves in some faceless retirement community or old-age home. Today's new trend of retiring with friends and forming some type of shared living arrangement is a way to comfortably transition into our older years, safe in the knowledge that we'll always be surrounded by familiar faces and kindred spirits. The basic understanding is that you'll take care of me, I'll take care of you, and together we'll have a good old time.

But how do we make it happen? That's what a growing number of boomers are trying to figure out. We're experimenting with new forms of shared living arrangements and tinkering with some of the old ones. In some instances we're reaching way back to our hippie days and the deep roots we planted then.

Welcome to the Twenty-First-Century Commune

At the forefront of the community trend is a growing phenomenon known as "cohousing," in which people in their fifties and sixties get together and decide they're going to live together in a circle of side-by-side houses all set around a big common space. Here the residents maintain separate lives with ample privacy but periodically get together to share meals and make joint decisions on how to run their new community. It's not exactly like a commune; each person gets to keep his or her own money and house. But everyone pitches in to fund the shared facilities. Unlike Woodstock, there's no "free love," but there is a great sense of community. For some of us weaned in the '60s, the concept echoes back to a happy point in our younger lives when we had real comrades.

I don't think you have to be an old nostalgic hippie to see the appeal of cohousing, to recognize it as a good alternative to the conventional retirement home. Charles Durrett, an architect and author who coined the term "cohousing" and has helped popularize it in the United States over the past decade, was first struck by its potential when he observed cohousing communities in Denmark some twenty years ago. Older Danes, looking for ways to avoid being shipped off to old-age homes, set up a bunch of shared housing communities among friends who wanted to age in place. They gardened together, cooked meals in groups, and looked out for anyone in the group who got sick or needed help. They describe themselves as "more than neighbors and less than family," says Durrett.

This model became the blueprint for a cohousing project that Durrett and his partner, Kathryn McCamant, organized in Davis, California, in the early '90s. Today there are more than one hundred cohousing developments around the country—most in California, Washington, Massachusetts, and Colorado—and they're starting to spread across the country at a rate of fifteen to twenty new ones a month. Surely the concept has come of age. Cohousing expert Tony Sirna states that most of the newer communities are being built by disaffected boomers who are "weary of car-dependent McMansion sprawl." Durrett adds, "The concept appeals to boomers because, by their nature, they need to be in control of their own lives—it's the only way they can be happy." But more than control, it's about the camaraderie. It's about the safety of neighbors keeping an eye out for one another. It's about the fact that there's always someone around to feed the cat when you're away. "We look out for each other," says Ellen Coppack, eighty, who lives in a Davis, California, cohousing development with several of her good friends.

To date, most cohousing developments have been multigenerational, but there is a trend now toward elder cohousing, which usually involves adults fifty-five and up. Houses are designed with step-free entrances and wheelchair-accessible doorways. The particular elder model that cohousing developers expect to take hold can be seen in Boulder, Colorado—Silver Sage Village is built right next to a multigenerational cohousing community named Wild Sage. The idea is that the younger residents can interact with the older ones, with the needs of each group being met with help from the other.

Can't Find the Perfect Neighborhood? Build It!

So how does a cohousing development get started? It usually begins with idle chatter among friends, talking about where they might like to live and whether they want to live there together. If the talk leads to action, it typically proceeds as follows:

1. **The group draws up some rough plans or sketches** of what they'd like their housing complex to look like.

2. They approach a real estate developer—either a developer who specializes in cohousing projects (you can find one of those on the Cohousing Association of the United States Web site at cohousing .org) or a general developer who can follow the established cohousing design model currently in use around the country.

3. Before anything gets built, a site must be found and acquired. If you're building a community in the wilderness, no problem; but if you want to build one in your favorite town or city, it can cost millions to buy up enough land for a group of houses. The cost is usually divided evenly among the community members.

4. Wherever you decide to build, you must get special zoning clearances from the local government. Some towns frown on these shared housing developments, whereas others (particularly in California, Colorado, and Massachusetts) tend to welcome them because they represent an efficient use of land.

5. The actual building of the complex typically incorporates the design plan of the residents—can we put a garden here, a tennis court there?—while also incorporating basic cohousing design principles, which specify that houses should face toward a central courtyard, with walkways creating a smooth flow through the complex and to the shared common house. Cars are generally parked in back of the properties, out of sight.

6. When everything is done and the new community members finally get to move in together, that's when the real work starts, as everyone begins the ongoing process of learning to live with one another while sharing community management responsibilities.

The "Golden Girls" Option

A typical cohousing community has fifteen to twenty households, and trying to create a whole new neighborhood of that size is not easy and can take years to get done. So instead some people look for a simpler, scaled-down approach to group retirement living and are opting for a group house. The big trend right now seems to involve divorced/unmarried/widowed female friends living together in what is affectionately known as a "*Golden Girls*" house.

Joan Forrester has set up this type of living arrangement with her sister, Lois McManus, and her friends Joanne Murphy and Nancy Rogers. Together the four women share two retirement homes—one in the northeast, the other in the sun belt. "One is on a golf course, the other's on a lake," says Joan. "By sharing, the cost of living in the two houses is greatly reduced." Both houses are owned by the two sisters, and the two friends pay rent. Should one sister die, they have an agreement that the other gets to live in the houses as long as she wants before they are passed along to heirs.

Joan says the disadvantages of house sharing include loss of privacy ("we all previously lived alone," she says) as well as the unavoidable reality that "sometimes, someone just gets on your nerves a bit. But for the most part, the interaction between people is a real benefit of living with others." Her housemates have a wide variety of interests and activities, Joan says, and she's sometimes "dragged along" and ends up meeting more people and doing more things than she would if she lived by herself. Plus, she says, "we read each other's magazines, we support each other when it comes to medical issues, and we have a ready-made foursome for golf."

Increasingly, as people form their own communities, they are doing it based on shared interests or a common lifestyle. Jon Parsons, publisher of an online magazine that tracks communities, says that there are six thousand people in the United States and Canada who now live among others with shared interests. This includes communities formed for gays and lesbians, aging hippies, environmentalists, vegetarians, bikers, boaters, and people who live in the buff. Doug Butler, a resident of the nudist community in Florida known as Caliente, says having a shared lifestyle with his neighbors "automatically gives you something to talk about and creates a bond. Before this, we lived in a suburban neighborhood in Virginia for eight years and only knew two of our neighbors. Here, everybody knows everybody."

Taking the More Conventional Route

When it comes to people retiring in shared communities, the most popular form is the so-called active adult community. It started in Arizona and Nevada decades ago but has seen explosive growth in recent years, with hundreds of them sprouting up in virtually every state. Many are restricted to residents fifty-five and older, but some have a mix of young professionals and active older adults.

The common denominator in these communities is the word "active"—earlier versions were centered around golf and tennis, but newer ones expand the menu of activities to include Pilates classes, hiking, and biking. With the increased diversity, it's now possible to find an adult community that's less generic and more suited to your personality and lifestyle, like the Anthem Ranch community outside Denver, which clearly caters to the adrenaline-rush crowd. Activities there—skydiving, white-water rafting, and hot-air ballooning—could scare anybody but the brave few.

These days many boomers tend to choose an active adult community because it's close to where they've lived, near family members, or near a job. Nearly one-third of people living in these communities still work. Perhaps the biggest plus of going to an active adult community is that it's all so easy. You don't have to assemble a group, create a neighborhood, or even figure out how to share a house. Everything's taken care of for you, from the amenities to the easy-care homes to the built-in social events. But to independent-minded boomers used to going their own way and making their own plans, this one-size-fits-all life-style can also be a turnoff. The connection among residents is much looser than in a shared home or cohousing complex; ger-ontologist Maria Dwight cautions, "It may be a 'community' in name only."

Active Adult Communities: Seven Grown-Up Questions to Ask

What kind of medical facilities do you have? Some active adult communities have an on-site medical room or doctor. If not, they should provide access to quick and easy transportation to a nearby hospital.

What does the annual home-owners' fee cover? It should, but sometimes doesn't, cover the use of the swimming pool and club-house, as well as all basic amenities excluding golf.

How long have you been open? Generally, the longer it's been open, the older the residents are.

Can you open up your books for me? Don't be afraid to ask the management of the community for financial information. Those budgets are public documents, explains Dave Schreiner, an execu-tive with Pulte Homes, which runs active adult communities na-tionwide. You especially want to look at how often they've raised fees on home owners; the hikes should be no more than the rate of inflation.

What kind of "mental" activities do you provide? Active adult communities tend to play up golf and tennis, but you can play only so much before your mind goes. The better communities now offer activities that involve arts, crafts, and continuing-education classes.

How do I get downtown from here? No matter how great the community seems to be, you'll need to get out among other people to maintain your sanity. Make sure that transportation to the nearest downtown area is accessible and quick.

Is everybody here local? The reason you're asking is because a good community should be a magnet that draws people from farther away than just the next street over. Also, if everybody is from the same area, the place may be cliquish.

Common Denominators

Whichever type of community you opt for, there are a few things to keep in mind. If you're going to live with friends, choose the core group wisely. Durrett warns that attempts to form small housing communities among a handful of friends often don't work out because some in the group are noncommittal; they stall, hem and haw, and eventually drop out. Also, he says, you can't look for the same things in a housemate as you do in a friend. Whether someone is fun matters less than whether he or she is responsible and cooperative. "When it comes to the good buddy that you like to have a beer with," Durrett says, "you might be better off just leaving that person as your friend."

If you want to test out living in a group beforehand to see how it works, you might consider trying something as extreme as what Joan Forrester did before forming her Golden Girls house: "The four of us took a two-and-a-half-month trip in a motor home traveling across the country," she says. "We figured that if we could get along in a twenty-nine-foot motor home for that length of time, we could probably manage to live together."

BEST PLACES TO JOIN A COMMUNITY

AUSTIN   Texas

Join the Hippest Trailer-Park Community in America

Austin is known for its music, its free-spirited people, and its pecan trees. The Pecan Grove RV Park has all three, plus a lake view and a location to die for. The RV park is a funky oasis smack in the middle of the most desirable neighborhood in one of the hippest towns around. Buy a condo in these parts and it'll set you back more than half a million dollars. But a simple lot at Pecan Grove, big enough to hold a forty-foot Airstream with room left over for a rock garden in front, costs just a few hundred dollars a month.

Forget your preconceptions about trailer-park inhabitants: Pecan Grove is home to movie stars (Matthew McConaughey has been part of this community in past years), young high-tech entrepreneurs, folk singers, certified public accountants, one professional clown named Doodle Bug, and a growing number of retirees. There are about eighty full-time residents in all. What draws everybody to this unassuming mobile-home park? For starters, it's those towering pecan trees, which create a cool, shady haven from the Texas sun and transform the place into what one resident calls "the emerald forest."

It also doesn't hurt that Pecan Grove is situated on gorgeous Town Lake, filled most days with kayaks and paddleboats. There's a tree-lined hiking and biking trail that circles the lake and crosses over the water by way of small bridges. Then there's the nearby Barton Springs Pool, one of the crown jewels of Austin. Three acres in size, the pool is fed from underground springs, and the water averages sixty-eight degrees year-round. Within walking distance is downtown Austin with its famous Sixth Street, a club-filled magnet for musicians and music lovers from all over the world. The Pecan Grove RV Park has been known to set up its own stage out back for impromptu concerts, known as "rash bashes" because there's so much poison ivy growing near the stage.

Some people at Pecan Grove come and go, but many just park their RVs here and never leave. Residents customize their little sites in quirky ways. One installed an inground fish pond in front of his RV, another built a complicated fountain, and someone else planted a cactus garden with upside-down wine bottles forming the border.

Jerry Brooks, sixty-five, is one of those settled in for the long haul, along with his wife, Maggie. "This is probably one of the world's best-kept secrets," he says. "It's also a close-knit community and we all look out for each other."

What It'll Cost You: Less than $500 a month, including electricity.
Inside Tip: Put your name on the waiting list now, as it may be a year or longer before a space opens up.
Sunny Days: 228/year.
Median Age: 32.

KNOXVILLE   Tennessee

For Boat Lovers Who Love Boat Lovers

"Boating in the Knoxville area is a well-kept secret," confides Don Eatock, a local resident who stays afloat much of the year. As Don explains, the interconnected flowing design of the local waterways in Knoxville is a boater's dream, and it all happened in response to a flood in the Tennessee Valley years ago. Today a boater can set sail from Knoxville and travel more than six hundred miles down to the Ohio River. Once there, you can turn south at the Tennessee-Tombigbee Waterway and go another 450 miles all the way to the Gulf of Mexico outside Mobile Bay in Alabama. All counted, that's more than one thousand miles of uninterrupted travel on smooth waters through several different states. There are parks, anchorages, and docking facilities all along the way with fellow boaters ready to welcome you.

The clean lakes and rivers of eastern Tennessee, with tall mountains as a backdrop, make this some of the most beautiful land in the country. The local boaters take full advantage, with many of them out on the water eight months of the year. In the off-season the lakes are drained and cleaned, making them sparkle the rest of the year. Boaters get together for float parties on the water, and when the University of Tennessee's football team plays at their riverfront stadium in Knoxville, an armada of boats sails to the arena to park and celebrate. They call it "boat-gating."

The rise of boaters in this area is a recent phenomenon. Eastern Tennessee was poor until the Tennessee Valley Authority came in and built dams. Then the areas outside of Knoxville began to blossom, and today a couple of those towns are becoming prime retirement spots. If you're a boat lover, you can't go wrong living in either Maryville, a gorgeous little town just twenty minutes from Knoxville, or Tellico Lake, about a half hour farther south.

Maryville has a nice mix of transplanted retirees, locals, and students. It has its own four-year liberal-arts college, and you can practically walk to the Great Smoky Mountains National Park and to the airport. Tellico Lake is pricier, but the lots are bigger and the lake itself is a pristine gem. Plus, there are four beautiful local golf courses.

A third option is to live right in Knoxville, which is on the Tennessee River with great boat access. The hottest new place in town is "The River Project," with luxury condos being built all along the water's edge. When the project is finished, it'll have its own river walk, with pedestrian bridges crossing over the river, and lots of upscale shops and outdoor markets. It will probably become some of the most desirable real estate in Knoxville. But for those among us in love with boating, the prime real estate will always be right on the water.

> **What It'll Cost You:** A three-bedroom house in Maryville costs about $170,000. Tellico Lake has lakefront lots starting at $300,000 where you launch your boat from your backyard. The average home price in Knoxville is $114,800.
> **Inside Tip:** The best buys are next door to Maryville in the Louisville area, says Lynn Waters of Realty Executive Associates. There you can get a waterfront lot starting at $100,000.
> **Bonus Fact:** Tennessee has the fourth-lowest tax burden of any state. There's no broad-based state income tax, and property taxes are low, too.
> **Sunny Days:** 204/year.
> **Median Age:** 35.

DAVIS   California

The Town of Schwinns and Shared Housing

The town of Davis, located just outside of Sacramento, is the ultimate biker's town—and I'm talking Schwinns, not Harleys. The League of American Bicyclists named it "the most bike-friendly town in America," and it's easy to see why. Davis has a perfect combination of flat terrain, moderate and dry weather, and a road system that makes plenty of room for two-wheelers.

You might expect that most of the people riding bikes in Davis would be students from the local University of California. But the fact is, *everyone*, of all ages, is out there pedaling. Men and women in full business attire cycle to work each morning, stopping for casual chats at stoplights in a way that drivers in their four-wheeled cubicles could never do.

Like many fun communities in America, this one was created by way of a grass-roots movement. Back in the '60s, the town was mad about cars, just like every other place in California. Local officials believed the bicycle was a relic that had outlived its usefulness. They saw no need for bike-friendly paths or traffic laws until a group of passionate bikers took on city hall and won. Davis became the first city in America to build a citywide system of bike lanes.

Today the city's whole identity is tied to biking. The city logo is a high-wheeler bike, there's a popular local radio show called *Bike Talk*, and there are bike picnics and a bike fair called "Cyclebration." Davis recently invested more than seven million dollars in the Putah Creek bike tunnel, connecting the south end of town to downtown and the college campus.

But Davis has more to offer than great biking. It also has lovely cherry trees and a vibrant art scene. Galleries and art-supply stores line the downtown streets. People are so devoted to nature that the town has even created a small highway underpass just for the benefit of local frogs! The community is a mix of farmers, university professors, students, natural-food lovers, and, of course, bikers. Everyone here is looking for a simpler, more down-to-earth way of life, and they all come together twice a week at the local farmers' markets, where the emphasis is on organic food.

Davis also happens to be the town where cohousing first got started in America. According to cohousing expert Charles Durrett, it remains an ideal place for anyone looking to start a new cohousing community with his or her friends. It's such an easy city to live in, and the local government takes pride in the success of local cohousing and truly supports those communities.

What It'll Cost You: As with most of California, Davis real estate is pricey. For single-family houses, the average price is $564,500. On the north side of town, new luxury condos will be priced at around $300,000 for a two-bedroom unit.

Inside Tip: If you want to be right in the heart of downtown, Realtor Ernesto Perez of Delta Homes suggests snapping up one of the

old downtown Victorians that come on the market occasionally.
They need refurbishing and are more affordable, meaning just
barely under $500,000.
Sunny Days: 267/year.
Median Age: 29.

GREAT PLACES FOR COHOUSING OR SHARED LIVING COMMUNITIES, BY REGION

Northeast: Beacon Hill in Boston, Massachusetts. The residents of Beacon Hill, a charming old-fashioned neighborhood in Boston known for its red brick sidewalks and nineteenth-century-style gas street lamps, have no desire to leave this adorable enclave, and who can blame them? With that in mind, local people have joined forces and come up with an innovative arrangement designed to help their residents "age in place." Beacon Hill Village is a nonprofit concierge service run by and for neighborhood residents aged fifty and up. With one phone call, you can get everything from help with shopping and medical appointments to handyman services to home-delivered meals. The three-hundred-plus members of the group pay annual fees ranging from $550 to $800, plus some small costs for other services. The Village's annual budget is up to three hundred thousand dollars, and the community continues to expand its offerings. Lectures, weekly lunches at restaurants, and trips to the Newport Jazz Festival have been added to the deal to foster a greater social connection among residents. The Village has also put together a handbook to guide others looking to set up their own concierge community (see its Web site at beaconhillvillage.org).

Mid-Atlantic: Riderwood Community in Silver Spring, Maryland. All the residents in this retirement community are over age sixty, but they sure don't act like it. On any given day, you'll find them building furniture for the poor, mentoring teenagers, and helping endangered turtles adapt to life on the community's eco-safe grounds. Most of all, Riderwood is a place where people seem to flourish, taking advantage of their unique talents. Maybe the setting helps—Riderwood is located on a beautiful, naturally wooded 120-acre campus. The community has attracted a disproportionate number of artists, teachers, entertainers, and creative types to live here, and that was part of the plan. Completed in 2007, Riderwood was designed with an eye toward endless stimulation and creativity. It has its own men's chorus and theater group, its own closed-circuit television channel with programming produced by the residents, and even its own clowns-in-training program. More than one hundred community-college classes are offered on site to the three thousand residents who live here. Apartments range from small efficiencies to large two-bedroom, two-bath units, and they're typically priced from $75,000 to $100,000 for the entrance deposit, with monthly fees of $1,000 to $1,500 after that. As one resident told the *Washington Post*, "I feel like I live on a cruise ship—without any seasickness."

Midwest: Zephyr Valley Community Cooperative in Rushford, Minnesota. If you don't want to wait around for years while developing your own cohousing community, there are lots of existing communities you can join as individual slots open up. Zephyr Valley Community Cooperative is a good example of a small, rural community open to newcomers. It consists of twenty-three people of all ages living in seven separate homes on 550 acres of stunningly beautiful land in southeast Minnesota. At the time of this writing, the community had six sites available for new homes to be added. The property includes a community center for occasional group meals as well as a spring-fed swimming pond and plenty of trails for walking and skiing. To see the property and find out more about the community, visit their Web site at zephyrvalleycoop.org.

West: Kiley Ranch in Sparks, Nevada. The term "master-planned community" (MPC) is often used loosely to describe just about any kind of housing subdivision. But in its truest form, a good MPC provides for all the living needs of its residents: housing, office buildings, and recreational parks and amenities, all in one place. Kiley Ranch, currently being developed in the hot little town of Sparks, near Reno, is a cutting-edge example of an MPC and is also part of a trend housing experts call "new urbanism." It's a suburban development designed to be its own self-contained village, with everything accessible by foot. Built on eight hundred acres with more than four thousand houses planned, the community has three activity centers: one where people will work, another where they'll shop, and a third where they'll socialize. All three are linked to the housing areas by an elaborate system of bicycle paths and walking trails, and the whole area will be densely packed with many different types of houses. The whole idea here is to create an easy living community while eliminating the typical problems associated with suburban living, such as houses that all look the same, inefficient use of land, and a car-dependent lifestyle with little opportunity for neighbors to interact. Kiley Ranch will be a few more years in the making, but if you want to check it out in advance, the Web site is at kileyranch.com.

CALIENTE   Florida

A Place for Nudes, Not Prudes

At Caliente, you won't spend any money on clothes. It's a nudist community, or what more politically correct people call "naturist," in the Tampa area. Either way, I think it's the best naked place around! There are other naturist resorts across the country that you can visit, but few are designed for year-round living and none offer the level of luxury you'll find here. In short, Caliente is the cream of the naturist crop. Residents live on a private 130-acre estate with more than 1,500 majestic oak and mature palm trees, three placid lakes, two lush islands, a massive lagoon pool, and a grotto waterfall.

Caliente, of course, means "hot," and the whole place has a mock Spanish flavor to it, with terra-cotta-tiled roofs and Spanish names for all the facilities. The houses here range from small casitas to huge mansions, and the central gathering spot is a massive 33,000-square-foot clubhouse, with a fancy restaurant, a cantina, a piano bar, and a discotheque.

Most people are nude all the time, but some wear wraps or open shirts. There are six hundred people of all ages in total, and needless to say, most are very sociable. "We've made some of the best friends of our lives here," says Doug Butler, fifty-eight, a retired home builder who moved here three years ago with his wife, Adele. "We've got doctors, lawyers, entrepreneurs, and Cuban émigrés. For some reason, people are much more willing to just come up and start talking to you at a nudist resort. It's like, if you're not wearing clothes, a lot of the other social pretenses are gone, too. Everybody just feels free to be themselves."

There's no golf at Caliente, but that doesn't stop people from riding around the community in little golf carts, many of them souped up and decorated to look like miniature sports cars. Everyone indulges in massages and body treatments at the club's giant spa. And the special events are, well, way out there! There's the annual on-premises nude auto show known as "Bare Bods and Hot Rods." There's a wild Halloween party ("you'd be amazed at the costumes," says Doug). And this year they'll be trying something new called "fluorescent tennis." Are you ready for this? At night, under black light, players will take to the courts nude, their bodies painted in glow-in-the-dark colors and the (tennis) balls painted, too.

What It'll Cost You: Pay $185,000 for a cozy one-bedroom with a little porch; fancier two-bedroom condos are in the $300,000 range; split-level town-house villas cost about $500,000. If you

> want to put up a million-dollar mansion, single-family lots go for
> $300,000.
> **Bonus Fact:** Once you've bought your home, membership fees
> are about $1,000 a year, which entitles you to discounts on all the
> clubhouse facilities.
> **Sunny Days:** 246/year.
> **Average Age:** 52.

VEDIC CITY   Iowa

Where Meditation Is on Everyone's Mind

Legend has it that in 1971, Maharishi Mahesh Yogi flew into
the middle of rural Iowa in a small pink plane and landed in
Fairfield, which he declared to be the new capital of Transcen-
dental Meditation (TM) in America. Maharishi is the man who
popularized meditation in America forty years ago by way of,
believe it or not, the Beatles. Back then, Maharishi served as the
spiritual advisor to the band and was sometimes referred to as
"the fifth Beatle."

Today, amid the cornfields of rural Iowa, Maharishi's chosen
spot has blossomed into the impressive Maharishi Vedic City, or
Vedic City for short. It currently has about five hundred full-
time residents, but the population is expected to double in the
next few years and eventually climb to about ten thousand
people.

It took a while for Vedic City to gather momentum, but now
it has its own university, a thriving cultural arts community, visiting notables, and an explosion of new housing geared to baby
boomers in search of a spiritually enlightened second act in their
lives.

At first glance the housing here looks like ordinary condos,
Cape Cod bungalows, and mansions. But "Vedic housing" has
its own completely unique design. *Vedic* is a Sanskrit word

meaning "totality of knowledge," and all the homes are designed with entrances facing east because that's where the sun comes up. The flow of a house is mapped out to correspond with the cycles of the sun and moon, and rooms are precisely sized according to mathematical formulas found in nature. The spacious central area of each home is designated as a quiet space, and there's a separate room specifically for practitioners of TM to meditate twice a day, twenty minutes at a time.

When you're not meditating, there's lots to do in Vedic City. The local Maharishi Vedic University provides lifelong-learning programs for retirees. There's also an international health spa, a newly built civic center with concerts and dance performances, and a "first Friday" art walk each month through the many downtown art galleries. Plus, there are two golf courses only ten minutes away.

Vedic City is full of surprises, and one is its entrepreneurial streak. Local people have opened shops and companies throughout the area, including lots of home-based businesses, ranging from finance to muffins to high-tech. City officials report that more than two hundred million dollars in venture capital has been invested in Fairfield and Vedic City companies during the past thirteen years, prompting outsiders to affectionately refer to this farming community as "Silicorn Valley."

What It'll Cost You: From $200,000 for a condo to $2 million for a Vedic mansion, take your pick.

Inside Tip: If you're looking for a bargain, you can forgo the Vedic-designed houses and buy a regular three-bedroom house right next door in Fairfield for less than $100,000. Then ride your bike to Vedic City and enjoy all the spiritual benefits.

Sunny Days: 199/year.

Median Age: 43.

SANTA FE   New Mexico

Somewhere over the Rainbow

Joy Silver opened RainbowVision two years ago as a place where gays and lesbians aged fifty and up can retire with like-minded souls—and with style. The place is designed to be, well, *fabulous*. With 146 condos on thirteen acres that overlook the beautiful desert mountains of New Mexico, there are rain-style showers and skylights in the condos and a glitzy "starlight lounge" with live cabaret shows. There's also a fitness center and spa named after Billie Jean King where you can get massages, try acupuncture, or bubble away in a hot tub. Other features include an arts studio, cooking classes with celebrity guests, and group excursions to the Santa Fe Opera.

Clearly, culture-rich Santa Fe is a great place for anyone to live, but it's also known as a gay-friendly city with an emphasis on diversity. It's no wonder Silver chose this town in which to open the first gay retirement community. It's been so successful, she's now planning to open a second one in Palm Springs.

Many of the residents at RainbowVision are in their fifties and still in their prime, but the community has been designed with assisted-living accommodations so that people can happily grow older here. I think it's a compliment that although Rainbow-Vision is obviously geared and promoted to the gay community, about 20 percent of RainbowVision residents are straight. They've picked the place because it's such a creative, fun-loving environment. One straight resident, who happens to be a ninety-year-old great-grandmother, explained her choice by saying, "I can't stand the regular retirement places. They're just for old people."

What It'll Cost You: Three-bedroom condos at RainbowVision are priced in the low $300,000 range.
Inside Tip: If you want to test it out first, there are rental units available.
Sunny Days: 313/year.
Age Range: 48 to 93.

Living Young

Emerging Cities and College Towns

*T*hirty years ago, when Joe and Debbie Karp were leaving New York City, Debbie cried as their car drove off by way of the Lincoln Tunnel. She loved New York and didn't want to leave. But warm sunshine and a safe family neighborhood beckoned in Florida. "As we drove away," Joe recalls now, "I said to Debbie, 'Someday we're coming back here, I promise.'"

It finally happened a few years ago as the Karps, in their sixties, began looking for an apartment in Manhattan. Most people move from New York to Florida to retire, but they found themselves going in the opposite direction—coming back from Florida so they could enjoy the best part of their retirement years in the heart of New York City. With their children grown, they decided the time was right to return to the place of their youth. "So we headed for the Upper West Side and found ourselves a good buy in a great building across the street from Lincoln Center," Debbie says.

"From there," adds Joe, "we can walk almost anywhere—and do we ever! We walk to Broadway shows—we caught the last showing of *The Pirates of Penzance* before it closed. The other day we walked *along Columbus Avenue to the flea markets and then stopped in at the little art cinema, where you can see the kind of film that never would've made it down to Florida." Down there, Joe says, "all you do is shop at the mall and then go out to eat and that's about it. And you're always stuck in a car. When people are so dependent on their cars, and then they get older and find they can't drive anymore, it's like they suddenly lose their independence—and Debbie and I don't ever want to be in that position. We want to be able to go where we want to go, whether it's by walking or hopping in a taxi or on a bus. At this point, if I never got in a car again, I'd be thrilled."*

Debbie regularly strolls over to Macy's to shop. She takes photographs in Central Park. She also likes to draw, so one day recently she went over to the Art Students League, paid a few bucks, and started drawing in a class with all of these New York artists. After that, she stopped into a Barnes & Noble, where a celebrity was plugging his new book. "I get to be a perpetual tourist," Debbie says. "Returning to New York at this point in my life really is the best of all possible worlds. I do precisely what I want, when I want, in a place that offers everything I want."

Who says you can never be young again? All you have to do is get yourself to the nearest fountain of youth. And don't bother looking for it in a stodgy suburb or a gated golf community. Instead, take a look in the downtown neighborhoods of a newly revitalized city. Or go to the nearest college town. Because the simple truth is, if you want to find someplace that'll make you feel young again, you have to go where the young people are.

Many of us have started to figure this out, which explains why the new trend of retiring to cities and college towns is picking up so much steam. If you're the kind of person who thrives on change and gets restless when things are too quiet and peaceful, this is the chapter for you.

I, for one, am hooked on city life, and I totally relate to Joe and Debbie Karp. For me, one of the great things about living in New York City is that even if you don't have ten bucks for a movie, you can get out and walk down any street and feel as if you've done something. The city keeps me moving, keeps my juices flowing, and frankly, it also allows me to be lazy. As long as the buzz is all around me, I don't have to do much of anything. I'm satisfied just to feel a part of the hubbub.

So many people make the mistake of thinking they need to slow down in retirement. They purposely remove themselves from the commotion of urban life. But I think a lot of us actually need that stimulation even *more* as we move into the next stage of life. The quiet suburbs are fine for raising kids. But once the kids are gone and we're less obsessed with climbing the career ladder, there are gaps to fill. And many of us learn to fill them by letting more life go on around us.

There's another reason why cities and college towns can become more appealing as we age. For all of us nostalgic boomers, it's a chance to turn back the page to a time when life was freer and more fun. Many of us spent the best years of our early twenties in a city or college town. We may have lived from hand to mouth at the time, but damn, we had fun, didn't we?

It was also a time in our life when we first got in touch with who we were as individuals. The historian William Strauss, an expert on differences between the generations, explains that when boomers go back to campuses and urban neighborhoods, "it's as if they are returning to their own personal beaches of Normandy." In other words, they're going back to the place that first tested them as individuals and helped to define them as adults. And so, in some ways, this desire to "live young" by moving to a more youthful environment is a movement of the soul.

But it's also practical. Cities and college towns offer many things that retirees need, such as transportation, walkability, nearby medical services, and an active work environment for those of us launching second careers. These places also foster learning in a rich cultural environment, which can be ideal for active boomers.

Living for the City

The college-town and back-to-the-city movements tend to overlap, particularly because some college towns double as mid-size cities, such as Ann Arbor and Austin. But there are also differences in what each locale has to offer retirees. College towns appeal to those who want a youthful lifestyle within a self-contained community, whereas cities tend to attract those who want a larger world without boundaries.

Kyle Ezell, the urban planner who coined the term "ruppies" (retired urban people), notes that where college-town retirees are sometimes returning to a place they've lived before, urban retirees typically venture into unfamiliar territory. "They may have lived in a city years earlier, but are likely to have spent the intervening years in the suburbs," Ezell says. "So when they come to the city, they have to make some adjustments." According to Ezell, some of the basic survival skills that downtown retirees must acquire include learning how to navigate public transport, getting used to walking again (Ezell recommends your first purchase be good walking shoes), and schlepping bags on your shoulder instead of loading up the car trunk. City retirees also need to adapt to living around a more diverse group of people, because everybody isn't just like you.

Joe Karp says that urban retirees also have to make an effort to "put themselves out there." Cities provide lots of opportunities for social interaction, but no one schedules bingo or creates other social activities just for you. "There's a risk that older people could become isolated in a city if they're not willing to make the effort to go out and do things," Joe says.

But the age-old image of the city as a cold, impersonal place is disputed by both city dwellers and urban-lifestyle experts. "Often, you're *more* likely in an urban setting to get to know local shopkeepers and neighborhood people, just because you're out walking around more than you are in the suburbs," says John McIlwain, a housing expert with the Urban Land Institute. And the social relationships that retirees form in cities tend to be more diverse and maybe even healthier, adds gerontologist Maria Dwight, who explains: "In suburban gated communities, you're kind of isolated with the same group of people and everybody knows each other's business. So there's a lot of talk about who's sleeping with whom or which neighbors are feuding, whereas in the city, you and your neighbors are part of a much larger world, where you talk about the theater or politics or just about anything."

I think there's more to talk about because the city affords a much fuller life. Aside from unlimited cultural opportunities, there's also more opportunity for full- and part-time work. As McIlwain notes, "Many retirees come to the city to pursue a second career—it's harder to do that if you're stuck in a retirement community in Sun City." And, too, there are more ways to help the many people all around you. You can find volunteer work wherever you live, but in the city the volunteer possibilities are endless, so you can find one that really suits you.

A Streamlined Lifestyle

Although city life offers lots more opportunities to get busy, it also means you can unload some of those jobs and chores that become especially burdensome for people as they age. Shoveling snow? Forget about it. Mowing the lawn? What lawn? As McIlwain puts it, "There's no house to take care of—you lock the door of your apartment or condo, and off you go."

McIlwain speaks from firsthand experience ever since he and his wife, both in their early sixties, moved from the suburbs to downtown Washington, D.C. "Our son left the house and moved downtown, and we said, 'Heck, we'll move downtown, too.'" The hardest part, he says, was giving up his suburban garden. "But that's part of the trade-off you have when you downsize for city living."

Spotting the Next "Hot" Neighborhood: Barb's Tips

When it comes to checking out an up-and-coming urban neighborhood, nighttime is the right time to snoop. You won't see much during the day because apartment dwellers are usually out working. But they're home by six or seven p.m., when the street life begins. Look for a few telltale signs, starting with the nightlife. You may have no intention of becoming a regular at the crowded disco where kids line up at the door each night, but be happy that it's there. It's a good indicator that the value of the local real estate is about to go through the roof. Don't worry if there are a few commercial tenants in the neighborhood. Young people move in first for cheap rent and bigger space. Then businesses follow. The first ones to open are the nightclubs and bars. After that, the restaurants and storefronts move in. Finally the yuppies come along, anxious to pay top dollar to live in the hip new neighborhood. That's when the old ghetto has turned "ghetto fabulous"!

When you check out a neighborhood at night, you can see if you feel safe. Size up the people you pass and look for young residents. The presence of a creative gay community is a sure sign that the neighborhood is about to emerge, assuring that the place you buy will explode in value.

There's one thing you can look for in the daytime while everyone's at work. I once asked a Harlem cab driver about the difference between two local neighborhoods, and he said one section was better than the other because in it were old people sitting on park benches, feeding the pigeons. That meant they weren't afraid to sit outside, he said, and the neighborhood was safe.

If you're moving to the city, downsizing is definitely part of the equation. Unless you're fabulously wealthy, you'll probably be moving to a much smaller space. But once you get used to the streamlined life, it can grow on you. "When we first left our house, we figured we needed a big spacious condo downtown," says McIlwain. "But now we've just downsized a second time by moving into a one-thousand-square-foot loft. With just the two of us, we really don't need that much space." And as for giving up that big backyard, Ezell says, "Think of it this way: your whole neighborhood is your backyard now."

Living Downtown: Who Says You Have to Be a Millionaire?

Most people assume that living in the city is more expensive than life in the suburbs. Who hasn't had the experience of being shocked by how much a night on the town can set you back? But when you're actually living in the city, it's a different story, says Joe Karp, who notes that his new life in a Manhattan co-op is no more expensive than his old suburban life in Florida. Here are some of the ways you save in the city:

Lower taxes. "The maintenance fees I pay for my co-op are cheaper than the property taxes I paid on my house," Joe says.

Lower insurance payments. "Home-owners' insurance has gotten particularly expensive in Florida—especially if you have wind-storm insurance."

Lower energy bills. Because he's heating and cooling a smaller space, Joe pays less to the utility companies.

No more paying at the pump. Joe figures the costs of buses and taxis are half of what he used to pay to fill up the car with gas.

Learn where the bargains are. Joe warns, "You have to budget yourself. When you're living in the city, you learn where the bargains are; know about the free activities and take advantage of them. And even though it's tempting, you can't eat out every night—that's a good way to go broke."

Going Back to School

If there's a retiree real estate trend that's just as strong as the back-to-the-city movement, it's the back-to-campus phenomenon. Take the vitality and excitement that a city has to offer, subtract the urban congestion, and add lifelong learning to the mix. When you squeeze it all down to a manageable midsize town, what you have is a college town. For a lot of us, it's the next best thing to heaven. That's partly because no one really retires in a college town, at least not in the classic "kick back and slow down" sense. Life among the ivory towers tends to be every bit as stimulating and challenging as big-city life, with a little homework added.

There are lots of obvious benefits provided by college-town life. For starters, you're surrounded by the palpable energy of youth and by incredible diversity. People come to college towns from all over the country as well as the world. It's an environment that tends to be very open and accepting. This means that when you move to a college town, you'll never feel like an outsider.

In fact, campuses value the input and wisdom of older people, and many towns offer them opportunities to share, teach, and be part of the youthful community of the college or university. "From the time we first arrived, we really felt we were welcomed here, and now we see ourselves as part of this community," says David Kimery, who, with his wife, Anita, both in their sixties, recently moved to Oxford, hometown of the University of Mississippi.

Like cities, college towns offer many employment possibilities for the retiree who wants to work as well as play. Not only do the universities create all sorts of jobs, but areas surrounding campuses often become thriving small-business hubs. And college towns are also very livable. They're compact and easy to get around. They generally have top-notch medical services, often affiliated with the university. This is why buying a home in a college town almost always proves a sound real estate investment, even though it may cost you 20–25 percent more than a home in a surrounding area. (See box below.)

Why College-Town Real Estate Gets an A

If you plan to retire to a college town but you're not ready to move just yet, you might want to send your money in advance and buy up some college-town real estate. There are few safer real estate bets than a college town with new students arriving every year, all in need of housing.

If you own a house or condo within walking or biking distance from campus, you can count on renting it year in and year out. In many college towns, the number of houses is limited by the size of the town itself, and some universities have actually been cutting back on student housing in recent years because of tight budgets. Meanwhile, college enrollment is enjoying double-digit growth and is expected to continue for the next decade as the children of the baby boomers pass through their college years. With housing demand outstripping supply, it's no wonder investment properties in college towns are usually 100 percent occupied, even in summer months. On top of that, property owners are able to raise rents year after year.

If you do decide to invest in property to rent, it makes sense to buy in the areas where the professors tend to live. They make better tenants than students and are not as likely to host a beer bash on your property. If you do rent to students, hire a weekly housecleaning service and include it in the rent.

If you value your sleep, you'll want to steer clear of fraternity row and the campus watering holes, but at the same time, don't stray too far from the action. One of the best things about college towns is that they're jam-packed with all kinds of cultural and entertainment activities—almost as much as you'd get in a major city. The differences are that tickets are more affordable here and you probably won't need to cab it from the show to the restaurant because most things are within walking distance. Restaurants are plentiful and usually cheap, with eclectic menus and lots of health-food joints geared to students. But guess what? Most students are either too broke or too busy studying for finals to enjoy all the great stuff. This means the "adults" get to have more than their fair share of fun in a college town.

Nonstop Learning

All of those lively activities aside, the main draw of college towns is simple. People go there to learn and grow, and it doesn't really matter what age you are. The idea that people over fifty would want to go back to school may have seemed like an oddity a few years ago, but not anymore. We've come to realize that there's no age limit on learning and the day you stop doing so is the day you get old.

As our generation embraces continuing education, colleges are returning the hug. Schools see retirees as a new opportunity to expand enrollment. "Colleges are inviting older people in, whereas in the past you used to have to work at getting into classes," notes gerontologist Maria Dwight. It's easy to audit courses without going through the rigors of the full enrollment process; often it's just a matter of asking a professor if you can sit in on lectures or perhaps join group discussions at the campus coffeehouse. But there are also more structured programs you can take advantage of, such as those sponsored by the Osher Lifelong Learning Institute or the Institutes for Learning in Retirement, which run separately from universities and are specially designed for older students. Classes are taught by university professors and local business leaders.

Some schools even offer special perks to draw older students into classes. Part of the reason David Kimery chose Oxford was because the university went out of its way to woo him by offering a package of free courses and credits not available to younger students. It worked: David, sixty-eight, is now reviving his old passion for mathematics, and he's not just auditing classes, he's going for a full degree. "And after I've done that," he says, "I may even go to graduate school."

BEST PLACES TO LIVE YOUNG

BURLINGTON   Vermont

Hippie Ideals Mixed with Hip Appeal

The popular image of Burlington is that of a cute Vermont hippie town, home to the founders of Ben & Jerry's ice cream. It's more than that, though—like Ben & Jerry's, this city has a lot of different and rich flavors.

Stroll through downtown Burlington and you'll witness a delicious blend of folksy and urban. The men with graying beards and ponytails mix easily with young rebels sporting tattoos. In between are countless other shades of humanity, drawn to Burlington because it provides the natural outdoor beauty they crave along with a great mix of culture and education. The city is home to both the University of Vermont and Champlain College, so it offers the benefits of a college town mixed with those of a small, thriving city.

Newcomers feel right at home when they move to Burlington. Part of the reason is that the high concentration of students injects youthful energy into the city. The median age here is thirty-two, a full five years younger than the national average, and the place manages to feel more like a village than a city. Everyone seems to know one another because everybody ends up on Church Street, a lovely European-style main street that is blessedly free of cars. Street performers do impromptu acts involving magic or music or some combination of the two.

Music is in the lifeblood of Burlington, which has launched bands that have risen to national fame, such as the rock band Phish. You'll have a hard time trying to pigeonhole the music here. Sure, there are lots of folk musicians, but it's also a town of classical-music lovers, and there's even a thriving hip-hop scene. One visitor from a big-city newspaper was astonished to discover that downtown Burlington also had jazz nightspots with sleek, minimalist décor, much like New York City's Tribeca, where people were sipping martinis and raspberry vodka gimlets. It's exactly that chic style that makes it attractive to sophisticated city folk.

Burlington is situated on a gorgeous body of water, Lake Champlain, with the Adirondack Mountains as a backdrop. And though Vermont gets cold in the winter, the lake effect actually moderates the weather a bit, making downtown Burlington a little warmer than the rest of the state. As soon as the weather warms in the spring, life emerges all around the lake. There's a glorious lakefront park and a fourteen-mile bike trail that winds along the lake's shore. As you circle Champlain, a number of small beaches serve as pit stops along the way.

In the winter, of course, there are many first-class ski mountains that surround Burlington, and that's another reason boomers here stay active and young. The ski resorts love having senior skiers, and all offer steep discounts on passes to keep them coming back.

When it's time to eat, keep in mind that Burlington is home to the nationally renowned New England Culinary Institute.

But save room for dessert: the Ben & Jerry's main factory is nearby, and the tour includes free samples.

> **What It'll Cost You:** The median home cost here is $253,000.
> **Inside Tip:** Downtown can get expensive, but the better bargains are found in the North End and New North End districts, according to Realtor Mary von Ziegesar of the local Lang, Lion & Davis firm. If you want mountain or lake views within walking distance of Church Street—nirvana, in other words—be prepared to pay $700,000 or more.
> **Bonus Fact:** Real estate prices in Burlington have seen a consistently steady appreciation of about 10 percent a year despite what's happening in other markets, so anything purchased here is usually a sound investment.
> **Sunny Days:** 157/year.
> **Median Age:** 32.

PANAMA CITY   Panama

Like South Beach on Sale

Everywhere you look, buildings are going up in Panama City: high-rise apartments, luxury condos, office towers. If you're searching for a young, emerging city, this is a textbook example.

The only mystery is why it took so long for Panama City, and Panama in general, to become a hot spot for people moving overseas. I guess you could blame it on the country's former political leaders, who've had a testy relationship at times with the West. In any case, the old obstacles are gone and the new Panama is not just embracing Americans, but is actually bending over backward to lure boomer retirees here.

For starters, when you move to Panama, there's almost no red tape to deal with. The country's *pensionado* (retirement) visa kicks in as long as you can show you have five hundred dollars in monthly income. You can buy property and not have to worry about paying any taxes on it for—*get this*—twenty years! And once you're living in the country as a pensioner, Panama showers you with lots of perks and freebies. You'll get 50 percent off public transportation, dinner checks, visits to the doctor, electrical bills, and even your movie tickets, which cost only two bucks to begin with! That's a big discount on a lot of stuff.

With all those incentives, you'd think the place was a hard sell, but it's just the opposite: Panama City is, as one American reporter recently noted, like South Beach without the velvet-roped lines and snobbery. It's become the fashion hub of Latin America, attracting more than its share of trendy celebrities, including Mick Jagger, who frequents the city's open-all-night Zona Rosa district. There's high culture here, including a new Guggenheim museum just going up, as well as casinos galore. Roam the lively streets of downtown and you'll find yourself in a melting pot of nationalities and cultures—Latino, but with a strong Caribbean island influence, lots of French, and a growing American presence.

Americans are more accepted here than in other Central American countries because of a long history of interaction between the countries over the Panama Canal. And speaking of the canal, it is one of the highlights of Panama City, an engineering marvel that still commands the attention of people who've lived in Panama City for years. The hundred-year-old canal is part of a rich and colorful history that goes all the way back to the days when the original version of Panama City was burned to the ground by the pirate Henry Morgan.

Today practically everything in Panama is a steal. You might be barely middle class in America, but here you'll feel as though you're rich. For a few bucks you can go down to the city's outdoor fish market and get a meal of seafood caught that day. Afterward you can wash it down with a thirty-five-cent ice-cold beer at a nearby bar.

One more thing to note about Panama: it's where the Atlantic and Pacific meet. On any given day you have your choice of two oceans. As one just-retired American puts it, "You can have breakfast by the Atlantic, and then go and have lunch by the Pacific."

> **What It'll Cost You:** Real estate prices are inching up a little, but tourist apartments average $60,000.
>
> **Inside Tip:** Some of the best deals are in the up-and-coming San Francisco district, according to Pedro Detresno of Pedro's Real Estate. A 3,000-square-foot house there can be had for $150,000.
>
> **Bonus Facts:** If you move here, you can import a car tax free. And about the weather, talk about consistency—average temperatures are 83° in January and 82° in July.
>
> **Sunny Days:** Approx. 216.
>
> **Median Age:** 26.

ST. GEORGE   Utah

Mecca for Action Junkies

This picturesque town in the southwest corner of Utah is made for action junkies of all shapes and ages, including lots of retirees who gravitate to St. George because they want to do anything but rest. St. George is definitely an emerging city, enjoying rapid growth in the past few years, and it also qualifies as a college town because of the local Dixie State College. But the real reason I think this is a great place to live young is because nobody sits still here. Everybody's too busy hiking, climbing, mountain biking, or golfing.

The town is in a valley surrounded by the Mojave Desert, the breathtaking Zion National Park, and Bryce Canyon National Park. In St. George, you get to pick your natural wonders. And here you've got lots of sunshine to play with, as long as you can stand midsummer heat that regularly tops one hundred degrees in July, though at least it's a dry heat.

St. George got its start as a cotton plantation run by Mormons, but the lack of water ended that enterprise pretty quickly. What survived, however, was a quaint little town built right smack in the midst of a desert valley. The Mormon influence is still a big part of St. George today, which, depending on your viewpoint, is either a blessing or . . . maybe not. But if the town was ever insular, it isn't anymore. Outsiders have been arriving in St. George in such large numbers over the past few years that today there's a diverse mix of people from all walks of life and just as many places.

When a town grows as quickly as St. George has as of late, it usually means it's time to look elsewhere. But this town has managed to absorb its growth well, and it still has a great small-town feeling. There are so many attractions within easy reach: it's a ninety-minute drive from Las Vegas for quick weekend getaways; there's year-round golf at more than a dozen area courses; and what really makes this place rock are the rocks themselves. In nearby Zion National Park, you can gape at towering sandstone walls and monoliths. In Snow Canyon State Park, just eleven miles from St. George, you can wander among volcanic cones and deep red sandstone cliffs—the same ones that provided the spectacular backdrop for the movie *Butch Cassidy and the Sundance Kid*. You can explore all of this at your own pace in your own time, or you can get the help of local experts. The area spas and retreats offer guided hikes to the top of the red rock cliffs and into Mojave caves where you can examine ancient artifacts. And St. George has lots of adventure-sports operations that'll help people of any age to risk their necks.

What It'll Cost You: Even with all the growth, the real estate prices are not too much out of whack (yet). The average home price is $210,000.

Inside Tip: Realtor Ellen Plante of Keller Williams says that if you opt for the underappreciated Red Cliffs neighborhood, you can get

a nice three-bedroom house in the low $200s. Condo town houses
are available in town for $160,000 and up.
Sunny Days: 255/year.
Median Age: 31.

CLEVELAND   Ohio

Its Soul Is Rock 'n' Roll

It had become the butt of national jokes, tagged as the "Mistake
on the Lake." Cleveland, a once-great American city, seemed
hopelessly lost. Until, suddenly, rock and roll saved its soul!

Well, maybe I'm making it sound too simple. There's no doubt
that the new Rock and Roll Hall of Fame—that big, bold, and
fabulous museum designed by I. M. Pei—helped boost the city's
spirits. But that's only part of the story of Cleveland's resurgence.
And the new, improved Cleveland is really just starting to re-
build, which means it's an opportune time for adventurous,
music-loving souls to get in on the ground floor.

This comeback city actually had some great qualities all along,
but they were either underappreciated or underutilized. Start
with the fact that it's a major city on a Great Lake—as such, you
would think it should've had loads of upscale waterfront housing.
But it didn't because the city had allowed much of its lakefront
property to languish or be used for industrial sites. Not anymore.
For the first time in a hundred years, Cleveland has begun to reclaim much of its lakefront for residential use, and it's doing the
same with prime riverfront property. The Cuyahoga River area
famously known as "The Flats" is now changing from industrial
development to mixed use, with trendy shops and luxury condos
sprouting up along the riverbanks.

Downtown, too, is hotter than it has been in years. Here the
music never stops, and that's not just true for rock aficionados.
There's the best of every type of music here, and you could enjoy

a different genre every night. If you were weaned on rock as many of us were, though, there's one museum in Cleveland made for rock 'n' rollers like you and me. It offers constantly changing exhibits filled with backstage stories and weird and fascinating artifacts from bands ranging from the Beach Boys to the Clash.

People who know Cleveland will tell you that even as it spruces itself up, its old-time authenticity separates it from newer cities. Its wonderful ethnic enclaves such as Little Italy and the Hungarian section of Shaker Square are still the real deal. People love to feast on walleye bites and potato pierogi, and good old meat loaf is still big here. You can bike a full circle around Cleveland to work off unwanted calories on what is known as "the emerald necklace"—a lush green path that surrounds the city and passes through parks and woodlands.

> **What It'll Cost You:** "For the next couple of years, Cleveland will be a value purchase opportunity," says Kevin Cahill of Keller Williams Realty in Cleveland. The average home price is $99,100.
> **Inside Tip:** Cleveland offers hundreds of opportunities for Great Lake escapes by way of quiet little cottages for sale or rent all along the hundred-plus miles of lakefront in Ohio.
> **Sunny Days:** 166/year.
> **Median Age:** 34.

STATE COLLEGE   Pennsylvania

Where the View Is Always Young

Penn State, of course, needs no introduction, being one of the largest and best-known universities in America. But what you may not know is that this university has, through the years, built up a wonderful little town around itself called State College. It has everything a college town should have, including restaurants and shops galore, a lively music scene chock-full of small clubs featuring homegrown talent, and top-notch medical facilities such as the Hershey Medical Center. But whereas some college towns can feel crowded and chaotic, State College has a definite laid-back, feel-good aura—in fact, it's been ranked as the city with the lowest stress in America by *Psychology Today*. People here like to stroll and chat, occasionally stopping for an ice-cream cone at the local creamery. No wonder the area is known as "Happy Valley."

When it comes to welcoming outsiders and allowing retirees to feel like an integral part of the campus community, nobody is doing it better than Penn State University. Penn State has gone out of its way to set up a community within the community, designed for the over-fifty crowd. It's called "The Village at Penn State," and it consists of two separate entities that exist side by side on the same lush plot of land. There's a planned housing community, where anyone of any age can buy a house (though it tends to attract lots of boomers), and next door to that, there's a "Life Care Retirement Community" geared to people sixty-two and older, where you can get a smaller one- to two-bedroom apartment or cottage. It's run by a nonprofit operation designed to take care of residents for life and provide long-term care as it becomes needed.

When you live in the pretty Village, you're in the middle of eighty acres of rolling hills, with views of horse pastures and scenic Mount Nittany. But you're also close enough to the heart of campus life to see the football stadium where Penn State's Nittany Lions play each week in the fall.

And when it comes to interacting with students, you're even closer because the Village brings the university to you. Students come into the retirement community each day to teach everything from fitness classes (tai chi, Pilates, and more) to computer skills. Student musicians stage classical-music performances on a regular basis, free of charge. Everyone likes the arrangement because students get course credit and life experience by interacting with retiree residents while the residents get constant contact with young people who "become like family to us," says Village resident Maddy Cattell.

Having a mixed-housing complex and senior housing side by side is ideal for younger retirees who might want to bring their parents with them or for boomers who want to make an easy transition from a mixed-age community to one offering more care and services.

What It'll Cost You: In the Village's multiage housing complex, a midsize three bedroom house goes for $250,000 to $300,000. Next door, in the Life Care Retirement Community, you can get a one- to two-bedroom apartment or cottage with entrance fees of $170,000 to $350,000.

Bonus Fact: This part of Pennsylvania is blessed with thirty-seven trout streams, meaning you can fish every day for a month and not fish the same stream twice.

Sunny Days: 178/year.

Median Age: 23.

OTHER GREAT COLLEGE TOWNS, BY REGION

Northeast: Ithaca, New York. With towering waterfalls, ice-age gorges, and amazing views everywhere you turn, you have to wonder how college students in Ithaca can keep their minds on their studies. Located on Cayuga Lake, the longest of the Finger Lakes, this scenic upstate New York town is home to two popular schools, Ithaca College and Cornell University. That means you tend to get twice as many college-town attractions such as visiting guest speakers and touring performers. If you're a film buff, Cornell Cinema is open to the public and shows about three hundred films a year, including all kinds of art films and silent movies accompanied by live music. There's also a downtown pedestrian mall, Ithaca Commons. But the natural attractions are best of all. Within a ten-mile radius of Ithaca, you'll find more than one hundred waterfalls! The attitude here is laid-back but very progressive. For instance, the cohousing trend discussed in the previous chapter is alive and flourishing in Ithaca in the form of an EcoVillage consisting of two thirty-home neighborhoods. The residents grow their own fruit and vegetables and even raise sheep.

Midwest: Yellow Springs, Ohio. This could be a great time to sneak into Yellow Springs at a bargain rate because the town's main draw, Antioch College, is temporarily shutting down for the next few years. The plan is to reopen it as a state-of-the-art college of the future, with a radical redesign that is under wraps for the time being. Once that happens, local housing rates could shoot up again and you'll be sitting pretty. And during Antioch's hiatus, you can take advantage of the other charms of Yellow Springs, a cute and friendly small town of four thousand people, named after a local natural spring that still flows. For more than a hundred years, the spring's curative waters drew people from far and wide and Yellow Springs was a popular health resort with hotels and spas serving travelers on the nearby stagecoach road and those brought in by the Little Miami Railroad. Today the spas are gone and the railroad has been converted into miles of scenic biking trails. It's so easy to get around by biking and walking that many residents don't even own cars. The compact downtown area manages to pack in sixty shops and a dozen eateries. In terms of cultural offerings, there's Shakespeare in the summer, artist studio tours, an acclaimed art cinema, and even a Buddhist meditation center. And the tiny town has a one-thousand-acre nature preserve right in its backyard, featuring springs, waterfalls, and limestone cliffs.

South: Oxford, Mississippi. As home to a long line of distinguished writers ranging from William Faulkner to John Grisham, Oxford has continually been seen as a bastion of Southern literature. If you have a passion for writing or even just reading, you'll feel right at home in a town that loves books, bookstores, writers' conferences, and anything to do with words. Oxford is home to the University of Mississippi—also known as "Ole Miss"—and the school has always encouraged retirees to come here, offering free courses each semester as part of its lifelong-learning program. Nestled among the rolling hills of north Mississippi, the town itself has all the cultural offerings and buzz of a midsize college town but still maintains its Southern charm. Magnolia and antebellum mansions are all around, and the locals are known for welcoming people who move here through an active newcomers club that meets monthly and hosts tours of the city as well as book and gourmet-cooking clubs.

Northwest: Ashland, Oregon. In Ashland, to quote Shakespeare, "the play's the thing." The town, home to Southern Oregon University, is best known for hosting the Tony Award–winning Oregon Shakespeare Festival. The festival runs through most of the year except winter and, combined with lots of other local stage productions, has made Ashland a magnet for theater buffs. But that's far from the only attraction. With its moderate climate and natural beauty, southern Oregon is a great spot for outdoor adventure. You can check out the country's deepest lake, Crater Lake, or ride the Mount Ashland Mountain Bike Trail, which winds through the foothills of the Siskiyou and Cascade ranges and offers stunning views. There are world-class fishing and rafting rivers, year-round golf, and top-notch skiing. After all that activity, you may need a healing dip in one of the city's many natural hot springs and a pit stop at one of the local wineries. That'll put you in a mellow mood for a night at the theater.

Chapter 6

Living Green

I don't just want to live green—I want to have fun while I'm at it!"

That's the philosophy of Ted Baumgart, who, along with his wife and family, decided to build an environmentally responsible house in a suburban Los Angeles neighborhood. Baumgart, a boomer who works as a production designer on TV commercials and films in his day job, has always had an interest in protecting the environment and living responsibly. But until he was near fifty, he says, "I never had the wherewithal to actually build a house that lived up to my own standards."

When he finally did it, he tackled the challenge with a vengeance, putting in solar-heating panels, reusing lumber from other torn-down houses, and even using recycled windows. The farmhouse he built is a model of environmental efficiency, right down to the super-water-saving toilets. But if you think green and efficient equals dull, you need to step inside Ted's fun house. He's built a dazzling indoor waterfall, using all recaptured water, of course, so there's no waste. He also grows plants right in the ground—inside the house. And just for kicks, he set up a miniature train system that runs from the kitchen to *the backyard pool. "I can put a snack or a drink on the train and send it to you at the pool," he says. And the food train is—of course—solar powered.*

Neighbors like to stop by and check out the house, as do lots of other curious people from outside the neighborhood. In fact, Ted now hosts ecotours of his house that sometimes draw a hundred or more people. "The more the merrier," he says. "I want to show people that creating an eco-house is very doable. And I also want to show them that you can have a blast doing it."

In the real estate business, you meet all kinds of people trying to make a personal statement with their house. Most of the time the message has more to do with ego than comfort. I always get a big kick out of the guys who strike it rich and build big trophy homes before the money is even in the bank. The houses always look like a cross between a king's palace and a circus tent. These over-the-top homes soon become the talk of the town, and never in a good way. And when it comes time to put this type of house on the market, it's the hardest property to sell because would-be buyers can't identify with it and can't see themselves living there. These houses always sell for far less than they cost to build, and in the worst-case scenario they end up becoming expensive teardowns.

Today there's a whole new way people use their homes to make a statement, but this time the statement is less about vanity and more about being socially responsible. It's the red-hot trend of living green. These homes are specifically designed to maximize energy, preserve our natural resources, and just maybe, in the long run, save the planet. A house that's been built green, using state-of-the-art design and materials, is also a kind of trophy property—but it's the best kind of trophy that many more people now want to own. The house makes a statement about your principles, not your ego. Your neighbors admire rather than resent it. And here's the bonus: as the green-living movement continues to grow in years ahead, these houses are going to become only more desirable and more salable. So in the end, the good guy who builds the green house comes out the clear winner. Along with the rest of us who live on the planet.

Until about a year ago, I hadn't grasped how large the green-living movement has become. It's gone well beyond a fad among idealistic college kids and graying hippies—it has gone mainstream in a big way. Almost three-fourths of the baby boomers we surveyed for this book told us that environmental considerations truly matter to them as they look ahead to where and how they'll live in the next stage of their lives. As someone who only just started taking the time to sort out the recyclables in my trash, I was a bit surprised. Most everyone is getting swept up in the big green tide. We now understand that caring about the environment isn't about distant, far-off concerns, but about the immediate ones that affect ourselves and our kids. We've started to realize that we can actually *do something* about it, on a local, personal, everyday level. So instead of feeling helpless or guilty, we can actually feel good about the way we choose to live our daily lives.

This is especially true for people who are about to retire or begin a new chapter in life. Why? Because if you're starting with a fresh new lifestyle, in a new place, it's a great opportunity to cast off old habits and clean up your act. It may be the first time in your life where you really are in a position to live in a manner that reflects your principles and ideals. You might finally have the resources, the time, and the wisdom to begin living in a more responsible, eco-friendly way.

All this talk about being responsible can make green living sound like such a chore. But the truth is, it can be fun, creative, and even quite glamorous. Green living has become the cause du jour among celebrities and socialites, the subject of cocktail-party chatter and *Vanity Fair* cover stories. Rick Hunter, whose Sage Homebuilders firm caters to baby boomers looking to green up their homes, says, "To a lot of people now, it represents a form of 'enlightened living.' It's a way of reacting against all the prefab McMansions and saying, 'I want to live in a more efficient, healthier, smarter house, with a cutting-edge design that makes sense for these times.'"

Finally, green homes come with bragging rights. Forget about marble steps or granite countertops that don't impress anyone anymore. If you really want to wow the Joneses now, just show them your all-natural, nontoxic bamboo floors shipped from easily replenished forests.

If saving the world and impressing your neighbors still isn't enough, then you can simply think of it as a healthy, common-sense way to live the rest of your life. A green home can protect you from pollutants and contaminants and shield you from sky-rocketing energy costs. If you're someone who wants to be more in control of your living conditions and takes pride in preserving your little piece of the earth, then read on, because this lifestyle and chapter are for you.

How do you begin to embrace the green life? It starts with where you choose to live. The good news is, you don't have to go off into the woods and live in a tree (though in Indiana, some people are doing just that, as you'll see later in our "Best Places to Live Green" section). Today you can live green in a house that doesn't skimp on creature comforts or on dazzling style. And you can do it just about anywhere, although some places are clearly much greener than others.

I think if you're making a commitment to live healthier and more naturally, it makes sense that you move to a place that has made a similar commitment. Some cities and towns make it easier for residents to walk and take public transportation instead of driving all the time. Some municipalities make stringent efforts to clean up local air and water by reducing polluting emissions and take strides to cut down on local use of electricity. Many towns encourage local builders to use eco-conscious materials and practices and strive to maintain a balance between new development and preserving open green space.

Where Are the Greenest Places?

The *Green Guide* magazine, a bible for the current environmental movement, rates top places around the country on all of these factors. The city that recently came out on top was Eugene, Oregon, profiled in this chapter. Austin, Texas (chapter 4), and Burlington, Vermont (chapter 5)—two cities that have made it into this book for reasons other than environmentalism—were also rated highly by the *Green Guide*. According to Paul McRandle, the guide's deputy editor, cities all around the country are making a bigger effort to be green because "it can attract retirees and tourists, increase property values, and bring in new business." That sounds like good common sense to me.

The best places for environmental living continue to be in western, northwestern, and mountain states such as Washington, Oregon, California, Colorado, and New Mexico—areas that tend to be associated with progressive attitudes and a healthy, outdoorsy lifestyle. These places were green long before it was fashionable.

But you might be surprised at some of the unexpected spots that are embracing the environment these days. Chicago has made great strides in toughening its emissions laws and putting up more energy-efficient buildings. St. Paul, Minnesota, and Huntsville, Alabama, both made the *Green Guide*'s top-ten cities list because of their efforts to reduce pollution while enlarging their parkland and nature preserves. And get this: one of the absolute greenest places you can live today is none other than the concrete jungle known as New York City. Why? Because New Yorkers drive less, walk more, and don't waste resources on watering big lawns and heating up giant mansions. The most eco-conscious New Yorkers even seek out "green high-rises" such as the one we profile later in this chapter.

Living "off the Grid"

Outside the big cities, there are also many small green communities, sprouting up all over the country. In these towns and neighborhoods, you'll find people living like homesteaders—generating their own power and proudly declaring their independence from the central power banks run by big utility companies. One example is the Three Rivers community, located just outside Bend, Oregon. It's made up of 250 homes that have all declared their independence by using solar panels and windmills to power their community. And if you think these folks live in tents, think again—the neighborhood includes lavish million-dollar homes that just happen to have shining panels on the roofs. The community's decision to stay "disconnected" is as much about aesthetics as it is about ethics. As one Three Rivers resident explains, "With power lines come streetlights, and there go your stars at night."

This type of self-sustaining, back-to-nature living is becoming more accepted. By one estimate, the number of people generating their own clean energy is increasingly by 30 percent each year. Some of these local communities go beyond energy conservation and also grow their own organic food, forming small "eco-villages" that live according to environmental principles that govern all aspects of life. If you check out Port Townsend, Washington, in this chapter, you'll get a glimpse of one amazing village.

As much as the green movement is spreading throughout the United States, it's growing even faster in some areas overseas. For those of us thinking about retiring abroad *and* living green, there are lots of exciting options. Brazil is at the forefront of creating green towns such as Curitiba, and Germany has staked out an environmental leadership position in Europe. The Netherlands is the home of the windmills. London just overhauled its environmental regulations and issued a bold mandate to become the "greenest city in the world," and New Zealand just set ambitious new national goals aimed at making it the "world's greenest country."

If you move to an area striving to be more green, you'll be awarded instant access to critical resources such as eco-conscious builders and home designers, retailers selling green materials and supplies, and everything else necessary for building and maintaining your own green home and lifestyle. And this is key, because living green starts with your house and home. Believe it or not, as much as 40 percent of greenhouse gases comes from homes, not cars, first through the manufacturing and building process and then through everyday living.

But all that changes if you apply the right materials and eco-design strategies to a house, either by building from scratch or renovating an existing one. And it's much easier now to find the help you need to do that. Although green building has been around for decades, home builders used to assume buyers would balk at the slightly higher costs, which average 5–10 percent more. They figured we'd rather put the money into fancy fixtures and countertops—that we cared more about appearances than environmental issues. And until now, they were right.

A Booming Market

But now that green is hip, the green home-building market is expected to triple in size by 2010, up to $38 billion a year. Builders are jumping on board as fast as they can, and so are real estate agents. Some agents have taken on the new label "eco-broker" and can help you figure out if a house on the market is as green as it claims to be. To that end, there are a number of checklists and certifications to run through when buying green (see box on the facing page).

Green House Hunting Made Simple

If you're looking for a green house but don't have the patience to build one from scratch, there's a growing supply of green houses on the market. In fact, there's something green for almost every price range and taste these days. But you'll have to keep an eye out for houses that promote themselves that way but don't deliver the goods. Here's how to check out a green house before you buy it:

1. Ask for third-party certification to ensure that the house meets basic green standards. There are three levels of certification. The lowest is "Energy Star qualified," which tells you that a house meets certain basic energy-efficiency levels. Next up are NAHB's (National Association of Home Builders) Model Green Home Building Guidelines, which mean a house was built using materials and methods that meet the building industry's new green specifications. The third and toughest level is the LEED (Leadership in Energy and Environmental Design) for Homes program. To be LEED certified, a house must pass a checklist of dozens of items relating not just to efficiency but overall environmental impact.

2. Check the utility bills. If the green house is doing its job, the bills should be half the normal amount for a house that size. And if the house has a working solar-panel system, the utility bills should be almost nothing.

3. Be on an east-west street, meaning the house should be oriented south and north to take advantage of passive solar energy. This makes a huge difference, and your air-conditioning bills will be cut by 25–50 percent.

4. Ask the seller for an "energy-cost guarantee," which means he or she will refund money if your monthly energy savings after the first year don't live up to what's promised.

5. Check if appliances are Energy Star qualified. This certifies their efficiency.

6. Look for shade trees on the property and minimum twenty-four-inch roof overhangs. They'll serve to shield windows from the sun and keep your house cooler for less in warmer climates.

The various jumbles of letters that signify green certification—from LEED to NAHB-GB guidelines—can be confusing, but it really boils down to just three basic principles. A green house is designed to cut energy costs, provide a healthier living situation for the occupant, and have a minimal impact on the environment. Deciding which priority comes first depends on whether you're out to save the world or out to save a few dollars, although there's no law that says you can't do both. In terms of money, green housing costs a little more up front, but experts agree that you'll recoup your investment and start to come out ahead within two years. The savings on your monthly utility bills happen right away, thanks to airtight sealing and higher-quality insulating materials, such as fiber cement board in place of vinyl siding. Top-quality composite or metal roofs reduce your energy bills, too.

If you really want to sock it to Con Ed, you can go solar—probably the most environmentally impactful thing you can do in a green home. It's also the most expensive thing to do. A solar-panel system costs anywhere from $25,000 to $50,000 and sometimes higher. But the good news is, you can immediately chip away at that cost with a two-thousand-dollar federal tax credit and other rebates offered by several states. The real savings come each month after that. Homes with solar panels sometimes produce more energy than they use, which earns you "credit" on your next electrical bill. Depending on how much you save each month, the panels could pay for themselves in ten years, particularly with oil prices so high and the cost of solar panels coming down. A solar-heating system can also increase the value of your home, adding as much as twenty thousand dollars onto your re-sale price because of the cost savings it represents.

Green home owners such as Georgia Goldfarb will tell you they're not in it for the money. Georgia and her husband built their California solar-heated home, with its multilevel glass walls and stunning ocean view, after decades of living in conventional housing. "The truth is, I've dreamed about something like

Building Green from the Ground Up

There are two things to know going into the green home-building process: it'll cost a little more (typically 5–10 percent) and take a little longer to complete. Here are the steps to follow along the way:

1. Start by finding a LEED-accredited architect, as they have the knowledge and experience of designing green homes. Go to the U.S. Green Building Council Web site (www.usgbc.org) to find those listed in your state and city.

2. Before you sign the land contract, hire an environmental assessor to check out the ground. You want to know about possible toxins in the soil or any other geological concerns. There's no point building a healthy house on unhealthy turf.

3. Generally, the more you can build into the ground, the better.

4. Choose the right insulating materials from the get-go, as they will make the house more energy efficient. Aerated concrete blocks and polystyrene-based products are self-insulating, and high-quality insulated glass with PVC frames also helps.

5. Use recycled materials wherever possible. The best green houses reuse lumber from torn-down houses, old wine corks to create cork floors, and rubber from tires to insulate walls. Green builders will recycle almost anything, including old blue jeans.

6. Think locally. Using materials that are made and sold in the local area means they don't have to be transported by exhaust-belching trucks. You'll also save on shipping costs.

this ever since my college days in the 1960s when I first got interested in the environment," says Georgia. But with her busy career as a pediatrician, she says, "I never had time to do anything like this until now." And now? "Now this house is my passion," she says.

For true believers like Georgia Goldfarb or Ted Baumgart, it can seem as if there is a deep spiritual connection to the house they live in. They tend to revel in the details of how the home was made and can tell you the whole "life story" of the various unorthodox materials used to create it—the tabletops made from compressed sunflower-seed shells, the insulation made from recycled tires, the lumber in the walls reclaimed from historic old barns. It makes the house seem almost like a living thing, with its own identity, integrity, and character. It says some pretty good things about the owner who lives there, too.

Six Easy Ways to Turn Your Home Green

If you're not ready to buy or build just yet, you can still work green wonders with the home you're in. According to the U.S. Green Building Council, here are six of the best ways to improve your home's energy efficiency and save some money:

1. Switch to compact fluorescent lightbulbs. They may look funny and cost more up front, but they'll end up saving you hundreds of dollars in electric bills. This is a simple thing that can make a huge environmental difference if enough people do it.

2. Get a programmable thermostat. It costs only fifty dollars at your local hardware store but can save you a hundred dollars in your first year alone.

3. Plug air leaks just by using basic weather stripping around doors and windows. Many older homes lose a quarter of their heat through leaks.

4. Tune up your heating and cooling system and wrap your hot-water heater. Wraps cost about twenty dollars and help your hot water heat up faster.

5. Reduce water use. Low-flow toilets and showerheads are a start, but if you want to make a bigger difference, you can change your landscaping to native plants and also reduce the size of your lawn.

6. Use low-VOC paints in your house. Unlike regular paints, which give off fumes for years, these paints are completely nontoxic.

For a more complete list of tips, go to usgbc.org.

BEST PLACES TO LIVE GREEN

EUGENE   Oregon

America's Greenest City

This bustling college town runs almost entirely on hydroelectric and wind power, which account for 85 percent of the juice that fuels it. On top of that, biking is the preferred mode of transportation in Eugene and there are bike trails winding their way throughout the city. In fact, when you cross the local Willamette River, there are more bridges for bikes than for cars! Eugene has also set aside a huge amount of acreage for parks, wilderness areas, and protected wetlands, which all add up to Eugene's *Green Guide* ranking as the greenest city in America.

The city itself is an urban forest. In the downtown area and on the University of Oregon campus alone, there are more than five hundred species of trees. And when you look up over the treetops, there are great views all around because Eugene is tucked into a valley surrounded by mountains.

The beautiful scenery makes for some head-turning bike rides, and while you're pedaling away, don't be surprised to see folks running past you. This is a hard-core runner's haven, known as Track Town, USA. The university has had a world-class track program for years, which is why Nike running shoes were invented here.

But Eugene isn't just about running and biking in the great outdoors. The city also has a wild-eyed hippie side, which is a big part of what makes it so green and so much more fun. The lingering countercultural spirit can seem like just a lark, but it's central to why Eugene is the way it is. Local hippies saved the city's trees from being cut down in years past by holding demonstrations called "tree-ins," and it's that same spirit that has given modern Eugene clean water, clean air, and a clean conscience, too.

Eugene is at the forefront of experimenting with co-ops and community projects, so if you're looking to start a commune or open an organic-food stand, this is the place. And if you enjoy marching to a different beat, you'll find plenty of company in a city that has its share of characters. There's one popular restaurant in town where, in order to get in on Friday nights, you must wear an extreme hat made from an old grocery bag. Everyone fits in here.

> **What It'll Cost You:** The median home price in Eugene is $256,000.
> **Inside Tip:** There are some good bargains on the west side of town, but just be aware that that's where the "anarchists" live. If you don't mind the occasional peaceful demonstration, it shouldn't be a problem.
> **Sunny Days:** 155/year.
> **Median Age:** 35.

THE SOLAIRE   New York

Living Green in the Big Red Apple

From top to bottom, the Solaire building is an amazing example of smart, efficient design in my beloved city of New York. It's twenty-seven stories high and stands in the heart of Battery Park City in lower Manhattan (who would have thought that New York's best green building would be built in a place called *Battery Park?*). The Solaire opened five years ago as the first green residential high-rise building in the country. Soon it was earning awards and accolades, including the hard-to-get gold rating from the Leadership in Energy and Environmental Design (LEED) program.

In the Solaire, all the air is filtered and freshly circulated through apartments, and the water to each apartment is also filtered. Many of the building's surfaces are made of naturally harvested wood. And the walls are so well insulated that electric bills are typically cut in half. The roof has solar panels that generate natural power and there's also a rooftop garden with a storage system that captures rainwater to reuse. The basement has its own water-treatment plant, and all apartments have compact fluorescent lighting that turns itself off when you're not in the room.

"I didn't really appreciate all of those green features until I was living here a while," says Polly Brandmeyer, who moved into the Solaire when it first opened and is now raising her children here. "On paper, the idea of filtered air may not seem like such a big deal, but when you're breathing it every day you can feel the difference."

And it's not just the building that's green—the whole neighborhood is, too. Battery Park City is a ninety-two-acre planned community along the Hudson River with direct views of the Statue of Liberty. More than a third of the area is dedicated to open space, with parks, gardens, ball fields, plazas, and walkways. People stroll along a waterfront esplanade that runs the whole length of the neighborhood, with sculptures and gardens along the way. If not for the full view of Lady Liberty, you would swear you're nowhere near New York City. There's a strong sense of community here, with kids horsing around on the playgrounds and even fishing in the Hudson River, casting their lines right off the esplanade.

The neighborhood—next door to ground zero—barely survived the tragedy of September 11. When the towers fell, Battery Park City felt the shock waves and was smothered in ash. I remember that many shaken New Yorkers abandoned the neighborhood in fear. But Battery Park cleaned itself up, even opened new buildings such as the Solaire, and kept people there with low-rent incentives. Now the neighborhood is booming, and blooming, more than before. Eight more green buildings will open here in the next two years, helping the community toward its goal of becoming "the most sustainable neighborhood in the world," as the Battery Park City officials proclaim.

What It'll Cost You: Monthly rents in the Solaire start in the $3,000-plus range for a one-bedroom and climb fast from there; you can pay $6,000 a month or more for a three-bedroom. If that seems extreme, it is, but it's also par for the course in terms of Manhattan luxury-building rents, so you're not really paying extra for those green amenities.

Inside Tip: Battery Park City offers some rent-subsidized apartments to those who qualify.

Sunny Days: 224/year.

Median Age: 36.

TRYON FARM   Indiana

Tree-House Living: You Can't Get Any Greener Than This

I've always wanted to live in a tree house, and I'm not alone. I built one with the other girls in my neighborhood when we were kids, though the boys took it over and made it a war camp. But there's a place called Tryon Farm an hour east of Chicago in Michigan City, Indiana, where some residents get to hold on to the tree house they build. It's a tranquil little retreat for nature lovers that combines woodsy architecture, sustainable living, and organic farming for a true back-to-nature way of life.

Tryon is one of the many new experiments in community living being developed around the country, and the spirit of green is what really defines this special place. It was started a few years ago by an architect, Ed Noonan, and his wife, Eve, with the goal of creating a community where people and their houses could live in peace and blend in with the natural surroundings. That's why Ed built a number of what he calls "tree houses," though these homes are actually planted firmly on the ground. But they're completely surrounded by trees that are within arm's reach, and the houses are the same colors as the tree trunks all around. In fact, it's hard to tell where nature ends and a house begins. Similarly, Ed built several "dune houses"—natural grass-rooted structures built right into the midst of grassy dunes—and here again, each house is almost indistinguishable from its natural setting.

By the time Ed and Eve are finished, there will be about 150 houses of various styles on this 170-acre plot of land. Most of the land will remain undeveloped to leave intact the open prairie space, the farmland, the ponds, the wetlands, and the woods of Tryon Farm. And the farm really is a working farm, producing sorghum, millet, alfalfa, and eggs.

The houses at Tryon Farm are clustered together into seven

groups, both to preserve the open space and to create a sense of community. The people who live here are a mix of retirees, young greenies, and city folks looking to escape the pressures of big-city living. They are all drawn to the peaceful serenity of rural living. Some have planted their own gardens, and at breakfast each morning you get your eggs from the henhouse. It's like "having a little house on the prairie," as one resident puts it, but you're also just half a mile from a train that can whisk you to downtown Chicago in one hour.

The people who move here also like the idea of living responsibly. At Tryon Farm, everything on the property has been designed with sustainability in mind. The houses are made with bamboo floors, and recycled denim is used for insulation. The septic tanks on the property are specially made to purify the wastewater that is recycled into the fields that feed the livestock. And best of all, your house can be built according to some of your own specs, allowing you to get the exact tree house you dreamed about when you were a kid.

> **What It'll Cost You:** More than the cost of lumber—it'll run from $200,000 to $500,000, depending on the size of the home you build.
> **Inside Tip:** Rather than buying the land, you get a 1/150th share in the entire settlement. The Tryon Farm Institute is a nonprofit and owns the open space. You pay taxes on your house only.
> **Sunny Days:** 175/year.
> **Median Age:** 35.

PORT TOWNSEND   Washington

Where Every Day Is Earth Day

Port Townsend is at the very tip of a peninsula that's in the far northwest corner of Washington—in other words, it's practically off the map. Everywhere else in the country, Earth Day comes and goes and nobody does much about it. In Port Townsend, Earth Day has been turned into a green Mardi Gras that goes on for days. Local people get together here and have rallies, ride around in experimental fuel-efficient cars, and set up field games where kids learn all about the life cycle of endangered salmon. They also have an all-day film festival featuring movies such as *Who Killed the Electric Car?*

That's just one reason why this small Victorian seaport is a good place to go if you're determined to live green. Here are a few others: The town is chock-full of volunteer groups and non-profit organizations you can join, and you can make friends dedicated to all kinds of eco-causes, from building green houses to preserving the gorgeous Olympic National Forest, just minutes away. If you decide to build your own green home—and lots of people here do—you'll get the support you need from several local companies that specialize in helping home owners go off the grid by using solar power instead of electric.

Or you can go further and join the local "EcoVillage," a small experimental community within the town. Here there are small cottages and duplexes on seven unspoiled acres. The community is still building, and the plan calls for twenty-seven dwellings in total. Resident farmers help the people who live here grow produce, and there are six hens laying eggs and thousands of bees producing honey that residents plan to bottle and sell. The group lives by community rules and the strict principle that nature is sacred. You can take a tour of the property and see if you like it by visiting ptecovillage.org.

Port Townsend was a very successful shipping port in the 1800s, and that financed the building of its beautiful Victorian mansions and brightly colored town houses. But the town was nearly abandoned during the railway era because the trains didn't go here. Still, the local fishermen stuck around, and so did that lovely Victorian architecture. The town has made a comeback in recent years as a big draw for retirees and artists of all types. In fact, it's now one of the best small-town art communities in the United States, with fifteen galleries and art studios packed into a compact and charming downtown area that hosts weekly gallery walks and year-round art festivals.

Though it's just two hours from Seattle, Port Townsend doesn't get that city's infamous wet weather. It is shielded from storm clouds by the nearby Olympic Mountains, which also provide breathtaking views. It gets less than twenty inches of rain a year and lots of sun for the Northwest—another plus if you're using solar panels to heat your house. The town of just fewer than nine thousand residents is crowded, but there's little traffic—people tend to walk and bike in Port Townsend, which is yet another reason why greenies love it so much. The only vehicle more popular here than a bike is an old-fashioned wooden boat; the town is famous for making them and showing them off at the annual Wooden Boat Festival.

What It'll Cost You: Median home cost in Port Townsend is a little more than $250,000, though you can easily pay twice that for a nice home with water views.

Inside Tip: To live in the EcoVillage, it costs $50,000 for property rights, which doesn't include the cost of building your own house there.

Sunny Days: 156/year.

Median Age: 47.

OTHER GREAT PLACES TO LIVE GREEN, BY REGION

Northeast: Portland, Maine. "In Portland, we don't talk a lot about 'going green' the way some cities do," says Portland hotelier Rauni Kew, owner of the local Inn by the Sea. "We've just always lived that way because we all love the outdoors, and we know that's what brings people here—so we're all into protecting it." Portland has always been stringent about keeping its water clean and maintaining a large amount of green space. People who live here are also big on indigenous plantings, which support wildlife and use less water. The local Hannaford grocery stores will be reopening with a new energy-efficient LEED-certified store design, and groups such as Efficiency Maine are helping to turn the whole city (and state, for that matter) on to compact fluorescent lighting. It's no surprise *Vegetarian Times* magazine named Portland one of the top green cities in the country. It's got a fantastic waterfront, lots of art galleries and museums, and great restaurants, but it's also managed to retain its authentic flavor as a port town, with fishermen still out there in full view and small local shops successfully fending off the invasion of the big retail chains.

Midwest: Madison, Wisconsin. Madison was recently named the "most walkable city" in America by *Prevention* magazine, and that award didn't come by accident. The city adopted a walker-friendly plan ten years ago, requiring that all roads accommodate pedestrians. Many local people walk to work and there's also easy access to parks. Madison loves biking, too, and has built an extensive system of more than one hundred miles of bikeways. In fact, biking is so popular that there are actually three bikes for every two cars in Madison! This explains why Madison's air quality is exceptional. On top of that, it's a great college town that's both vegetarian friendly and gay friendly. So what's not to like? Even the chilly winters don't stop the locals from getting out there and walking.

South: Myrtle Beach, South Carolina. Retirees have always come to Myrtle Beach for the weather, the water, and the golf, but now the area seems to be reaching out to more environmentally conscious boomers. Withers Preserve is a large community (3,790 acres) built on an old Air Force base, and it's laid out so that you can easily walk everywhere. It has more than 40 acres of lakes, four miles of nature trails, and 120 acres of open park space. There's one specific neighborhood of sixty homes that is being set up as a green neighborhood of the future. It's in partnership with General Electric as a product of its "Ecomagination" program. The homes will be built with extra-energy-efficient GE products, including appliances, lighting products, solar panels, and a digital command center providing feedback on electricity and water consumption. This is a place where you can live green with the utmost control over water and electrical use and CO_2 emissions. Withers Preserve town houses start at four hundred thousand dollars and single-family houses at five hundred thousand dollars.

Mountain: Ridgway, Colorado. If you're looking for a place to park your Earthship, Ridgway is a fine old spot. And what is an "Earthship"? Well, it's a house that's actually built into the earth, with earthen walls providing natural insulation and solar-powered panels on the roof. The funny thing is, it really does look like something from outer space, but it saves a lot of energy. The late actor and environmentalist Dennis Weaver (aka McCloud) was one of the first to live in an Earthship house, and he built it in Ridgway (the house was recently put on the market for three million dollars). Others have kept Weaver's mission alive, building their own extravagant earthen houses and advocating a healthy environment along with a prosperous economy. Not everybody in Ridgway is an environmentalist. It's an authentic Old West town with lots of ranchers and a smattering of creative types. The chic ski town of Telluride is forty-five minutes away, but it might as well be a world away. Ridgway has old gravel roads, no movie theater, and absolutely no pretension. What it does have is amazing views of towering mountains on all sides, a natural hot springs where clothing is optional, and folks who love the earth so much that many decide to make their houses out of it.

Chapter 7

Losing Yourself

*F*or Ken and Roseann Layne, it all started with an image on their computer screen. It was a picture of a small converted farmhouse located in a remote village in Mexico. A friend who was traveling had stumbled upon the town, saw the little casita that was for sale, and later told the Laynes about it, directing them to a Mexican real estate Web site showing a picture of the house.

"And then," says Ken, "for the next few weeks, I noticed that Roseann would tiptoe upstairs to the computer and stare dreamily at the little casita. So I figured I'd better look into it."

Ken subsequently found himself in the village of El Quelite. "It was awash in color," he wrote in his journal. "Houses are painted bright hues of red, yellow, green, the complete rainbow." Ken looked around and saw a different world with its own unique customs. Each morning, after the rooster's call, the women of the town would sweep the streets with hand brooms, then mop those streets and patios till they were sparkling clean. The men rode through town on horses while the children played an Aztec sport called ulama, using their hips to strike a ball. And everywhere he looked were translucent lizards, prized by the villagers because they helped keep insects at bay.

Soon after Ken's visit, he and Roseann made an offer on the little casita. It was a bold move for the northern California couple. "We were about to become the only two gringos in this town of twenty-five hundred natives, only a handful of whom speak English," says Ken. "Our friends thought we were crazy." With Ken recently retired from book publishing and Roseann coming up on retirement from her schoolteacher job, why not go to a more conventional retirement community? But the Laynes were itching for something different—and you couldn't get much more different then El Quelite.

"In this village, you're far away from all the modern diversions," Ken says. "You become part of the slower pace. There's more time for talking, reading, writing. And you begin to notice all the rich things going on around you. You learn something every day."

For example, Ken has learned that in this village, "everybody, from eighty-year-olds to the eight-year-olds, all dance to the same beat of banda *music." Something else he's learned: "Lizards make good watchdogs, really."*

Have you ever taken a trip to somewhere exotic and allowed yourself, just for a little while, to become completely immersed in that culture? For those who have, I'll bet it's one of your most vivid memories. It's probably more memorable than any pampered and predictable luxury vacation you've been on. Years ago my husband and I traveled through Nepal and allowed ourselves to settle into that world for a few weeks. Today the experience lives in my mind as if it happened just last week—the vivid colors and exotic smells, the people's warmth and inner peace—as it was so different from anything we'd experienced before. I never once thought about my "normal life" back home—I felt like another person living a whole new existence. When you immerse yourself in a totally different world, everything becomes fresh. Nothing fits the patterns your mind has grown accustomed to, and your senses come truly alive.

But what if the experience isn't just temporary? What if you decide to live the rest of your life in a place that's radically different from where you've lived before? What happens if you choose to embrace a way of life that's a total departure from what you've always known?

Today more of us are taking this kind of exciting midlife detour and trading our old familiar place in the world for something strange and different. That's the focus of this chapter: places to lose yourself. You have to be a bit of an adventurer and risk taker to do it because it involves giving up the world as you know it.

To my mind, it matters less *where* you go than *that* you go. You can venture abroad to live in a foreign country or seek out a remote deserted island. Maybe you're trading in an urban or suburban life for the "exotic" experience of rural or small-town living. Or taking yourself up into the mountains to live, or leaving the land behind and living on the water. It can be far away or close, but what it must entail is a complete break from your old way of life. That's the key that turns the lock that allows you to go through the door to a totally changed life, where you can meet up with a fresh and different version of yourself.

For some of us, moving is our best shot at true reinvention. A simple change of scenery may break the old patterns and routines of your day-to-day life, but you can *really* shake things up by transplanting yourself into completely new and unfamiliar soil. It forces you to adapt, and that's just what you need to transition into a whole new second life.

There are several things driving boomers to seek out radical change for the next stage of their lives. Ours is a generation of achievers who have worked their butts off to attain success. Now we want to decompress and slow things down. Professor Geoffrey Godbey of Penn State University studies the way different generations approach leisure. He says, "A lot of boomers have been surprised and dismayed to discover that they are slaves to the system and the workplace—working more hours than they should, always wearing a pager or answering a cell phone. And for a lot of them, that is triggering a desire to unplug and escape."

Jim Uffelman is a good example. After thirty years of living in Manhattan and building a successful business, he recently cashed out and then promptly checked out—relocating to a remote spot in rural Connecticut, where he built himself a big quirky house on top of a hill. "I was looking for the most secluded place possible," Jim explains. "I wanted to be able to look all around and not see another soul. I liked the idea of being able to step outside and not hear a sound—no horns, nobody's dog barking. I wanted to be able to run around naked by the swimming pool. Or go into the woods around my property and play God with my chain saw, cutting down some of the oaks so the maples could grow. I guess what it comes down to is, I wanted to live on *my* terms, not somebody else's."

Rob Goldenhill felt pretty much the same way. He'd scaled Wall Street to the heights of success as a high-powered bond trader, with more money than he could spend and a life of luxury and chic dinner parties. But on reaching midlife, he had an itch to live in a more simple way. As he told *Fortune Small Business* magazine, he longed for something that felt real to him. So he chucked his big-city job and wandered to Vermont, landing in a tiny town with not much more than a general store. Rob purchased the store and a couple of horses and now spends his days baking fresh bread in the Williamsville General Store. When the day is done, he heads back home to his horses. It's an escape for sure, but it's more than that. Rob says he's a different person now, with new skills, new habits, and a whole new outlook on life.

The Urge to "Zoom"

Heading for the hills, as Jim and Rob have done, is enough of an escape for many of us. But others feel the need to go farther away, and they do. There's a major trend now for people of our generation to leave the country and start a new life abroad. Of the four million Americans living abroad, almost a quarter are retirees. These "zoomers" are zooming all over the place, but some of the spots becoming attractive are Panama (featured in chapter 5), Nicaragua, and Southeast Asia, particularly Malaysia and the Philippines. Others are finding exotic spots without leaving the continent, as Ken and Roseann Layne did by going to a Mexican village. And still others go in the other direction and lose themselves up north in the wonderfully removed and underappreciated area of Nova Scotia (profiled in this chapter).

What makes all of these spots attractive is that they are actively courting American retirees by offering great pension benefits and tax breaks, and they still have that feeling of being somewhat undiscovered with cultures different enough to be utterly fascinating. These are the kinds of places where nobody cares if you have the coolest cell phone because people are too busy making pots by hand.

If you move to a country that's in the up-and-coming development stages, rather than one that's already overdeveloped, you wind up in a place that wants to grow and attract new people. You're more likely to be welcomed into these worlds with open arms. But don't confuse that with thinking you'll automatically feel comfortable there. Ruth Halcomb, editor of the Living Abroad Web site (liveabroad.com), says a lot of people who move to foreign countries make the mistake of not spending time there first. "You have to do your homework," she says, and that includes living there part-time in various seasons as well as talking to lots of people who already live there. In general, it's no piece of cake to just pick up and move to another country. There are lots of adjustments to be made, starting with the fact that you have to be smart about buying property abroad (see the box below).

How to Feel at Home When Buying Real Estate Abroad

If you want to lose yourself in a foreign culture, don't lose your shirt along the way. Here are a few things to keep in mind before you plunk down your money on a property overseas.

1. Get the lowdown on residency restrictions. Different countries have different requirements for people who want to live there. For example, you may be required to have a pension or there may be health stipulations (some countries don't want anybody with a medical condition). You can get all the information you need by checking with a U.S.-based consulate office for the country you're interested in. Just Google "Panamanian consulate," for example, and you'll be able to find a Web site and phone number for that office.

2. Hire an independent attorney. Before you even begin looking, hire a local and credentialed pro who knows the law of the land. Ideally, he or she should speak English and be completely independent of the sales agent or developer you might be working with.

3. Use a *real* real estate agent. There are lots of "cowboy vendors" out there, each hustling his or her brother-in-law's house to an American tourist. Instead, look for someone associated with a real estate company, preferably with more than one office. As for the developer, check to see if he or she is part of the Federation of Overseas Property Developers, Agents and Consultants (FOPDAC), which means he or she is a credentialed pro with a track record.

4. Never buy blindly. It may sound crazy, but people do buy property sight unseen on the Internet. Usually they're pressured, the deal's "too good to last," or they don't have enough time to visit. But you absolutely *must* see it before you buy.

5. Make sure the owner is really the owner. Sometimes people sell what's not theirs, especially to unsuspecting Americans. The owner must have a clear title to the property, and you should have your local attorney check it out.

6. Keep what you buy. Local laws of succession determine if you'll be able to will your property to your family when you die. Also review local "eminent domain" issues with your attorney as, in some countries, under certain circumstances, the government has the right to just swoop in and take your land.

7. Open a bank account in the country before you buy. It will save you lots of time and red tape when you find the house you want.

8. Always do a survey—even if you have to bring your own reliable surveyor along on the plane with you.

It can be almost as big an adjustment when you stay in the United States but move to a totally different setting—whether it be rural, small town, or even a secluded Alaskan island. Wherever you wander, the key to successfully immersing yourself in a new world is to be open, flexible, and willing to give up some of your creature comforts. Phil Keoghan, a lifelong adventurer who regularly circles the globe as host of the TV series *The Amazing Race*, has made a study of how people adapt to strange environments. His book, *No Opportunity Wasted*, has a chapter dedicated to the art of "getting lost." He believes that venturing into new and unfamiliar turf appeals to the ancient seeker inside all of us. "We all have a deep longing to explore that goes back to early man," Keoghan says. "That's why it can be so satisfying when you put yourself into a strange environment—because you're using these innate explorer skills that you just don't tap into in your normal everyday life."

But as Keoghan points out, life in an exotic environment is also demanding. You may not be able to get the wine you're used to drinking or find that there's only one bank, with very long lines. And forget about high-speed Internet connections. But if we allow ourselves to focus on what the new place lacks, we'll be miserable. Keoghan says, "Instead of expecting a new and different place to conform to your every need, *you* have to learn to adapt your tastes. The best adapters are the people who actually revel in all the local differences instead of griping about them."

Will Your Nest Egg Go Further Overseas?

People often assume that only the well-to-do can retire abroad. But if you pick the right spot, you can enjoy the huge savings and extend your retirement nest egg much further than you would in the States. Here's what to look at as you do the math on how far your money will go.

1. Cost of living. In Southeast Asia and Central America, cost of living can be half of what it is in the United States. On the same budget that would force you to scrounge here, over there you can live by the water, eat at the best restaurants, and have maid service. Keep in mind that a source of savings can be utility bills, particularly in a country with a more moderate climate.

2. Exchange rate. Just make sure those great prices you read about hold up *after* you exchange your dollars. The strength of the dollar fluctuates over time, so it's worthwhile to check out the recent performance of the dollar in a given country to find out how stable it's been.

3. Local retirement benefits. Many countries these days try hard to draw in retirees by offering discounts and special benefits to pensioners who move there. Incentives include everything from tax breaks to discounts on medical services. Check a country's Web site or go to its tourism office to find out about the perks.

4. Taxes. Sometimes you can save a bundle on property taxes because many countries encourage foreigners to buy land by eliminating all taxes for a decade or two—sometimes forever! Check out whether the United States has tax treaties with the country you're moving to as that determines whether or not the income you earn in that country is exempt from U.S. taxes.

5. Health care. As you won't be able to rely on Medicare overseas, be prepared to cover your own medical expenses or buy local insurance when you get there. The good news is that good medical care is much less expensive overseas, and in some countries it's downright cheap. Often you can join a state-sponsored medical plan for a few hundred bucks a year, or you can opt for a higher-quality private plan that costs more but is still a bargain compared to U.S. medical insurance.

Stretching Family Ties

If you're like me, what you might miss most when you leave your old world behind are the people. It's a big issue for would-be zoomers and the main reason many of us won't take the dramatic step into another life. It's always difficult to separate from your family and friends, yet people who've done it point to a surprising discovery: if you transplant yourself into a cool and exciting new world, the people close to you will want to visit and spend time there. So what you lose in casual, everyday contact with loved ones is compensated for by more quality time spent together.

Ed and Diane Lane, the couple that moved to a Maui art enclave to pursue Ed's passion for painting (chapter 3), say that even though they don't see their children and grandchildren as often because of the distance, the get-togethers are now longer—frequently two weeks at a stretch—and more fulfilling. Ed explains, "You form a different kind of relationship. It's a trade-off, but it has its benefits." Diane also points out that in a dramatically different environment, people form new relationships more easily because the situation challenges you to make the effort to meet new people and engage them.

On the other hand, part of the joy of losing yourself is the feeling of *disengagement*—the sense that you've cut the cord that tied you to old familiar ways. Jon DiLude spent his career as a sales rep in Boston and opted for a retirement home in rural Georgia precisely because it felt so removed from the plugged-in, modern city life he had grown so accustomed to. He settled into the small Georgia town of Cleveland, which, he says, "felt to me exactly like a New England town from the 1950s—no interstate, no chain stores, and a small-town way of life that seemed like something this country has lost." And it just so happens that the town is located near the foothills of the Appalachian Mountains. Jon starts his days by hiking on wooded trails with hardwood trees, streams, cascading waterfalls, and, often, no one around but him.

BEST PLACES TO LOSE YOURSELF

PRINCE OF WALES ISLAND   Alaska

Gone Fishin'

If you're dreaming of a place where you can escape and just go fishing, it's hard to find a better place than Prince of Wales Island, Alaska. This is one of Alaska's best-kept secrets, maybe because it takes some effort to get here. First you fly into the Alaskan city of Ketchikan and then take a three-hour ferry to the island. When you arrive, you'll be amazed to discover that you've landed on one of the biggest islands in America, big enough to contain the largest national forest in the United States.

On the island, you'll encounter amazing wildlife—including big black bears by the hundreds—as well as some of the best salmon fishing in the world. But you'll have a hard time finding many other people—there are just 4,500 of them on an island of 2,200 square miles. That means in the average square mile here, there are likely to be only two people. And one of them might be you.

The island is divided into eleven communities, some of them original native villages. But don't think the locals are backward: the people of Prince of Wales Island are all wired into the Internet and are very aware of what is going on in the world. They welcome newcomers, especially if you have something to contribute to their growing local communities. Resident Mark Jaqua says, "One thing we really appreciate is that new people can bring expertise here—whether it's an artist setting up a studio, or a chiropractor opening a practice. Any talents people bring are needed here. And I think this is a place where you can do whatever you want to do. There's room to build a mansion or maybe just a log cabin, with logs you cut yourself. You can work in the arts, start a small business, or become the town mayor in a few years. It's just open-ended potential."

On the other hand, you can also just kick back and enjoy the solitude and the natural beauty here. It's easy to find a secluded lake or stream and have it all to yourself. And Prince of Wales is a great place in which to wander and explore. There are seventeen million acres of forest, with trails throughout, and hundreds of caves, many of them gorgeous limestone grottoes with archaeological treasures. In fact, the near-perfect remains of a 45,000-year-old bear were found here. You can also see lots of authentic totem poles on various parts of the island, each pole telling picture stories of the Northwest Coast Indians. And the birding is great here, too: blue herons and bald eagles soar by, scoping out the fish swimming in the waters. And those little fish lure in big ones—in the springtime, whales swim up near the island's shoreline to feed on herring.

Of course, it's not all just fishing and easy living here. The mild summers and cool autumns eventually turn into hard Alaskan winters. "If you don't have an ability to independently entertain yourself, you're probably not going to last the winter," says Mark. But if you're okay sitting by a fireplace, "having potluck dinners with friends and playing Scrabble," he says, you'll make it to the spring—and then it's all worth it again.

What It'll Cost You: Land is dirt cheap here. You can get a couple of acres for less than $50,000 if you want to build your own cabin. The average price of a prebuilt house is $291,600.
Bonus Fact: Taxes are very low in Alaska. There's no sales tax and no state income tax, and there are big property tax breaks for retirees and seniors.
Sunny Days: 98/year.
Median Age: 36.

THE WORLD

An Endless Cruise to Anywhere and Everywhere

This next option is for the few who can afford it. Buying a condo on a cruise ship was introduced five years ago, and it seems to have caught on with a surprising number of wealthy people. *The World* is the first ship to offer these floating luxury condos. The ship is a massive 644-foot vessel owned by ResidenSea, and the buy-in price starts at more than one million dollars for a small onboard cabin and goes up to seven million dollars for a three-bedroom condo.

Buy a condo on *The World* and you essentially live everywhere as the ship circles the globe, making constant stops along the way, timed perfectly with major events such as Carnaval in Rio or the Cannes Film Festival. Then, after being a perpetual tourist by day, you return to your not-too-cozy cabin at night.

I guess you could buy a yacht and have a similar lifestyle, but you won't be pampered the way residents of *The World* are. There's a staff of 340 to look after you and a concierge that makes arrangements for you at every port. The amenities on a boat such as this almost defy belief. The individual condos are styled by top European designers, featuring wood or stone floors, grand living rooms with coffered ceilings, Internet connections, and wide-open ocean views. There are the usual gourmet restaurants throughout the ship, a state-of-the-art health club, and large swimming pools, but that's just for starters. The ship has revolving art exhibitions and a live-performance theater, a retractable marina that is pulled out to allow for water sports alongside the ship, a helicopter landing pad on board, and a medical center with an operating room and three recovery wards. And that's not all. If you're a golfer, there are three artificial-grass putting greens, a simulator that mimics the playing conditions of fifty of the world's top courses, and a driving range on the top deck where you whack your balls into the ocean—and don't worry, the eco-sensitive balls simply dissolve in the water. Now, who would have thought of that?

The World holds up to 650 people but usually has only 150 to 200 on board. The residents tend to be in their fifties, most of them successful entrepreneurs looking to get away from it all. Some are full-time, whereas others come and go. But there's no time-sharing or fractional ownership on board *The World*—you have to buy your condo outright, and the residents obviously have enough money to do so. However, there's soon to be a new cruise ship named the *Magellan* launching in 2008 that does offer fractional shares, allowing you to buy a month per year on the ship. And *The World* has another competitor named the *Orphalese*, which offers the same full-ownership option as *The World* and has a lot of the same amenities with one added feature—there's an eighty-thousand-square-foot shopping mall on board. Oh, it's so nice to have money.

What It'll Cost You: The old line, "If you have to ask, you can't afford it," applies here. At press time there was a $6-million residence for sale on *The World*, but lower-priced units, when available, are mostly in the $2-million range. The *Magellan* and the *Orphalese* both start as $1.8 million for a small condo. Ship maintenance fees vary tremendously but can run from a few thousand a month into the tens of thousands.

Cost of Just a Slice: A one-month fractional share on the *Magellan* goes for $156,000.

Sunny Days: Varies.

Median Age: Mid-50s.

KENNET AND AVON CANAL
United Kingdom

Living on a Narrow Boat

In England, narrow boats are as common a local sight as red double-decker buses. They measure just six or seven feet wide but are up to seventy feet long. They're tailor made for squeezing through the large connected network of British canals. And they are sometimes used by tourists or weekenders enjoying a pleasure-boat ride. But more and more people are moving in and calling these boats home.

Some are doing it to save money. With property prices in prime areas throughout the United Kingdom continuing to rise, many people—retirees as well as young professionals—find they can live a lot cheaper on a boat. But that's only a small part of the appeal. What really draws people to this lifestyle is the opportunity to disconnect from everyday life and adopt a simpler, quieter, free-floating lifestyle. They say you can really lose yourself out there on "the cut," which is what boat owners call the canal because it cuts through the whole country.

Among the many canals running throughout the country, the most scenic is the Kennet and Avon. This canal in southern England extends from the Thames River to the Avon River, creating a continuous waterway that runs all the way from London to the Bristol Channel. Along the way, it winds through some of the loveliest spots in England, including West Berkshire, the Cotswolds, and Bath. The canal has great fishing, and you can hop off your boat anytime and walk the hiking and biking trails. It's also a wildlife conservation area with hundreds of species of birds, including the big heron and kingfisher.

Narrow-boat life is slow and easy, as the boat drifts at the same speed you might walk. Boats are typically decked out with all the comforts of a home, including a television, washing machine, dishwasher, and sometimes even a Jacuzzi. The full-time boaters get to know one another, especially in the winter when all the tourists have left. "That's when the cut becomes like one long thin village," says one narrow-boat blogger.

It may seem like a permanent vacation, but there's also some work involved, as you have to maneuver your boat through the locks and pull it into the moorings by rope. And you need to have your own residential mooring at a marina if you want to be able to park your boat for any length of time. Moorings are sometimes difficult to acquire, and it's best to put yourself on a waiting list. If you can't get one, you can just get a license to be a "continuous cruiser," meaning you keep moving through the network, never stopping for more than two weeks at a time at the spots you most enjoy.

What It'll Cost You: A boat is $150,000 or more if you buy a new one, maybe half as much if you buy it used. Be sure to buy a steel boat.

Add in the Expense: A residential mooring, which, if you can get one, will cost a few thousand dollars a year depending on the size of your boat.

Inside Tip: It's smart to hang on to your house for the first year to make sure you like life on a narrow boat. Some people just can't get used to living adrift, but the ones who make it past the first year tend to become lifers.

Sunny Days: Approx. 170.

Typical Age: Mid-40s.

NOVA SCOTIA   Canada

Remote Is Closer Than You Think

One good way to lose yourself is to find a truly exotic culture and then totally immerse yourself in that strange new world. You might think you have to go halfway around the globe to do that, but in fact you don't have to leave the North American continent at all. Just make your way to an overlooked corner known as Nova Scotia.

Canada's southeastern coast has a rugged natural beauty not found anywhere else in the world. Its rich culture is steeped in Scottish, Irish, French, and Aboriginal influences. It's a place where people speak Gaelic and still play fiddles and bagpipes. But you won't feel like an outsider here. Nova Scotia invites newcomers in with open arms, often with the Gaelic phrase *Ciad mile failte*, which means "one hundred thousand welcomes." The government shares that sentiment and has set up multiple programs to help new people move and settle here. The low real estate prices are another strong enticement to move here.

Yet, for reasons I find hard to fathom, Nova Scotia remains largely undiscovered and underappreciated by non-Canadians. That's probably because most people have no idea what they're missing. Nova Scotia is wrapped in more than four thousand miles of coastline, with unspoiled beaches, untouched bays, and the world's highest tides. All along the shore you'll find little fishing villages and lighthouses, offering dozens of possible havens. But if you really want to wade into the full cultural experience of Nova Scotia, try heading northeast to the island of Cape Breton.

There are some four thousand islands off the shores of Nova Scotia, but Cape Breton is by far the largest, and it's the heart of Scottish culture here (*Nova Scotia*, by the way, is Latin for "New Scotland"). Scottish and Irish immigrants first came here en masse two centuries ago. And as Cape Breton Island was somewhat cut off from the rest of Nova Scotia, Gaelic culture and music endured here unchanged. Cape Breton is a land of kilts, fiddles, bagpipes, Gaelic storytelling, traditional dance, and a cappella singing.

Cape Breton Island also has beautiful highlands that bring Scotland to mind, and it has some of the most pristine beaches in all of Nova Scotia. You can take in much of the beauty of this island by driving the Cabot Trail, one of the most scenic drives in all of North America. The road winds along the mountain-side, and as you drive you look down on the Gulf of St. Lawrence, where you can see pods of whales offshore. The Cabot Trail winds along for almost two hundred miles and then climbs into Cape Breton Highlands National Park. Here you can stop driving and start hiking and exploring. There's enough territory to spend a lifetime doing just that. But when you hear how cheap real estate is here, you'll want to leave the park and go house shopping.

> **What It'll Cost You:** The average home price is $176,146. It is one of the least expensive housing areas in all of Canada.
>
> **Inside Tip:** The only thing that's not cheap in Nova Scotia is the "harmonized sales tax" (HST) of 14% on most goods and services.
>
> **Sunny Days:** 83.
>
> **Median Age:** 39.

REGIONAL SPOTS WHERE YOU CAN LOSE YOURSELF (WITHOUT LEAVING THE MAINLAND)

Northeast: The Northeast Kingdom, Vermont. About fifty years ago, a Vermont senator came out to this vast northeastern corner of the state bordered by Canada and New Hampshire, looked around at the rolling hills dotted with little red farm-houses, and declared the area a "kingdom." The name stuck. This is where Vermonters go when they want to escape to the wilderness to find peace. Outside Vermont, it's still a well-kept secret. It's vast in size but sparsely populated. There are only one hundred or so small villages tucked among all those rolling hills. When you step into these villages, you step back in time—and into a time of classic architecture and local craftspeople making quilts, pots, and maple sugar. The Kingdom has two hundred lakes and ponds and various deep forests to explore, many of which you can have all to yourself. In most of the vast areas that make up the Kingdom, you'll be unreachable by cell phone. For those of us who really want to lose ourselves, that should be just fine.

Midwest: Flint Hills, Kansas. The Flint Hills are a series of gorgeous hills that extend from eastern Kansas all the way down into Oklahoma. Here you can get lost in what has been called "the last great swath of tallgrass in the nation," which includes the Tallgrass Prairie National Preserve. This is what most of our country's heartland looked like before it was cut, plowed, and farmed. Picture it: waist-high grass bending in the breeze, with thousands of bright wildflowers and a big, beautiful, wide-open horizon. The Flint Hills Tourism Coalition rightfully refers to the area as "the grass roots of America." And the only reason the prairies have survived here is because the hilly soil isn't good for farming. But it's great to look at and great to wander through. The towns in the Flint Hills area are small, friendly, and full of Midwestern character. You can go to the Flint Hills Rodeo in Strong City or work at the local cattle ranch in the tiny town of Clements. In Chase County, there's the Tallgrass Spiritual Retreat Center, which leads groups of women on long, rejuvenating walks through the grass.

South: Tybee Island, Georgia. Fewer than twenty miles from Savannah, Tybee Island is a small seaside community that feels like an old Southern beach town stuck in a time capsule. The island is just a couple of miles long, and it's filled with restored cottages from the 1920s, freshly painted in the bright colors of banana trees and morning glories. The same Southern families have been coming back for generations. The town's claim to fame is that every year the Tybee Island residents engage in the world's largest water-gun fight, sometimes resorting to horses in order to soak anyone and everyone within shooting distance. The other big-time pleasure is hunting for turtle tracks on the beach. And that's about all you'll do here. But if you're looking to lose yourself in a place that's like a quirky little Mayberry on the beach, Tybee Island might be for you.

Mountain/West: McCall, Idaho. If you opt to settle in the mountain town of McCall in central Idaho, you can leave your usual world behind. You can even enter a contest to select the man with the fullest beard and the woman with the hairiest legs. Yes, this is one of those towns with each foot in a different world. It was originally on old Western logging and mining town back in the 1800s, and it still maintains that simple, hardscrabble flavor. It's five thousand feet up in the mountains, in the middle of the deep woods and on the shore of a glacial lake. If you're in the mood to roam, you've got 1,400 miles of streams for fishing and three nearby wilderness areas totaling more than a million acres for hikers and campers. But the area's great skiing has drawn just enough outsiders to give it a nice eclectic feel. The town provides Internet cafés, good food, and upscale clothing shops. You've got to love the snow if you're going to love McCall. The place gets three hundred inches annually, keeping several area ski resorts thriving and also making snowshoeing a way of life. Yuppie skiers have been snapping up lakeside properties, but the median home cost is still a reasonable $230,000, or you can get a waterfront lot in nearby Cascade for $99,000 and build yourself a nice log cabin.

Finding Your Purpose

*W*hen Roger Forrester retired from his job at the University of *Minnesota and moved to sunny Arizona, he never expected to discover a new mission in life. "I really just went there to take it easy, play some golf and tennis," he says. "And that was all right for a while. But it wasn't enough for me."*

The funny thing was, Roger, in his late fifties at the time, discovered that lots of the people around him were feeling the same kind of restlessness. In the active adult community where he lived, around the pool or out on the golf course he was hearing the same thing over and over. "The retirees I talked to were all saying they really wanted to work again, that they felt they needed to do something, but they didn't know where to turn. I discovered there were no employment resources in the area of people over fifty. And then the thought occurred to me— I might be able to help these people!"

Roger had been the director of human resources at his old university job and knew the ins and outs of matching up talent with jobs that needed to be done. And so he used his experience, along with his own seed money and all of his free time, to open a tiny employment service for people over fifty called the Mature Worker Connection. In his first full year of operation he placed more than three hundred people into local jobs in the Tucson area. Now Roger has visions of taking the concept nationwide because, as he says, "this is an issue facing people all over the country."

Roger's operation is strictly nonprofit. "I call myself an altruistic entrepreneur. I honestly feel like I'm doing something I was meant to do by using my skills to help all of these people. It's the most enjoyable work I've ever done. Just hearing the news that 'So-and-so got a job today'—that really makes my day."

Many of us expect to whistle a carefree tune when retirement rolls around but instead find ourselves humming "Is That All There Is?" It's happening to boomers a lot these days. As a group, we're asking ourselves soul-searching questions such as whether we're doing our fair share to help our communities or if we're really making a difference.

If you're the type of person accustomed to creating change rather than being on the tail end of it, or if you're someone who's more comfortable giving than taking, this chapter on finding purpose is for you.

Boomers are often depicted as being self-absorbed. But if that was ever true, it's changing now. Many more of us have a growing hunger to become part of something bigger than ourselves. We're looking for a cause, a mission, a movement. There's a think tank called Civic Ventures that focuses on the over-fifty set, and they've found that more than half these people are eagerly looking for ways they can work to improve their communities and serve the people around them. Of the boomers we surveyed for this book, a whopping 80 percent expressed an interest in getting involved in a cause that could help others. They expressed a desire to do everything from teaching kids to feeding the hungry to making life easier for the elderly, mentoring young entrepreneurs, or protecting animals. In short, they want to help.

Coming Together to Make a Difference

Of course, we're not the first generation to want to give back. Volunteering has always been something that people do more as they get older. But I think the desire is even stronger with our generation. We grew up with the idealism of the Peace Corps and JFK. And as a group we're more educated and affluent then previous generations. We have more knowledge and material wealth to give back. We're also high achievers, quick to take on challenges and find solutions. Many of us have done it most of our working lives and want to apply that same energy and drive to something beyond making money. Greg O'Neill, director of the National Academy on an Aging Society, puts it another way: "The boomers are now looking to make the transition from *material* to *meaning*, and from *success* to *significance*."

Social experts tell us that the ramifications of the new "boomer activism" could be huge. If all the talent and experience of our massive group could be channeled into addressing the world's needs, there would be few problems we couldn't solve or at least make a little better. But many of us are still in the wishful-thinking stage because we haven't figured out *what* we're going to do to contribute to society or *where* we're going to do it.

People sometimes think of serving the community and finding a great place to live as separate issues, but they can go hand in hand. Every place on earth needs volunteers of some sort. Wherever you happen to be, someone could use a helping hand and worthy tasks need doing. I think that's why so many people volunteer right in their own town or neighborhood. But I also think that volunteering or community involvement as a life cause can be a doorway to a whole other world when done in an exciting new place.

I've researched instances of people who stumbled upon a cause or a job that needed doing in a place they'd never dreamed of living. But once they got involved in the cause, they became part of the community and soon were living a whole new stimulating life filled with deep personal satisfaction. Take, for instance, Jane Newman, a successful ad executive. She retired early from the ad business a few years back to search for the next thing to do in life. She traveled to Africa and did some short-term volunteer work there. On one of her trips, her car broke down and as she sought help, she met a few locals trying to set up modernized schools for the nomadic Sereolipi children of northern Kenya. Jane jumped right in, realizing that she could use her Madison Avenue skills to raise money and help with the various management and organizational problems. Today Jane leads the Thorn Tree Project helping to educate a thousand Sereolipi children who previously had little or no formal education. Jane made this her life's passion and made Africa her new home.

You don't have to go halfway around the world to find areas in need. Paige Ellison, a forty-five-year-old sales rep in Alabama, traveled to Mississippi right after Hurricane Katrina to help her sister move out. But while she was there, she witnessed the urgent need for child-care services. Paige took a leave from her job to devote herself to setting up local centers to help the kids of Mississippi. Now she runs Project K.I.D., a nonprofit group dedicated to setting up child-care centers in devastated areas nationwide.

Stories such as these are inspiring, though they seem extreme to the average person. Not all of us are up for moving to an impoverished part of Africa or a devastated American town—it takes a hardy and very adventurous soul. And most of us want to maintain a level of comfort for ourselves even as we try to comfort others. I believe you can have the best of both worlds. You can indulge your own selfish dreams of having a great place to live while also being of service to the community surrounding that special place.

WHERE THE "DO-GOODERS" ARE

These five cities lead the pack when it comes to volunteering. The percentage shown indicates how many adult residents engage in volunteer activities.

City	Percentage
1. Minneapolis-St. Paul	40.5
2. Salt Lake City	38.4
3. Austin	38.1
4. Omaha	37.8
5. Seattle	36.3

Playing Up Your Strengths

When you match up things you love to do and are good at doing with an appealing place that offers volunteer opportunities suited to you, you can make a beautiful life for yourself. For example, if you're a hiker, you can move to the gorgeous mountains of New Hampshire and get involved in managing and maintaining some of the world's best hiking trails. An animal lover can be part of one of the country's best wildlife-rescue programs while also enjoying one of America's most livable cities, Atlanta. And if you're a nature lover, there's an area in Costa Rica where you can help plant and expand the rain forest—all while getting to live along the lush beaches of Costa Rica! We profile each of these places in this chapter.

My point here is simple: whatever you're best suited to do, there's a place that's ideal for doing it. Enjoy the mundane task of pulling weeds in the yard? In lovely Asheville, North Carolina, they need your help controlling invasive plants in the Pisgah

National Forest. Love to watch birds and enjoy their music or just love exploring animal worlds more thoroughly? The Mountain Birdwatch project out of Vermont desperately needs spotters to help gather information on songbirds through the Northeast, and the Massachusetts Audubon Society needs your help keeping track of butterfly and turtle populations. And if you consider yourself a beach bum but feel guilty just lying still, you can help clean up the beaches in the Great Lakes area and learn all about marine life there.

If none of these suits you but you still want to lead a good guy's life, there are about a million other possibilities, in any place you might choose to go. Finding the right opportunity in the right place is as easy as going online. At Web sites like VolunteerMatch (volunteermatch.org), just punch in any location you're interested in and you'll get a description of all the volunteer projects that exist there.

If you're having trouble figuring out which activity or cause is best for you, I suggest taking a look at your own résumé. Experts say the best and most productive volunteers are the ones who tap into their past experiences and skills and apply them to a new cause. And I think we all know that doing something you're good at always brings the most satisfaction.

"Voluntourism"

Another way to find the right cause in the right place is to test the waters first. "Voluntourism" is a cute name for a new and growing trend in which people take vacation trips that incorporate local volunteer work as part of the experience. It's a smart way to find out if you really, truly enjoy doing a particular kind of volunteer work in a certain place before you commit to moving there.

How to Be Good at Doing Good

- ❑ **Read your own résumé.** It can help you figure out what you might enjoy and what you'll be good at.
- ❑ **Research the volunteer organization** before you commit. Ask for references and talk to other volunteers.
- ❑ **Bring your résumé with you.** It can help the volunteer group better match you up with tasks that make the most of your skills.
- ❑ **Ask about results.** VolunteerMatch's Jason Willett says, "A volunteer organization should be able to tell you the specific impact of what they're doing—how many people are benefiting and how."
- ❑ **Start small.** Dedicate just a few hours a week or month and build from there. Trying to do too much too soon can leave you feeling overwhelmed.
- ❑ **Diversify.** You don't have to keep doing what you started out doing. Changing tasks of shifting to a new cause will keep things fresh, and you'll also be helping a cross section of the community.

"You can use the Internet as a good tool to begin your search for volunteer actively, but ultimately, if you really want to find the right activity, you have to get out there and interact with people and experiment," says John Gomperts of Experience Corps, which helps match up the over-fifty-five crowd with volunteer opportunities. To that end, more people are taking what are affectionately called "deprivation vacations." The idea is to grab a shovel and actually work for a local cause while you're on vacation. If you want to give it a try, the Global Volunteers program (globalvolunteers.org) offers lots of possibilities.

I think it's perfectly acceptable to be picky when it comes to volunteerism. No one's paying you to volunteer and so you have every right to expect satisfaction. The experts say that boomer volunteers are more demanding. They say we're willing to serve, but we want to do it on *our* terms and want to see results. "In the past, retirees would be willing to do simple and basic volunteer work just to keep busy," says the Experience Corps' Gomperts. "That's not sufficient for the boomers. They really want to feel that they're making an impact."

The generational historian William Strauss echoes that, describing many boomer volunteers: "They don't want someone telling them, 'Go stand over there and serve the mashed potatoes.' They're looking for more self-definition in the volunteerism they do. And in some cases, instead of trying to fit into somebody else's mission, they're more likely to go out and create their own charity."

Social Entrepreneurs

Lots of us do just that—take matters into out own hands by creating nonprofits. Roger Forrester did so when he set up the Mature Workers Connection, and so did Paige Ellison with Project K.I.D. These days, if you have a great idea that serves a need in a community, there's a good chance you can get funding from what today are called "venture philanthropists." They're backing more and more nonprofit start-ups. Many grants are available from groups such as the Skoll Foundation, Ashoka, and the Blue Ridge Foundation New York. Some groups such as Civic Ventures offer annual hundred-thousand-dollar cash awards to the top social entrepreneur over age fifty.

Marc Freedman runs Civic Ventures and describes the wave of new social entrepreneurs as former businesspeople "who now worship a different bottom line—a better society." According to Freedman, today's boomers are very different from the retirees who used to volunteer in dribs and drabs, just to fill the hours after a career was over. Today people are turning activism into *part of* their careers. Civic Ventures calls this "the encore career," a ten-to-fifteen-year period of work, often done when people are in their fifties and sixties, that usually involves some form of pay and is geared toward social change and community service. Freedman stresses the importance of pay in all this because a paycheck—even if it's a modest one—is often what separates nonprofit work from volunteerism, and it can make the difference between being fully committed to an endeavor or just doing it in your spare time.

But even if there is a paycheck involved, no one gets rich when working for a cause. The real payoff comes in other forms: a deep feeling of fulfillment, new friends (because volunteering is absolutely one of the best ways to connect with people), a deep connection to a new community, and a whole new outlook on life. Not a bad deal. Best of all, you get to live as the genuine good guy you always thought you were.

Volunteer Organizations: Our Top-Ten List

There are a zillion volunteer groups out there, but here are ten that are particularly relevant if you're thinking about combining volunteer work with a move to a new place.

Experience Corps. If you long to teach, this program can match you up with great places around the country where part-time teaching help is needed (see the profile on Tempe, Arizona, later in this chapter). experiencecorps.org

ReServe. Restless retirees are placed in part-time positions with social-service and government bodies that need the help.

ReServists are paid ten dollars an hour for fifteen hours a week. reserveinc.org

VolunteerMatch. This great resource shows what volunteer opportunities exist in any city or town where you might wish to live. volunteermatch.org

SCORE. This program consists of retired executives who help young entrepreneurs develop sound business plans. There are local SCORE offices all around the country. score.org

Volunteers in Medicine Institute. Started by a group of retired doctors, the program sets up free health clinics around the country. If you have any medical experience, it's a plus, but the group also needs help just running the local clinics. vimi.org

Habitat for Humanity. Everyone's familiar with this one—hard hats, Jimmy Carter, you know the drill. It's great for people who like to get their hands dirty and actually build something meaningful they can see immediately. habitat.org

Reef Check. If you love to dive, this group will teach you how to do the underwater inspections that help save the endangered coral reef along the California and Florida coastlines. reefcheck.org

Sierra Club. This is the place to turn if you're a nature lover. The group can hook you up with volunteer opportunities in our great national parks. sierraclub.org

The Humane Society of the United States. Why not walk a shelter dog? It's also a great way to get to know your new neighborhood. hsus.org

ProLiteracy Worldwide. Love to read? Share the joy with others who need your help. literacyvolunteers.org

BEST PLACES TO FIND YOUR PURPOSE

NEW ORLEANS   Louisiana

Help Raise the Entrepreneurial Spirit Here

New Orleans these days is attracting lots of young volunteers, and they're helping with the hard work of teaching at under-staffed local schools and rebuilding houses damaged by Hurricane Katrina. But this city also needs a different kind of help, one that boomers with business savvy are well suited for—New Orleans needs business mentors. The local residents know that even if all the houses are rebuilt, people won't come back to the city to live unless there are jobs, services, and everyday businesses and products available.

That's why the city is aggressively reaching out to experienced businesspeople who want to lend a hand in the Herculean effort to relaunch New Orleans as an entrepreneurial boomtown. If you happen to have the right business skills, local nonprofit organizations such as the Idea Village (ideavillage.org) can hook you up with local businesses that need your help. From local restaurants and shops to larger companies, they have the will and the dream but often need outside expertise in marketing and business strategy. "What's needed are high-level thinkers and problem solvers," says Tim Williamson, president of Idea Village. Personally, I think there's nothing more satisfying than mentoring someone in business. You get to pass on what you know and then watch someone grow and reach his or her potential. And if you're doing it in New Orleans, you're also playing a historic roles in helping a great American city return to its old glory.

On top of all that, you'll be in one of the most stimulating places on earth. New Orleans hasn't lost its charm or its spirit, even after all the hardships of Katrina. Bourbon Street is still the best place to hear jazz music. The local restaurants are back to serving some of the spiciest food around. And the city is a warmer, more inviting place than it was before. Lots of people left, but those who've stayed have bonded and they're embracing newcomers willing to help with the rebuilding effort. "As soon as people hear that I've come from outside the city to volunteer, the first thing they say is 'Thank you for coming down here,'" says Maria Kramer, who recently moved to New Orleans from Seattle to teach underprivileged kids. Maria, an empty nester looking for something meaningful to do, initially planned on just a short-term volunteer stint in the city, but she found she loved it so much that she couldn't leave. Look into other revitalizing and rebuilding opportunities with Hands On New Orleans (handsonneworleans.org).

The areas hit hardest by the storm are still in bad shape, but neighborhoods such as the French Quarter and the Warehouse District are pretty much back to normal, though they are less touristy and have stronger senses of community. People chat on the streets outside the jazz clubs and everyone goes to the costumed carnival parades and crawfish boils. Art is flourishing in the city, and the rebuilding challenge is attracting top architects, urban planners, and the help of celebrities such as Brad Pitt. There's a great sense that history will be created here, making it the perfect place for a big and meaningful second act in your life—if you're up to the challenge.

What It'll Cost You: Rents are surprisingly high in New Orleans because of the shortage of temporary housing, but housing prices are very affordable. The median house price is $147,000. In the fancy uptown neighborhoods filled with grand Victorian homes, many prices have been slashed by 25 percent or more.
Inside Tip: Expect to pay a ton of money for home-owners' insurance, as much as $10,000 a year, or decide to go without it.
Sunny Days: 216/year.
Median Age: 34.

SOUTHERN NICOYA PENINSULA
Costa Rica

Grow Your Own Chunk of the Rain Forest

Everybody knows that Coast Rica has been a popular destination for lots of American and European retirees and that in the overdeveloped southern part of the country, real estate prices are up over the treetops. But people don't know that in the west-central area known as the southern Nicoya Peninsula, life is more affordable, far less touristy, and more eco-conscious. It's the best place to go if you want to help the environment and still enjoy one of the most beautiful tropical islands in the world.

The Nicoya region has more than its fair share of earthy, hippie, and creative types. That's why you'll find plenty of organic-food markets, dance and yoga studios, wildlife conservation projects, and acupuncturists here. The area is now trying to attract social entrepreneurs who can help build and maintain a better ecosystem. There are programs to organize recycling efforts, teach local kids about wildlife conservation, and work with endangered native species. One program is helping to save sea turtles by operating hatcheries to guard the turtles' precious eggs. What they all have in common is that they all need help.

But I think the most unique opportunity here is the chance to grow your very own bit of rain forest. There can't be too many places in the world where you can do it, but the conditions are just right here. You simply snap up a patch of barren land and do your plantings. With help from dirt-cheap local gardeners, you'll start to see tropical growth, exotic birds, and maybe even a few howler monkeys within a few short years.

To get the most affordable jungle land, you need to be at least fifteen or twenty minutes inland, but that's still a short hop to the beach. And those beaches have eighty-degree water all year and some of the world's best waves. This lesser-known part of

Costa Rica is all about the *pura vida*, or "pure life." Here you can revel in stunningly beautiful surroundings and wildlife, go on jungle hikes, and pick your own fresh fruit. Not a bad way to save the world.

What It'll Cost You: Jungle lots can be bought for $50,000 to $100,000, and building your own place is affordable because the local labor is cheap. The average price of a house already built is $350,000.

Bonus Fact: Property taxes are super low in Costa Rica (0.25 percent), and you won't pay any income tax on pension or foreign income.

Inside Tip: Before you buy anything, check the national registry to make sure the property is free and clear. And if you leave your property unattended for long periods of time in Costa Rica, you may end up with friendly squatters who will not happily move on.

Sunny Days: Varies.

Median Age: 26.

MALAWI   Africa

Lend a Hand at the Malawi Children's Village

This is one of those volunteer challenges that are for the hardy and brave souls among us. In Malawi, a small, impoverished, yet beautiful country in southeastern Africa, hundreds of thousands of children have lost their parents to AIDS. These orphans are stigmatized and extremely vulnerable, and many of them live on the street. The Malawi Children's Village is trying to give these kids a chance.

The Village is a nonprofit organization in the district of Mangochi. Its staff are mostly local volunteers tackling the immense challenge of providing medical care, food, education, and on-site housing for 3,500 orphans who have no guardians. The local volunteers are young men and women from nearby villages who travel here by bike. They wear crisp blue uniforms and are the backbone of this place. But the Children's Village relies on help from outside volunteers as well—people of all ages from all around the world. Tom and Frances Vitaglione are a retired couple from North Carolina who came to Mangochi a few years back so they could return to what they'd done decades earlier when they worked in the Peace Corps. Another volunteer, Sheila Ravendhran, is a young pediatrician who recently graduated from New York University and came to Malawi for a real-world education.

The things you can do in the Village are almost limitless, as help is needed with everything from looking after babies to teaching kids basic reading or vocational skills. Many of the local volunteers are young and inexperienced themselves, and they sometimes need support as they try to deal with the children's problems. It's hard work for everyone, but the Village is a very upbeat place with so many kids smiling, playing, learning, and healing.

Some outside volunteers are here only for short periods, but others stay long-term. You can live cheaply and reasonably well in Mangochi, which is on a beautiful lake and near a resort. The area is known for its dramatic "monkey bread trees," which look as if they're upside down because the branches resemble roots, and incredible wildlife safaris are just an hour away. The village itself is very safe, with high-quality medical care at the nearby Mangochi District Hospital. There are even a couple of Indian restaurants here because the Children's Village has many volunteers from India.

All that said, none of this softens the hard realities around you. Malawi is very poor and underdeveloped. The roads are rough, people get by with the bare minimum, and it's heart-wrenching to witness up close the devastation AIDS has wrought onto this part of the world. But if there's a front line in the world of volunteering, this is it. "There are few in this world who need help more than these orphans," says Sheila Ravendhran. "And there's nothing more rewarding or fulfilling than seeing those kids smile at you."

> **What It'll Cost You:** "For twenty to twenty-two dollars a day you can live in nice digs and get served good food," says Sheila.
> **Alternative Option:** If you're not ready to move to Malawi full-time, you can volunteer for a few weeks and still make a difference. You can also help the Village by making a donation. Learn more at the Web site malawichildrensvillage.com.
> **Sunny Days:** Varies.
> **Median Age:** 16.

TEMPE   Arizona

Connect with Kids and with Your Peers

If you're itching to teach kids, you might want to go to Tempe. This city, in the heart of the Valley of the Sun, is all about education. For starters, Arizona State University is here, one of the biggest colleges in America. But Tempe is also a great place to teach young kids, thanks to a program that pairs you with grade-schoolers who could really use your help.

The local program is called Experience Corps, and it matches up adults over the age of fifty-five with needy students at several local elementary schools. Experience Corps provides training beforehand and then sends you out to teach a kindergartner or a first-, second-, or third-grader how to read. You work one on one for about fifteen hours a week, which means you really get to know the kids and have a huge impact on them. The tutoring programs of Experience Corps are in place in about twenty cities around the country, but Tempe stands out because this is also a great city for connecting with people your own age.

Tempe hosts a separate program that matches up boomers in

the area with second-career opportunities. This experimental program, created by the Civic Ventures group, is call Tempe Connections and the Connections Café (tempeconnections .org). People age fifty and older gather, learn, and work in a big Internet coffee shop at the Tempe Public Library. The wireless café offers the usual coffee and scones while providing coaching sessions, help with résumés, classes (in partnership with Arizona State University), and opportunities to volunteer. The program can also match you up with paid positions in the areas you're interested in, such as small-business consulting. If you combine the Experience Corps part-time tutoring program with the many opportunities available through the Connections Café, you can have a new life that balances volunteerism, paid work, and new friends.

Tempe is smack in the middle of Arizona: Scottsdale borders on the north, Mesa on the east, and Phoenix to the west. You can get to each of these neighboring cities in a flash, especially when the area gets a new light-rail line running in 2008, connecting Phoenix to Mesa by way of Tempe. But you'll find most of what you need right in Tempe, which has a revitalized downtown area adjacent to hundreds of acres of parkland and a 220-acre urban lake. There are also 150 miles of bike paths, and you'll have plenty of chances to enjoy them because the sun shines all the time here.

What It'll Cost You: The average home price in Tempe is $157,381.
Inside Tip: There are some good buys on condos downtown—the brand-new Riverwalk condo development has two-bedroom units in the $200,000 range.
Sunny Days: 300/year
Median Age: 31.

GREAT PLACES TO FIND YOUR PURPOSE, BY REGION

Northeast: "Adopt a trail" in the White Mountains, New Hampshire. If you love to hike and you're a volunteer at heart, think about adopting a hiking trail in the majestic White Mountains, home of the highest mountain peak in the Northeast. Adopting a trail is kind of like adopting a pet. Once you've been given responsibility for a trail, you're expected to monitor its condition by sprucing it up, cleaning drainage, and clearing brush. This important maintenance allows the historic trails in the Appalachian region to survive and be used by hikers and nature lovers from all over the world. The work is a great excuse to go hiking in the beautiful White Mountains as you help make the trails a little more beautiful for all of us. If you like company, the Appalachian Mountain Club will let you lead their nature walks. The club has an office in Gorham, New Hampshire, a picture-perfect town nestled in the heart of the White Mountains. Check out this opportunity at outdoors.org.

Midwest: Restore the Great Lakes while enjoying Chicago, Illinois. You probably don't associate lake restoration with life in a big city such as Chicago. But the truth is, Chicagoans have been committed to protecting Lake Michigan ever since 1970, when city residents stood on the lakeshore and declared: "We can take steps together to restore the lake we love." What started as a local effort to clean up one lake has expanded to include other parts of the Great Lakes basin. Today, the Alliance for the Great Lakes (greatlakes.org) is responsible for conserving and restoring the world's largest freshwater resource—and the center of the action is still Chicago, where many of the Alliance's volunteers are based. Members do hands-on work such as restoring the lake habitat and providing public education.

As a bonus, Chicago also has a program called One Brick that adds a fresh twist to volunteering by making it a social event, with get-togethers at restaurants and cafés after each volunteer effort (onebrick.org). And although everyone knows the Windy City has plenty of stimulation to keep you going, it's also becoming a city where people can age in place. Chicago is already easy to maneuver around, and now it's putting up more senior housing than any other city in the country, including stylish luxury high-rises just for retirees.

South: Rescue wildlife in Atlanta, Georgia. These days, Atlanta is known as a booming business center and a magnet for young professionals. It's even showing up on lots of lists for "hot places" to live or work. But Atlanta also has a lot of heart, especially when it comes to helping animals. Though the city has lots of great animal shelters all in need of help, the program that really caught my eye is AWARE, which stands for Atlanta Wild Animal Rescue Effort (awareone.org). I know what you're thinking: wild animals in Atlanta? Well, we're not talking lions and tigers here—more like baby birds that get abandoned, squirrels that have fallen out of trees, and injured rabbits or raccoons. AWARE gets thirty to sixty calls a day, according to founder Michael Ellis. Volunteers go to the troubled animal, nurse it back to health, and then release it into the wild. The AWARE center, located on seven beautiful acres in the Lithonia area, trains anyone interested in how to be an animal caregiver. A lot of the work is a blend of nursing and mothering skills. With a baby animal, you may actually have to nurture it back to health using specially prepared baby formulas and a syringe nipple. In addition, broken limbs and wings need mending and cages must be cleaned. It's hard work, says Ellis, and you must be prepared for the fact that lots of injured animals don't survive. But most of the time, they do. "People who work here save lives *every single day,*" says Ellis. "There's nothing better than seeing an animal get better because of your help—and then being there for the release. It bring tears to my eyes, every time."

Mountain/West: Build adobe homes in Taos, New Mexico. One of the best-known ways to volunteer anywhere is to sign up for Habitat for Humanity. It's satisfying work no matter where you do it, but if you want to put a unique twist on your home building, you might join Habitat in Taos, New Mexico. Taos is a lively arts town that's rich in Native American culture and offers plenty to do and see when you're not building homes. Besides that, the homes you'll build in Taos aren't just regular houses. The Habitat operation here builds most of its houses in the Pueblo Indian style that's unique to New Mexico. The main material used in Pueblo housing is adobe, which is basically mud mixed with straw, shaped into bricks, and dried in the sun. A house made of adobe is made from the earth, which means it's organic, energy efficient, and affordable. And there's a real feeling of craftsmanship in making an adobe house because it's done entirely by hand in an architectural tradition that goes back not just to the Pueblos but also to the Aztecs and Incas. "We train everyone from secretaries to business executives," says Paul Hesch, the director of the local Habitat office (taoshabitiat.org). "You get a great feeling of accomplishment building these houses, and you get to learn new skills. And when the work is done, you get to go out and enjoy Taos."

Chapter 9

Living the Boomerang Life

*C*harlotte Hart is leading a double life. Though she's officially retired from a career in the software industry, she serves on two nonprofit boards and is also president of the Boston Club, a group that helps women in business. When not shuttling across the Boston/Cambridge area to attend meetings, Charlotte also helps reform the local school system. In what spare time she has, she enjoys a robust social life and goes to the theater often. I'd say she's pretty busy.

But Charlotte has another world to which she escapes on a regular basis. She owns a condo on the Caribbean island of Bonaire, where she becomes a beach bum. There, her only concern is shore diving among the island's beautiful reefs. "When I get to Bonaire, I downshift," she says. "I become part of that culture—I know all the island people; they're my friends now. And I've decided to learn about marine biology."

By owning a place on the island, Charlotte says she's able to feel at home there in a way that a visiting tourist never could. The place Charlotte owns is in a "condotel"—a hotel that sells condo units—which means she gets hotel-style service and doesn't have to lift a finger. If she wants to rent the place out when she's not there, she *can. "But I usually just send my friends down to use it when I can't," she says.*

So why not just retire there full-time and give herself over completely to the easygoing island life? "I have too much going on in my city life to just leave it behind," she says. "There are people who depend on me and things I still need to do. Besides, as much as I love Bonaire, I really don't want to live there full-time. There's no theater, no downtown—I want all that. I want to have both the slow life and the faster life. I think it gives you great perspective when you have two completely different lifestyles and can go back and forth between them."

I'm a big believer in going to new places and finding new adventures. But I don't think that means you can't come back home to your old place. Many of us absolutely love the life we live and the place we are and don't want to give up the good things we have. We enjoy being close to family and friends, or maybe we're raising a second family. Some of us are in the thick of a career and we're not quite ready to let go. Or maybe we just don't want to leave the city or neighborhood we cherish. I couldn't imagine leaving New York City and all the things I love about it. For me, there are just too many friendships and emotional connections that bind me here.

But does that mean I can't have a rejuvenating second life in a new place? Heck no! We all need and deserve that escape to Nextville, and we can do it on a part-time basis, too.

This chapter is for the people who want to keep loving what they have but also dream of adding a whole new dimension to their lives, complete with a new place, a new lifestyle, and even a new identity. Simply taking more or better vacations won't do it for you. After all, that's not a new life, and it won't allow you to discover another you. Vacations only turn you into a tourist version of your same self for a week or two.

If you really want a slice of paradise, you'll have to own that slice or make it yours in some way. You'll need to put down new roots there while keeping your old ones back home. Then you can go back and forth between the old and the new—that's what makes your life a "boomerang."

Why is the boomerang lifestyle a growing trend for retirees today? Because our lives are more complicated, and sometimes the solution is not as easy as "just moving away." Many of us aren't willing to give up our first lives entirely. Our connection to work can sometimes make it harder to just pack up and go. But the biggest factor is usually our connection to family. We're marrying and having kids later, and sometimes marrying again. We're combining families, and after the kids are grown, there may be grandkids involved. We may want to be in the thick of enjoying them in our current home. And there's also the community aspect. In chapter 4 we looked at the boomers eagerly searching for a sense of community, but the flip side is that some of us have found it already—and it just happens to be in the place where we already live.

So the question becomes, how can you keep the old life while adding on a whole new one? Well, if you're willing to make the effort and do a little bit of juggling—because maintaining two lives and two homes can be tricky at times—then there are lots of great possibilities. Although the idea of having a second home is nothing new, there have never been so many low-maintenance ways to do it as there are now, such as fractional ownership, condo hotels, private residence clubs, house swapping, slow travel, and more.

What all these options have in common is that they require some level of personal commitment. I'm talking about a commitment of regular time spent there to become a real part of the new community and, of course, a commitment of money.

People assume the biggest obstacle to having the boomerang lifestyle is not being able to afford it. But having a second place doesn't have to break the bank. There are some very affordable options and ways to offset your costs by generating income with the property.

Park It Here

Let's start with the cheapest and most intriguing possibility for a boomerang—making your second home a trailer. I know if you're over fifty, trailer-park living may sound déclassé, but the truth is that it has become popular with the young and chic. Today it's a smart way to get the benefits of a second home in a great location at an incredibly low cost.

Trailers are evolving with the times by becoming sleeker, more stylish, and more customized. The most popular type is the "park model," so named because it's designed to be parked in one location, as opposed to being moved around. Park-model sales are going through the roof, and people park them in campgrounds, beachfront areas, gated communities, and anywhere else it's permitted. To see them, you might not even know they're trailers because they're now made to look like log cabins and English country cottages. And they cost a fraction of what a house goes for. You can get a nice one for only fifty thousand dollars and the cheapest model for half that price.

For Luanne DeMatto, it's the perfect retirement home. Luanne, fifty-five, isn't quite retired yet—she still plans to work a few more years at her bank job in Mystic, Connecticut. But Luanne says that even when she does stop working, she still plans to keep her house because it's close to family members. "I can't imagine being away from our grandkids," she says.

At the same time, though, she wants to have a nice little getaway spot to enjoy now and throughout her retirement. So she and her already-retired husband bought a park model, which they keep just five minutes away from the beach in Westerly, Rhode Island. "If you wanted to buy a beach house in Westerly," she says, "it would cost you a million dollars. This is a nice alternative." Luanne's trailer is customized with the kind of windows, bookcases, and ceramic tile floors she's always wanted, and she's surrounded it with a flower-filled garden. "It's our little slice of heaven," she says.

The great thing about a parked trailer, as opposed to tooling around in an RV, is that you can put down roots in one place. Luanne says that in trailer campgrounds like the one where she's parked in Westerly, "it's an old-fashioned way of living, where you can sit on the porch and talk to your neighbors, because everybody's always out walking around. In suburban neighborhoods, it seems like you don't get to know your neighbors nearly as well."

But people who opt for more mobile RVs, driving them around and using various campgrounds as their bases, also find a strong sense of community at each location. Some RV owners use one site as their primary location—their home away from home. The best of these places can be amazing worlds unto themselves, as is the case with Slab City, profiled in this chapter, where RV owners come together each season to indulge in a thoroughly offbeat way of life by dancing around bonfires and living like gypsies. It's not unusual for RV owners who travel a lot to find several different RV-park communities that soon become their favorites. And just when you think you've heard everything, the true aficionados of this lifestyle even keep separate RVs or park models in a couple of different locations so that they can boomerang from one trailer to another.

Fractional Ownership

One downside to using an RV or parked trailer as your second home is that you're stuck maintaining it all year round, even though you might use it only seasonally. And as nice as the newer models look, it's still a trailer with a more transient feel than a luxury condo or town house. If a luxury condo is more your style, the good news is that today you can get a million-dollar condo at a fraction of the cost—if you're willing to share.

Fractional ownership is the new buzzword when it comes to

part-time shared vacation homes. Think of a higher-quality version of time-shares. Time-shares earned a well-deserved bad reputation over the past twenty years because of high-pressure sales tactics and stories of people stuck with places that didn't live up to salespeople's promises. But the growing fractional condo/town-house market is a different story because reputable companies are managing the new developments, including big hotel names such as Hyatt, Marriott, Ritz-Carlton, and Four Seasons.

These companies have squarely addressed a couple of problems associated with the old time-share model. Time-shares really just sell you time, but when you buy a fractional unit, you get a title of ownership, broken down as, say, one-twelfth of a share (three weeks to one month a year). Fractionals also provide more luxury and more flexibility. You get points that can be traded in so you can stay at other locations run by the same company. And fractionals typically come with high-quality amenities such as spas, restaurants, and prime access to beaches and ski slopes. In some cases, all of these amenities are contained in a country-club setting called a private residence club.

For all of this, of course, you'll pay a premium. A one-twelfth share in a two-bedroom town house with prime ski-slope access can cost you three hundred thousand dollars for three weeks' time a year. That's ten to twenty times as much as you might pay for a time-share, though with the time-share you'll get less time (typically a week) at a lesser facility shared by more people with no deed in your name. This is not to say time-shares aren't a good option for some of us, especially for those on a tight budget. But if you go the time-share route, just be careful and read my box on the next page for tips of what to watch out for.

Fractional Versus Time-Share: Six Things You Need to Ask

If you're confused about fractional ownership versus time-shares and the pros and cons of each, here are some things to ask up front:

Where's my deed? With fractional ownership, you actually own a share of the property and you get a deed. With time-shares, you don't really *own* anything—you've leased a specific amount of time each year. So, unlike with fractionals, you can't build equity in a time-share.

Can I trade it? With time-shares, you usually have a fixed week in a fixed location. You should check out how easy it is to swap that with other shareholders in different locations. With fractionals, you're more likely to have a points-based share, which enables you to use the points for alternative locations or even for hotel stays and airline flights. But, like time-shares, fractionals usually require booking well in advance, and you should find out how far in advance you'll need to plan.

What's it worth? Find out about recent sales of similar time-shares and fractionals from other share owners. And always check for resales on the Internet before you buy. Buying your slice online is almost always cheaper.

Who's in charge? The time-share business has attracted a lot of fly-by-nighters through the years. Research the companies offering shares online—find out how long they've been around and whether there are complaints filed against them for failing to properly maintain properties. You can check with the Better Business Bureau and with the local Timeshare Owners Association for the city or country. Stay clear of high-pressure tactics and come-on prizes—they're always a bad sign.

Are there any hidden fees? With fractionals, the annual fees are typically stated up front, much as if you were buying a condo. With time-shares, there can be hidden fees disclosed only in the fine print. The best way to know what they are is to ask and to have a local attorney review the documentation before you buy.

How many people share the place? If a half-dozen people are sharing a property, it's manageable. But if fifty different people use it over the course of the year, it'll look like a dump in a few short years.

Fractional ownership has gotten so popular that it's spreading well beyond luxurious condos and town houses. Today you can go online and buy a fractional share of a French vineyard from Lifestyle Vineyards (buyavineyard.co.uk) or, for a mere two million dollars, you can buy a fractional share of a yacht, which entitles you to five weeks per year when that 132-foot beauty is all yours. Just click on yachtplus.co.uk to have a peek.

Owning It Outright

Not everyone likes to share. If you want to keep your vacation property all to yourself, there are some great new options out there. A condo hotel unit, such as the one Charlotte Hart owns in Bonaire, is just like buying a hotel suite. You get the full concierge service of a hotel, but the unit is yours and yours alone. A unit like this can cost anywhere from $250,000 to a million or more, but the good news is that you can rent it out as much as you like and it can actually earn back a substantial portion of that outlay. But beware—when you rent out your unit, you usually get only half the income. The hotel takes the other half for managing and maintaining the rented room in your absence.

A condotel unit can be ideal for a boomerang because it makes things so simple. There's no need to take care of the place—everything is done for you—and no need to worry about security while you're away. As Charlotte Hart says, "It's the easiest way to go—you feel as if you're on vacation all the time."

Buying a private residence at a resort is a step up from the condotel. Instead of buying a hotel room, you're buying a full house within a resort development, though you still get all the hotel-room amenities. The cost is much higher, from half a million up to ten million dollars. If you buy from a destination club instead (see destinationclub.org), you can get a similarly luxurious package, but the difference is that you're not buying anything outright. Instead, you pay an up-front membership fee of one million dollars or more, with annual dues in the $20,000–$25,000 range. I think of it as a country-club membership that comes with a house you can use for a month or two each year.

Now, if you're someone who likes to take cruises, you can actually buy a condo on a cruise ship (and we're not talking about *The World*, the multimillion-dollar adventure profiled in chapter 7). Several companies offer this option, the largest being Condo Cruise Lines International (condocruiselines.com). These suites can cost from three to six hundred thousand dollars, with another ten thousand dollars a year in condo fees. But you can make a lot of that money back by renting the suite at a going rate of three to five thousand dollars a week, with the cruise management splitting the income with you. Rent it out enough times and eventually you'll be cruising for free.

The Basic Vacation Home

With so many new alternatives, does it still make sense to simply go out and buy a vacation home? I think it does, but only if you plan to make full use of it. The whole reason for going the fractional route is to avoid having a vacation house that sits empty and unused much of the year. But if you buy a second home that's easily rented and you have someone on-site to manage it for you, owning a vacation home can be relatively stress free. The property value of vacation homes typically appreciates the most over time, so that's an added bonus.

When you buy a second home, make sure it's not too far to get to. Lots of us like the notion of retreating to someplace remote, but the reality is that too "remote" translates to "no one will visit," so make sure you like being alone before you buy it!

A vacation home should be refreshingly different from your primary home. As a city dweller with a busy life and crowded place, my ideal is a small cottage on a quiet island such as Harbour Island (profiled in this chapter). There I could live like a no-good beatnik with nowhere to go and no one to see. But it's also accessible enough for my close friends and family to visit.

That brings us to the subject of families. A big emerging trend in vacation homes is the creation of family compounds. Families create them by buying or building an extra-large vacation home or by putting a cluster of smaller homes together and having each family member chip in for a share. Again it's the fractional approach, but here it's kept all in the family. Family members (and sometimes friends) divvy up the weeks and weekends, but the best part is when stays overlap and the whole gang is together. A family compound can be a great way to maximize the use of a vacation home, share the costs, and strengthen family ties. But I think the key to making it successful over the long haul is to have the compound professionally managed and the ownership structured with good tax counsel—just like the Kennedys.

If You're Just Not Buying Any of This . . .

Some of us don't want to feel encumbered by second-home ownership, not even in a partial or fractional way. Some of us like to constantly explore new and different places, and for that carefree traveling is the only way to go. But I suggest taking the travel experience up a notch and immersing yourself more deeply.

You'll change your experience completely if, rather than being a typical tourist, you feel as if you're actually living in the place you're visiting. There are a couple of ways to do this.

One is by house swapping. When you house swap, you get to live in someone's home instead of a tourist hotel for a week, a

House Swapping in Seven Easy Steps

Step 1. List your home on an Internet swapping site. Most of them charge an annual fee that ranges from forty dollars to seventy-five. Here are a few good ones: diggsville.com, HomeLink International (homelink.org), and Home Exchange (homeexchange.com).

Step 2. Pick a few places you'd like to visit and list them on the swap site you've chosen.

Step 3. When you find a swap partner, you'll exchange information by e-mail, but also arrange to speak on the phone. You'll get a much better sense of the person and can go over a lot more details by phone.

Step 4. Sign a contract with your swap partner. Samples are provided by house-swapping Web sites. The contract should specify who's paying for phone charges and any other financial details.

Step 5. Lock up your valuables before you leave. There's virtually no theft in home exchanges, but it will give you peace of mind.

Step 6. Tell a neighbor that there will be someone staying in your house. You don't want your guests to get arrested!

Step 7. Leave detailed instructions at your house. Include emergency numbers and any relevant details about the nuances of your home.

month, or sometimes a year. You get to enjoy that person's neighborhood, shop his or her stores, and often meet the neighbors, and the house sometimes comes with a car and a pet. It's a more authentic experience. If you've never swapped before, it's easy, and Web sites that organize swapping report that homes are consistently well cared for.

Another option is "slow traveling," which has become very popular of late and is particularly ideal for retirees who have more flexibility with their schedule. The idea here is, again, to live like a local resident by renting a home or apartment and spending more time in the city or country you're visiting. Most of us have grown used to the frantic one- or two-week vacations where we try to see and do everything and end up experiencing very little. With slow travel, you get to spend a month, or maybe three months, or maybe six—enough time to feel as though you've really lived somewhere. You meet people, make your own discoveries, and get into the flow and rhythm of a place—all the things a tourist doesn't get a chance to do.

You can slow travel just about anywhere—the more far-flung the better—and there's a slow-travel Web site (slowtravel.com) that provides lots of tips and information on rentals. In this chapter I've singled out New Zealand as our destination. Because it takes so long to get there, it just makes sense to stay awhile. It's a country and a culture that need time to be thoroughly enjoyed. Soon enough—but not too soon—you'll feel like a full-fledged kiwi, and when your time is up, you can come flying back to where you started, just like a good boomerang should.

SORTING THROUGH THE BOOMERANG OPTIONS

Option	What You're Buying	Pros	Cons
The RV life	A recreational vehicle that you use as a mobile vacation home	Low cost (less than $100K for the RV, plus fees for spaces in RV parks); ability to change locations whenever you want	Transient environment; year-round maintenance; may be cramped and less homey than a house or condo
Vacation home	A second home that's all yours	No restrictions on when you can use it; can fix it up the way you like; full equity ownership; can be a good investment	Expensive because you're not sharing costs; may sit empty and unused for long periods of time; have to maintain it yourself
Time-share	Usually one week of time, at a fixed date in a fixed location	Inexpensive—many cost less than $20K; lots of locations and properties to choose from; some flexibility in terms of swapping with other locations	Limited time; fixed date not always convenient; no equity ownership; resale value iffy; lots of people using the place, resulting in heavy wear and tear
Fractional ownership	A partial-ownership share in a condo or house (e.g., a one-twelfth share gives you one month)	Access to higher-quality properties; equity ownership with a deed	Moderately expensive—at least $250K to $300K or more for a desirable property; fixed location (though you may earn points that can be used to stay at other properties from the same owner)
Destination club	Membership in a club that gives you access to mansionlike homes and resort services for several weeks a year	Top-quality, luxurious properties; concierge services	Expensive—may cost $500K to $1 million up front, plus thousands in monthly fees; no equity stake; often guaranteed only a partial refund if you quit the club
Condo hotel	A room or suite in a resort-type hotel	Prime locations and top-notch facilities; hotel-style concierge services; ownership; split revenues with hotel as it rents out the room when you're gone	Only a room or suite, rather than a house or full condo; less privacy; moderately expensive ($200K to $500K): may be limits on your usage of the room (typically, thirty days per year maximum)

BEST PLACES FOR THE BOOMERANG LIFESTYLE

BEAUFORT   South Carolina

Beach? City? Small Town? Have It All!

For lots of us, the trouble with committing to a vacation home is that it locks you into one type of getaway spot. Suppose you can't decide where your second life should be based. A relaxing beach area? An exciting city? Or maybe a friendly small town? If all three of these possibilities appeal to you, I suggest looking at Beaufort, South Carolina. It's smack in between the great beaches of Hilton Head Island and the urban chic of Charleston, South Carolina. And Beaufort itself is a classic Southern town with loads of charm.

Buying in Beaufort is a great way to "borrow" many of the amenities of Hilton Head without actually living there. You'll have easy access to Hilton Head for day trips, where there's so much great golf and wonderful biking throughout the island. And of course there are those glorious beaches, with gentle waves and hard-packed sand you can ride your bike on—there's nothing better than cycling along the beach and jumping off your bike and into the water when you get too hot.

When you're feeling more of an urban vibe, head off from Beaufort in the other direction and in ninety minutes you'll be in Charleston. This city has one of the most walkable downtowns anywhere, with lots of mansions to poke around in. Charleston has a serious buzz about it, partly because it has some of the top restaurants in the country right now. It could easily have made my list of up-and-coming "Living Young" cities for chapter 5. And although you could get a nice little getaway apartment there, you may not always be in the mood for the bustle of a growing city such as this one or Savannah, which is also close by (just a forty-five-minute drive from Beaufort). But with Beaufort as your base, you can alternate between these two great cities, enjoying them for an afternoon or a night out before heading home to quiet Beaufort.

Beaufort has a unique mix of old-world charm and small-town friendliness. When you're not up for the city or a day at the beach, this is the place where you'll want to kick back and relax. It's got antebellum mansions to rival Charleston's, and instead of busy traffic you've got horse-drawn carriage tours rolling through the historic downtown streets. The trees here are amazing: moss-draped oaks, tropical palms, and palmettos. And you don't have to trek to Hilton Head for the water. Beaufort is a coastal town and the surrounding county has two thousand small islands, all great for boating. There's a big annual shrimp festival for lovers of the crustacean, as well as a local festival celebrating the Gullah culture, a living legacy of the region's African American history ("Gullah" refers to both the native Beaufort country islanders and their language). There's also a brand-new film festival that started in 2007, appropriate because Beaufort has long been Hollywood's go-to spot when it comes to filming in a charming Southern town. More than twenty movies have been shot here, including *The Big Chill* and *Forrest Gump*.

What It'll Cost You: Beaufort is still surprisingly affordable, with a median home cost of $156,000. The mansions may be out of reach for most of us, but there are lots of bargains on small vacation homes.

Inside Tip: If you're interested in a top-notch gated community in this area, check out Dataw Island, a private gated island where residents are in love with two things: golf and volunteering.

Sunny Days: 216/year.

Median Age: 31.

NEW ZEALAND

A Nice Place to Visit, But You May Never Want to Leave

The Lord of the Rings films really kicked up interest in New Zealand, as the movies showed off the stunning natural beauty of this country. But though more people now have New Zealand on their list of places they'd like to see, most never go because it's so far away. You'll lose a whole vacation day going and another one coming back, which is why I say New Zealand is an ideal place for slow travel.

You won't find a better world to immerse yourself in than New Zealand. The culture is truly unique, with its worship of kiwis, its irreverent down-under worldview, its love of wild adventure, and its strong indigenous Maori influence. It's also familiar and friendly enough that you can easily settle in and feel at home. And there's so much to see and do that you'll need a minimum of two months to do the place justice.

Another great thing is that New Zealanders will welcome you into their homes. In some areas local farms take in visitors for very reasonable rates, which is a great way to experience how New Zealanders live, work, and eat. On slow-travel Web sites you can find the places that offer "farm stays" (try truenz.co.nz/farmstays). Another way to live like a native New Zealander is to house swap with a kiwi. Right now New Zealanders are as interested in coming here as we are in going there because America really appeals to their big and bold approach to life.

Once you've spent time in New Zealand, you'll find it's really not that big a country after all. It's comparable in size to Colorado but has great cities such as Auckland, Christchurch, and Wellington and countless sights to see, many of them reachable by legendary walking trails. One-third of the country is protected national parkland and there's incredible variety in the landscape and vegetation. There are world-class mountain ranges with skiing landscapes you'll find nowhere else in the world. There are sweeping plains, lush rain forests, some of the world's most dramatic waterfalls, steaming volcanoes, geothermal pools, limestone caves, and glacial valleys. In short, the country has nature in just about every form except ice caps.

New Zealand is the world capital of adventure sports—the first man to climb Mt. Everest was a New Zealander. Bungee jumping was invented here, and in the free-spirited town of Queenstown, people jump off bridges, dive down waterfalls, and ride three hundred feet high on zip cables (I did the latter with my kids and I'll never do it again). New Zealand also has wineries everywhere and more golf courses per capita than anywhere else in the world. The whole country is like one big playground, and the New Zealand laugh is the most robust laugh I've ever heard.

What It'll Cost You: You can do farm stays for as little as forty dollars a day, and house swapping lets you stay for free. The average home price in Queenstown is $243,692.
Sunny Days: 187.
Median Age: 35.

HARBOUR ISLAND   The Bahamas

A World Away, But Easy to Reach

This little gem of an island is one of the best-kept secrets of the Bahamas. It's great for the boomerang life because you can get here in a one-to-two-hour flight from the United States and yet feel as if you're entering an entirely different world. After your flight, you'll take a water taxi to this tiny spit of an island that's just four miles long and half a mile wide with mature palm trees, shallow crystal clear waters, and natural dunes tumbling down to the pale pink sand the island is known for.

What I love best about Harbour Island, called "Briland" by its inhabitants, is that there's nothing fancy about it. There are a couple of big plantation houses on the tip of the island, but most of the residences are modest, simple cottages. Inside these cottages you'll find wealthy people from all over the world. Many are boomers, and most have been coming to Harbour Island for twenty years (while telling no one else about it). So there's much more of a community feeling here than on a typical tourist island.

In the center of the island is Dunmore Town, with old Victorian-style architecture mixed with the bright pastel colors of the Bahamas. There are a few restaurants in Dunmore with sophisticated fare and no ice-cream or T-shirt shops. If you walk along the bay, you can get a salad made from freshly caught and chopped conches—natives crack the shells right in front of you! The island has roosters strutting everywhere, and there are leashed goats in fields and backyards where local people and children play. There are thousands of colorful songbirds, but no mosquitoes. No one uses air conditioners here because it's so breezy, and no one has screens on their windows. You can fall asleep to the sounds of the ocean through the open windows and then wake up to the songbirds.

There are no cars on Harbour Island—they allow only old golf carts that are noisy but charming as they putt-putt down the streets. And there are no parking rules, so you can drive and park them anywhere. There are no fences on any of the beaches and no police on the streets, and you can walk anywhere at night and be perfectly safe. Harbour Island is a place with an amazing anything-goes attitude, which makes it the perfect spot in which to relax and let go.

What It'll Cost You: The few mansions here can easily run five to seven million dollars, but the average home price is $400,000.
Inside Tips: There are plans on nearby Eleuthera Island to build a Jack Nicklaus deluxe golf course, which could attract wealthy

duffers who've stayed away because Harbour Island has no golf. So if you plan to buy here, you might want to get in before the golf course does. Also, lots of loyal people just rent here, year after year. So if you plan to do that, be sure to book your house a year in advance.

Sunny Days: 340/year.

Median Age: 28.

DUBAI   United Arab Emirates

Vegas Meets Disneyland in the Desert

Picture 20 percent of all the construction cranes in the world parked in one place, all putting up buildings at the same time. Not just ordinary buildings, either. Dubai is erecting the world's tallest skyscraper (two hundred stories, twice as tall as the Empire State Building) as well as the first fully rotating building (each floor will rotate 360 degrees independently). There are shopping malls that look like the Taj Mahal, where you can buy everything from iPods to gold necklaces discounted and tax free. When you need a break from shopping, you can stop and go skiing on one mall's artificial refrigerated ski slopes. There'll soon be a gigantic theme park that will make Disney World look like a Mickey Mouse operation. And to top it all off, the imaginative builders of this great city have created the world's two largest man-made islands (with a third planned) right off Dubai's shores. These twin islands, each about twelve square miles, were raised up from the bottom of the water and are sculpted in the shape of giant palm trees! They are filling up fast with super-luxury hotels and multimillion-dollar villas.

If all of this seems excessive, it is—and that's what Dubai is all about. If you're looking for subtle and understated, it's not the place for you. But if you want to be surrounded by dazzling architectural wonders everywhere you turn, and if you thrive on mega-shopping, nightlife, exotic culture, and endless forms of lavish man-made amusement, then you'll never get bored in Dubai. And if you enjoy an eclectic mix of people, there are more than eighty nationalities living here.

Dubai's long thirteen-hour flight from the United States makes it a better place for a boomerang than for a tourist. If you visit Dubai as a tourist, you lose too much of your vacation time traveling and, once you get here, you'll pay rock-star hotel rates sometimes as high as two thousand dollars a night. But if you're smart and follow the lead of Middle Eastern investors, you'll buy yourself a share in a condo or condo hotel room. You can get a piece of Dubai for as low as fifty thousand dollars for a time share or two hundred thousand dollars for a condotel. Real estate has been a great investment in recent years, with double-digit returns the norm. Even with a shaky real estate market in other parts of the world, this one has a better shot at maintaining momentum in the next few years because of all the world-class buildings and attractions opening here between 2008 and 2010.

What it all boils down to is this: if you get a condotel in Dubai, you can stay for a stretch of three to four weeks, enough to make the long trip worthwhile. Then leave the room/suite to the hotel to rent out the rest of the year, splitting the proceeds. If all goes well, you should get all your purchase money back in six to seven years. Not a bad deal.

There are time-shares and condotels all over Dubai, and you can spend a month-long vacation just looking at all of them. One that's worth a look is the Cube, a five-star tower right in the heart of the new Dubai Sports City complex. The Cube is yet another Dubai dazzler—the architects cut out a huge cube area right in the middle of the building and turned the hole into an open-air artificial park with palm trees and a giant pool. It will open in mid-2009.

What It'll Cost You: A studio in the Cube goes for $200,000 and a one-bedroom for $290,000, and you can use the room a total of thirty days a year. Joel Greene of Condo Hotel Center says an owner of a $200,000 room would typically get back 13 to 18 percent, or about $30,000, a year.

Bonus Facts: Dubai makes so much money on oil and gas that it can afford to be practically tax free—no income tax, sales tax, or capital taxes. Also, Dubai is known for having very hot temperatures, and one-hundred-degree weather is not uncommon.

Sunny Days: 338/year.

Median Age: 27.

GREAT DOMESTIC SPOTS FOR BOOMERANGS, BY REGION

Northeast: Ski in and ski out at a condotel on Hunter Mountain, New York. What's great about Hunter Mountain is that it's close enough to New York City to drive here in just a few short hours. That makes having a condotel here a great option for a big family with a boomerang lifestyle. Hunter used to be where young city types went to ski by day and party by night, but it's undergoing an interesting evolution and is now more of a wholesome family environment with a lot fewer daredevils crowding the slopes. If you've always wanted a ski chalet but don't want to take care of one, you can buy a condo in the Kaatskill Mountain Club, a ski-in, ski-out hotel that has small studios and larger suites up to two thousand square feet. You'll get full-service treatment—including bell service and housekeeping—plus extras everyone in the family can enjoy, such as the slope-side outdoor heated pool. A quarter-share of a condo, entitling you to thirteen weeks each year, can be purchased for a onetime price that ranges anywhere from sixty thousand to two hundred thousand dollars.

Mid-Atlantic: Fly in and fly out to a second home in Burnsville, North Carolina. Everyone seems to love Asheville, North Carolina, and because of that love affair, it's gotten a little overcrowded and overpriced these days. But Burnsville, just the next town over, is a younger version of Asheville—a tiny bit hip but still very small-townish. Within Burnsville there's a gated community called Mountain Air that lives up to its name. It's perched on top of a mountain five thousand feet up with amazing views of the surrounding Blue Ridge Mountains and a lot of privacy. The 1,300-acre community has its own award-winning golf course as well as some more unexpected amenities, such as an organic community garden and a "nature cove," where the community's in-house nature guides lead field trips and nighttime salamander hunts. But here's the coolest thing about Mountain Air: it's got its own landing strip, so you can fly in and out on your own schedule. All you have to do is buy a condo or single-family house here, starting at $225,000. And then buy yourself a jet.

South: Become an artist in Fairhope, Alabama. If you're ready to pursue a passion in art but not ready to give it all up and move to Tahiti, you might consider an accessible little art community named Fairhope, where you can go for occasional doses of inspiration. Fairhope is a great place for aspiring artists to get a small second house or a time-share. It is located on the eastern shores of Mobile Bay and was founded a century ago as a renegade colony—a group of utopian dreamers were seeking "a fair hope" of a utopian life. Today Fairhope provides that life for the many artists who live here and get inspired each day by the picture-postcard beauty of this little town. To begin with, there are seasonal flowers everywhere—the locals even go out of their way to beautify the downtown's wooden trash receptacles by topping them with flower boxes. The Southern-style architecture, with wrought-iron balconies overlooking shady streets, makes this a great place to stroll. Sunsets over the bay are amazing, which is why Fairhope has been named one of the most romantic towns in America. There are local customs not found anywhere else, such as the annual jubilee held each summer when fish and crabs migrate to the shallow waters and the locals catch them by hand. There are galleries galore all over town where you can show your work along with other local artists, and there are small Southern cafés where artists, writers, farmers, and shopkeepers all talk together about how good life can be. Median home cost is $237,000; visit cofairhope.com.

Mountain: Set up your family's compound in Star Valley, Wyoming. Anybody who goes to Jackson Hole usually falls in love with it, but the problem there is that you can't get enough space for your family's buck. However, if you look just outside Jackson, you can find great, inexpensive Wyoming real estate perfectly suited for a family compound. Star Valley is an authentic home on the range, with big ranches, grazing cows, and wide-open Wyoming skies. The valley is surrounded by mountains with great fishing rivers running through them. There are just a few small towns here, and one of them is Afton, welcoming you with an arch of antlers on Main Street that stands eighteen feet high. The townsfolk claim it's the tallest elk antler arch in the world, and who am I to argue? From Star Valley, Jackson Hole is only twenty minutes by horse, and prices for large parcels of property are all over the place, allowing most of us to find a parcel to fit our family budget (check the listings at real estatejackson.com). Besides the fact that Wyoming is drop-dead gorgeous, it's also one of the few states that does not collect income tax, a gift tax, or taxes on interest and dividends—all good reasons to set up a family compound.

West: Join a gang of RV gypsies at Slab City, California. It's only fitting that the last item on our list should be a little wild and crazy. I talked earlier in this chapter about how people are using their RVs to live boomerang-style, often by finding a great

RV community that can provide a home away from home and a whole second life. Well, if you want that second life to be truly offbeat and different, check out Slab City, a seasonal RV camp set up in the desert of southeastern California about an hour from Palm Springs. The site used to be a military base, and when the base was abandoned, all that was left were large slabs of concrete in the desert. Then a bunch of RV campers arrived and gradually transformed the area. Everything, from the makeshift performing stage to the little shack of a library, is made from scraps and cobbled together by hand. Most of the people at Slab City are retirees, but they don't act like it. They come here to cut loose, singing around campfires, dancing under the stars in tuxedos and sneakers, flying hippie flags, hosting prom nights, riding around in sand buggies, and building giant sculptures that no one but themselves will ever see. It's kind of like a quirky tribal experience, a chance for regular folks to be real gypsies for a few months each year. And this is not just a few individuals having a good old time. At peak season, in the midwinter months, there are several thousand people in the camp. But when winter ends and the desert heat begins to rise, most of the snowbirds take off, going back to being grandmas and grandpas, church-goers, and good citizens, until next year when they come back to the Slabs, ready to get wild all over again.

Chapter 10

Going Nowhere (and Loving It!)

U p to this point, I've cited more than seventy great places in which you can begin the next act of your life. In this chapter, I focus on the last place on our list. It's difficult to categorize— could be a big city, or maybe a small town. Could be in the Southwest or the Northeast. But one thing for sure is that traveling to this place is a cinch. In fact, you're already there. Because for some of us, Nextville is the place where we're living right now.

Here's the way I look at it: if you've already found paradise, why keep searching? There's no law that says you *have* to head out of town to enjoy the next chapter. In fact, today more people are staying put. It's part of a growing trend known as "aging in place." Why? Because as I mentioned earlier, our generation has more things keeping us connected to our "first life"—longer careers, families starting later, friends too precious to leave behind. And as community is of huge importance to our particular generation, there are many people among us who feel they've made themselves part of a great community already and simply don't want to yank themselves out of it just because they're older.

Now, if you consider yourself a boomerang like in chapter 9, the solution is to maintain your connection to your first life at home while also starting a fresh second life somewhere else. But there's another approach, and that's to decide this: "Hey—why not just create a new and exciting second life right here, in the place I love so much?"

It's not a cop-out and it's a perfectly good option for many. But it comes with one challenge: *How do you stay where you are and still feel as though you're starting over?* I believe that whether we're venturing off or staying put, we all need that sense of beginning a new chapter in life to feel emotionally satisfied as we age. And from a practical standpoint, our needs and desires change from midlife on, and the place we choose to spend the rest of our life should be able to fulfill those needs.

There are lots of ways to reinvent the place where you're already living, and that's what this chapter's about. It could be a matter of renovating and retrofitting your house so it's a better fit for the next stage of life. Or you may leave that big old house behind but choose to remain in the same area. Lots of us are downsizing to condos or apartments, moving down the road or just across town, and in doing so, we simplify our lives, lower our expenses, and usually stash away some of the profit on the sale of our house. We also keep what's most precious to us—remaining part of the community we've learned to love.

To Move or Not to Move

Even if you stay in the same community, the question of whether or not to change homes should be addressed up front. Much as you love the house you've lived in all these years, it's good to be realistic when you ask yourself, "Is this really the best place for me to live for the next ten, twenty, or fifty years?" And the best way to answer this is to do some looking ahead and soul-searching. Just like boomers who are planning to move to a whole different country, there's no escaping the fact that you'll need to do your homework to figure out what's best for you.

In a funny way, a lot of the issues I've already raised about moving still come into play even when you're staying put. Take, for example, "pursuing your passions." If you're planning to pursue that passion in your hometown, you still need the right house. Maybe you'll need a studio where you can produce artwork in a professional manner, or a suite that can serve as an office for a new entrepreneurial venture, or a gourmet kitchen where you can totally indulge your culinary passion. Whatever your pursuit, when it comes to making a life change in a meaningful way, your old house probably won't fit.

The same is true if you think back on the chapter about community—it's still relevant here because even if you're staying in the same physical community, there are going to be some changes in terms of the people you associate with on a daily basis. Your kids may be gone, but now there could be grandchildren requiring different kinds of rooms that allow for larger gatherings. Again, you'll need to adapt your living situation to fit those changes. And let's think back on the "living young" chapter. I talked there about the need to keep ourselves in the mix by having easy access to activities, stimulation, and the flow of everyday life. Does your house, in its present location, provide the opportunity for that kind of lifestyle? Or is it more likely to keep you isolated in the burbs and burdened by too many household chores?

Downsizing is a major consideration for any retiree, but it's especially so for boomers. A 2005 study on boomers by Pulte Homes, a leading developer of retirement communities, found that about half of people in their fifties plan to downsize their living arrangements when retiring. And why not? You get rid of empty rooms that need cleaning and big yards that need tending.

You also free up some of your time and money because a smaller living space usually costs a lot less to buy and maintain. And in shaky real estate markets, downsizing makes sense because it lowers your risk by taking some money off the table. If your local market takes a tumble, big houses have more to lose than smaller ones.

But the real dividend of downsizing is the freedom you feel when you can just lock the door and go, whenever you want, without worrying about the lawn or dust or a million lights on timers. It's perfect for the travel-filled boomerang lifestyle. And if you buy a condo, you usually move closer to the downtown area and closer to good medical facilities. The location is often more walkable, giving you easy access to destinations you wouldn't get to if you were still living in your big house.

I think for most of us the hardest part of downsizing is getting rid of our stuff. All of us are weighed down by too many things we never look at or use. But as everyone discovers, the temporary pain of letting go can end up being very freeing. "I thought it would be difficult to part with all my stuff, but it was a very good experience once I got started—it was almost as if I was shedding the past," says Marion Wishnefski, who recently downsized from a large three-bedroom house to a condo about half the size.

Opting for something smaller and more manageable doesn't mean you need to live in a box—the cramped "senior apartment" doesn't appeal to any boomers I know. Nanette Overly, an Ohio-based condo developer, describes how boomers are hunting for condos and town houses with "ample space, tall ceilings [that] create a sense of volume, verandas and screened porches, garden-style layouts that minimize staircases, studio areas for pursuing hobbies, and luxuries such as Jacuzzi tubs and gourmet kitchens." Wow! That's a long list of particulars. Overly says we still want it all to look like a house, and this explains why many newer condos are striving for an exterior design that looks more like a detached home when seen from the street.

Moving to a condo can also be good for us from a sociability viewpoint. We'll have more interaction with our neighbors through shared facilities, particularly in newer developments that are going all out with features such as health clubs and hiking and biking trails.

Your Local Active Adult Community

Lots of boomer retirees are opting for local active adult communities, mentioned in chapter 4. And today many of us are choosing an active adult community in our hometown or within short driving distance of it. That's a big change from days of old, when retirees would pack up, wave good-bye to all their friends, and move to Sun City, where they'd have to begin building new friendships all over again. In the new more localized approach, you still get the new group of people you can meet and interact with at the active adult community, but you get to keep your old network, too. It can prove to be the best of both worlds, but only if we take full advantage by not relying too much on our old friends and family as a crutch. It's not an easy task, and it takes a determined effort to reach out to new neighbors and make them our friends. I think we have to ask ourselves if we're well suited for the challenge, as some are and others are not.

Because there are so many quality active adult communities opening up around the country, there's a fair chance you've got a good one in your general area. But I caution you not to assume the one you find is a good one until you do your due diligence and address my questions in chapter 4 on choosing the right community. You can also check to see if the place you're contemplating made it onto any of the various lists of best active adult communities. For example, the magazine *Where to Retire* publishes a list of the one hundred best retirement communities around the country each year. Another tool at your disposal is local word of mouth. When you're moving close by, it pays to talk to everyone you know to find out the real scuttlebutt about the local active adult community.

Exploring Home Upgrades

If you say, "Forget the condo—I want to stay right in my own house," that's just fine. It means you can focus your energy and resources on turning your house into an ideal retirement haven. It can cost you as little as twenty thousand dollars if you do it on a small scale or as much as six figures if you're thinking big, but either way think of it as an investment in your future. To finance big renovations, you can take out a home equity line of credit or consider getting a reverse mortgage. Reverse mortgages sound scary, but I think they're an ideal and secure solution for those of us who have large equity tied up in our current home and want a gradual, low-risk means of accessing it.

Using a Reverse Mortgage to Pay for Your Home Upgrade

The beauty of a reverse mortgage is that instead of you paying the lender—which is what we're all used to doing—it's the other way around and the bank pays you. You have to be at least sixty-two years old to qualify, and you can opt for a lump-sum payment or monthly payments for as long as you stay in the house. And you don't have to pay it back until you sell your house or die. It's a great option if you're house rich and cash poor or you want to retrofit the house you love but don't have the cash to do it.

Let me try to explain how it works. If you own your house outright, it means you have that amount in equity. With a reverse mortgage, the bank starts making loan payments to you, and as it does, your equity in the house is gradually reduced. When your home is sold, the bank recoups all it has lent you, including interest. Whatever remaining equity there is in your house will then go to you or your heirs. Because of the way the arrangement is set up, you don't have to worry about ever borrowing more than the house is worth.

The downside to a reverse mortgage is potentially overpaying on rates and fees. Origination fees can be up to 2 percent of your home's value, plus another 2 percent for insurance on the mortgage. Combined with closing costs, fees can climb up to 5 percent, or $15,000 on a $300,000 home. You have to shop around for the most competitive fees and always demand that the mortgage broker break down all the fees, separately and clearly, up front.

The amount of cash you get up front depends not only on your home value but your age, too—the older you are, the more you get. The AARP has a site to help you calculate how much you will get (rmaarp.com). There are "jumbo" mortgages that provide more up-front money, but they also carry higher interest rates.

If you want to pay less interest, don't choose the big up-front payment. Even if you're doing renovations, steady monthly payments may be sufficient to help finance the improvements done step-by-step over time.

The real question for many of us is not so much how to pay for the changes, but what kind of changes to make. There are two considerations. The first is how to redesign our home to reflect our fantasy lifestyle. That's the fun part. The second is the more practical part of retrofitting our home so that it can meet our everyday needs as we age. And for those among us who think we'll never get old, the second part ain't no fun at all! But if you're committed to staying in your house for the many years to come, now's the perfect time to prepare for that future. By making both the fun and practical changes, you'll have the dream home you deserve now and an adaptable home where you can be comfortable in the future.

I can't tell you what changes to make to create your ideal house—you know better than anyone what you've been dreaming about. You know which rooms you'd like to enlarge or combine and what luxuries you'd like to add. All I'll say is, reach for a house that is inspirational! Let it make room for your passions, the community of people you most want to be with, and the colors that make you feel happiest. Consider making it "greener" if that fits with the new you. But make it inspirational!

Retrofitting

I do want to address the more practical matter of retrofitting your home. How to do it is pretty simple and straightforward, but it's important to do it well if you plan to live a long and comfortable life.

In a recent report, the AARP found that a whopping 84 percent of boomers want to age in their own homes rather than move to assisted-living facilities or nursing homes. That's typical of our self-sufficient, independent approach to life. But if we're going to be realistic about aging at home, we have to take the necessary steps to modify our homes early. Specific accommodations—such as creating better lighting, situating bathrooms and bedrooms on the first floor, widening hallways and doorways, and creating step-free entrances—may not seem important now but will almost certainly matter later. These features are sometimes referred to as "universal design," and a growing number of contractors today specialize in this type of work. If you're hiring a contractor, make sure you check for universal-design credentials (see more of my tips in the box on the next page).

Barb's Tips on How to Hire the Right Contractor to Renovate Your Home

1. Check out his truck. A contractor's truck is his office. If it's a mess, the job will be run the same way. Get up out of your chair and walk the contractor back to his truck.

2. Hire someone local. Local contractors have a reputation to uphold and they know the local ordinances and authorities. Also, they can't run away.

3. Get a personal recommendation. Ask neighbors and friends, your neighborhood real estate broker, and the local building department.

4. Get three competitive bids. Don't hire the contractor whose bid is substantially lower than the other two.

5. Speak to the people he's recently done work for. Other customers will always tell you the truth.

6. Put it in writing. Make sure your written contract includes permits and fees, change orders, cleanup, and the number of workers that will be on the job each day. Don't forget to get proof of insurance.

7. Hold one-third of the money. Pay the contractor a third on signing, a third halfway through, and the last third when *everything* is done. Nothing is more aggravating than chasing a contractor to finish a job.

Universal Design

In its most basic form, universal design always includes wide doorways, at least one entrance without steps, and a first-floor bathroom. A house with these three features meets the standard of "visitability," which means anyone, regardless of age or disability, can visit the house. There is a "visitability movement" under way right now in a growing number of states across the country, requiring that all new homes be built with these same features.

But we all know there's a huge difference between visiting a house and living in one. To make a house suitable for truly comfortable living for the next many years, you'll need to go beyond the basics. The ground-floor bathroom should be accompanied by a bedroom. And it's not just the doorways that should be wider, but the hallways and stairways, too. Floors throughout the house should be level without thresholds to climb over, and tubs and showers should be made so that they're easy to get in and out of, with handheld showerheads as well.

Further, a universal-design house tends to have everything in just the right place and at the right height. Ever think about how often you stretch or bend to reach up or down in your house? With smart design, that doesn't happen. Appliances such as ovens are placed at just the right height so you don't have to stoop or bend, and kitchen counters are low enough to sit at when chopping veggies, with enough overhang to fit your knees comfortably under the counter.

Then there are all the little things, such as lever handles on doors and plumbing fixtures that are easier to use than knobs. There's pinpoint task lighting focused on where you're reading or cooking and subtle but distinctive color coordination throughout the house so that counter surfaces clearly contrast floor surfaces. The list, of course, goes on and on. But with help from the National Association of Home Builders, I've boiled it all down to a top-ten list on the next page.

Ten Best Retrofitting Improvements to Make on Your House

- ❏ **At least one bedroom and one bathroom on the first floor**
- ❏ **No-step entrances**
- ❏ **Wider doorways and hallways** (thirty-two inches for interior doors)
- ❏ **Easy-to-reach light switches**
- ❏ **Task lighting**
- ❏ **Raised appliances**
- ❏ **Curbless walk-in shower**
- ❏ **Tub and shower grab bars**
- ❏ **Handheld showerheads**
- ❏ **Lever-type handles** on doors and sinks

On one hand, these changes make perfect sense because most of them make life a little easier for everyone, including kids, parents, and grandchildren. But on the other hand, there's a stigma associated with them. Certainly, none of us want our home to look like a senior center or a hospital, and many style-conscious boomers worry that retrofitting will have that effect. And years ago that concern was merited.

But today, when universal design is done right, it's just as appealing to the eye as any good home design. Easily distinguished surfaces and borders not only add depth perception, they also add sophisticated pizzazz when the colors and finishes are well chosen. Even the most detested features, such as grab bars and benches in the bath, take on a whole new look with beautiful material and contoured styling, turning a useful bath into a luxurious spa. In fact, designers have begun using the term "accessibility chic," which means the features are all there to help when you need them but are unobtrusive.

Universal design today is smart, and it's even trendy. A recent survey of architecture firms by the American Institute of Architects named accessibility as the number-one and fastest-growing trend in home design. So even if you think you'll never get old, you can embrace the trend just because, well, everybody's doing it. Or you can make changes now for the benefit of a parent who might later live in your house or for older relatives or friends who may visit—even if you don't get old, other people do. It's also a way to protect the investment you've made in your home by ensuring that the house will age as gracefully as you.

Before you arrange to meet with potential contractors, it's helpful to get a sense of the retrofitting possibilities available. There's a clever online survey by the company Lifease (lifease .com) to help you envision some of the ways you might adapt your home. It makes suggestions for retrofit features and also provides relevant product information. (The survey costs about twenty dollars, but you can sample it for free.)

Expanding Your World Without Leaving Your House

We all realize that technology will continue to change how we live the next chapter of our lives. Boomers will be the first generation of tech-savvy retirees, and this opens up all kinds of opportunities that previous generations didn't have. We'll not only be able to network and work at home, but we'll be able to pursue far-flung passions in a virtual way.

But cyberspace can be particularly useful if we're planning to stay put. If your Nextville is right in your own home, then cyberspace can expand your world and open the doors to new communities—without your ever leaving the house. For that reason, I'm giving cyberspace an honorary slot on our list of seventy-plus great places to begin our next act.

One of the many great things online access brings is the opportunity to seek out and connect with not just new people, but new people who become kindred souls because they have similar ideas and interests. It can also give us that sense of community many of us are looking for. Before the advent of the Internet, people had to move in order to immerse themselves in a community of, say, bird-watchers. But online we can find bird-watcher groups and chat rooms where we can mingle with like-minded people and share tips and information. The Internet enlarges our social world because it builds a larger network of compatible friends to enjoy, and as more people make arrangements to actually meet their online friends in person, the boundaries are sometimes erased between real life and cyberspace.

These days the Internet is awash in boomer sites. We've tried to sort through some of them for you in our accompanying top-ten list. It isn't meant to be definitive, as there are thousands of sites that may be of interest to you based on your particular passions. Part of the fun is in finding them. Jeff Taylor, founder of the popular boomer site Eons, points out that we are a generation that has so much to offer and share in terms of our many interests, our passions, and our knowledge of a wide range of subjects, and cyberspace is a place where we can put our interests, passions, and knowledge to use. "I really think when you're talking about great places for boomer retirees to go and explore, cyberspace has to be high on that list because of all the possibilities it offers," says Taylor.

So for those of us who are planning to stay put, be sure to add a "virtual wing" as part of the renovation—a room that opens out onto the whole larger world of cyberspace. And for those of us moving to someplace new, I don't need to explain how valuable the Web will be in helping us find our way.

Expand Your World in Cyberspace: Barb's Recommended Sites

☐ **Eons (eons.com).** Social networking for boomers and community groups you can join

☐ **Third Age (thirdage.com).** Focus on the needs of midlife adults as they move "from limitation to possibility"

☐ **More (more.com).** The online companion to *More* magazine, for women over forty, with a focus on pursuing your second act in life

☐ **What's Next (whatsnext.com).** What you can do with the next stage of life, with lots of first-person experiences shared

☐ **ELDR (eldr.com).** Entertaining and edgy approach to aging

☐ **Gather (gather.com).** Another place to connect with people who share your passions

☐ **eHarmony (eharmony.com).** Relationship advice for adults

☐ **AARP (aarp.org).** A treasure trove of articles and resources

☐ **ElderTreks (eldertreks.com).** Adventure travel experiences for people fifty and over

☐ **Elderhostel (elderhostel.org).** Opportunities for lifelong learning

☐ **Ideal Places to Retire (ideal-places-to-retire.com).** Analyses of cities, from the inexpensive to the exotic

☐ **Find Utopia (findutopia.com).** Information on cities' cost of living, housing prices, and retirement communities

Chapter 11

Beginning the Journey

Ten Questions to Answer and Ten Rules
to Remember

I hope by now you've read through all the themes in this book and have taken my little quiz in chapter 2. You should have a good sense of where you might belong. Maybe some of the seventy-plus Nextvilles listed here are perfect for you, or maybe you're already looking for some potential Nextvilles of your own. So what now? What's stopping you from taking the big step and moving to the perfect place to begin the best chapter of your life?

Well, if you're like most people, the big kahuna is almost always fear. Change is scary and major change even scarier. And with so many unanswered questions associated with making a big change, it's natural for us to put it off. But when it comes to starting the next act of our lives, I don't think we can hold back. Life, as they say, is short, and life after fifty is even shorter. Every month counts, and the only thing we should really be afraid of is that one day we might look back and realize we should have made the move when we had the chance! The happiest people I know are always those brave souls who seized opportunities, while the saddest are those who stood by and watched. So here's my time-tested method to get you over your fears.

First, make a list of all the things that scare the heck out of you about starting all over. Most of our lists will read the same way, starting with life-threatening events that could go wrong. Big concerns usually involve our family and our friends. Then there are the physical hassles of selling our house, getting rid of our stuff, and buying a new house. Fears about making the wrong choices and the fear of making a big mistake always land on the list. Write it all down—take your time, and make sure the list is complete. Because once it's all on paper, you're halfway there. Ready?

Now let's go through another list—my ten questions that address the fears that stand in the way of most people trying to begin their life someplace new. After we answer them, I hope we'll have addressed all your concerns.

Question 1: How Do I Get on the Same Page as My Spouse?

If you're single, you're lucky and you can skip right to question two. But if you have a mate, you can't even begin to plan a move without first getting in sync with your partner. Men and women are different in the way they generally view retirement. Men more often see it as a time to kick back and relax or play, whereas women are sometimes more focused on a second career or finding more meaning in life. So, how do you bridge the gaps? The usual—compromise. You'll need to find the place and the lifestyle that offers something for each of you, and the only way to do that is to start exploring all the options together.

My real estate quiz in chapter 2 can be the perfect icebreaker. The results may point you in different directions, but you might also find some overlap where the themes of passion, community, living green, and living young, for example, apply to you both. And if you don't find any common ground, then look back to the chapter on the boomerang lifestyle—you can decide to bounce back and forth between your spouse's and your versions of paradise. You might even enrich your marriage as a result.

Sometimes you may have a strong desire to pursue your dream and your partner is ambivalent. If that's your situation, you might say something like, "Listen, Ambivalent, either come up with your own dream and we'll discuss it along with mine, or get on board with my dream and maybe you'll find yours along the way." Sometimes your partner really does find his or her passion along the way (like Diane Lane from chapter 3).

Question 2: What Will the Kids Think?

For many of us, this is a big one. How exactly do you tell your kids you're starting a new life somewhere else? It brings two sets of challenges. If your kids are still growing up, there's the difficulty that always comes with uprooting children. But it's also an issue for grown kids, who might feel protective of you and be concerned that you're moving too far away, especially if you live close to begin with. I believe the best thing to do is to start talking early and let them in on the decision process. Don't spring it on them. You might even get them to do some of the research and scouting for you. It's important to address the distance issue—specifically, who's going to visit whom and when. You need to make it clear that you're not cutting yourself off from them and give them time to adjust.

Also, grown kids are often interested in the practical issue of what will happen to the house. If you're planning to sell it, it's sometimes a big deal for them. You'll want to give them an early heads-up and enough time to gather all their things from your attic. If you're planning to give one of your kids the house— maybe he or she is just starting out or can't afford a different one—I have one word of advice: don't. If you give a child the house, you'll both get slammed with gift taxes. If you want your child to have your house, then loan him or her the money to buy the house instead and then forgive the legal portion of the debt each year. That way there's no gift tax. Read my tips in the box below and hire a competent tax accountant to do it right.

How to Give Your Kid the House

1. Decide if it's really the right neighborhood for your kid. The neighborhood you raised your kids in may have aged. If your child plans to raise his or her kids there, are there other young neighbors with kids? Are the schools still good?

2. Do the necessary due diligence. Just because it's a friendly transaction doesn't mean you shouldn't follow normal protocol of the usual inspections, an independent appraisal, and an engineer's report.

3. Beware of the too-friendly appraisal. The IRS watches home sales to family members closely. If there's a difference between the fair market value and actual sale price of the house, the difference will be taxed as a gift.

4. Set ground rules up front. Sometimes when you turn over the house to a kid, you feel as if it's still yours. It's not. Talk through issues such as how often you may be visiting. If you're emotionally attached to the house and don't want to see it changed, that needs to be discussed.

5. Gift the down payment. Your child is entitled to receive up to $11,000 tax free per year from both you and your spouse. "Child" includes each of your kids, each of their spouses, and each of your grandchildren.

6. Forgive the mortgage. You can loan the money for the entire purchase price to your child, put a mortgage on the property for the full amount, and then forgive the mortgage up to $11,000 per person per year until the mortgage is payed off. Note: you must charge interest on the mortgage, and this is set by the federal government, usually 1–2 percent less than regular mortgage rates.

Question 3: What About the Dog?

This is not a silly question, as it ranks number three among our biggest concerns about moving. If you're moving to your next home and are wondering how to get Max there safely, one of your first online stops should be the Independent Pet and Animal Transportation Association (ipata.com), which gives great tips about transporting animals. Did you know, for instance, that transporting a pet by air is better than over ground? There's also a list of accredited pet shippers and plenty of practical tips for easing the stress of the move for your loyal furry friend.

Before you move, check to see if your new place has any breed bans or pet limit rules in place. Some condo associations or townships place restrictions on the type or size of the dog (you'll also want to check if there are rules about other types of pets you may have, such as cats, birds, or snakes). You'll find that information in the condo bylaws or at the municipal office in your new town. And check the leash and muzzle laws while you're at it. If you'll be renting, talk to the landlord in person about any pet issue, as it's harder to say no face-to-face. It's smart to bring a folder of info on your pet, complete with references from neighbors, a previous landlord, the vet, or the trainer. Offer to sign a pet agreement and to pay a higher deposit against damages.

Just because you might be downsizing to a smaller place or one without a yard doesn't mean you have to give up your dog. Dogs will adapt to any situation, even living in the desert, as long as they're with you. But if conditions are such that you can't keep the dog, then you'll have to work hard to find him a new home. Tell everyone you know: friends, relatives, veterinarian, church, pet stores, trainers, etc. Again, prepare a dossier showing Max at his finest. Consider paying to board him at a friend's or relative's home until a permanent home is found. Advertise on the Web, or contact a volunteer-run animal rescue organization that can take your dog as a foster and find him a new home.

If you're truly a dog lover, you'll want to factor in your pet's needs when selecting Nextville. Many of the places cited in this book are a dog's paradise, offering more room to run, parks to frolic in, and birds to chase. After all, your dog deserves a great next life, too.

Question 4: What Do I Do with All My Stuff?

This issue stops a lot of people from even thinking about moving. For too many of us, our possessions own us, but it doesn't have to stay that way. I think of getting rid of old stuff like casting off an old shell. It's often a freeing experience that allows us to move on to finding our next place. You have to be ruthless about getting rid of a lifetime of clutter, but you don't have to do it all by yourself.

Today there's a growing number of "senior move management" businesses that specialize in helping you sort through your stuff and figure out what to do with it. If you've already found your new place, one of the first things a specialist does is help you figure out how much of your furniture and possessions will actually fit there, and they'll also help you pack everything you're keeping. As for everything else, they'll help you sell it if it's salable or connect you with charities so you can give it away. When it comes to the real junk, they'll help you break it down and dispose of it, using paper shredders if necessary. When everything is sorted, sold, trashed, or packed, the same company can usually do the actual moving job for you, too. To find one of these specialists in your area, simply check with the National Association of Senior Move Managers (nasmm.com).

When you begin the process, it's important to set a firm deadline—if your kids or anybody else want to pick through your stuff, they can do so by a given date. But when giving items to your family members, be careful about starting squabbles among offspring and siblings. It's best to talk things over first to get a sense of who's interested in what. It can help a lot to give your stuff to family and friends because you know it's ending up in good hands, but only if you can manage to divvy your things up peacefully.

If you're selling some of your stuff on your own, you can skip the old-fashioned tag sale and go the more modern route of selling your stuff on eBay; just follow the tips in the box on the next page to get the best results.

One last thought: most house sales benefit from getting rid of a third of the furniture and two-thirds of the clutter prior to listing the house on the market. But if you have something that really adds to the appeal of the house, think about including it as part of the house. I'm not talking about junk, but a high-quality item that could easily be sold separately. Sometimes a throw-in is a way to wow buyers and make them feel that this really is a deal they can't get elsewhere.

Selling Your Stuff on eBay

Want to lighten your load before the moving truck shows up? You could do the usual—run ads, post signs, and hope people show up at your yard sale. But you can cast a much wider net by using an online auction service such as eBay (ebay.com). If you're an eBay newbie, there are three ways to get help selling your stuff:

Attend a "how to sell" seminar at "eBay University." They're held in different locations around the country and also online. The cost is minimal, about sixty dollars per course.

Hire a trading assistant. eBay lists consignment sellers (type in your zip code to find one near you), and they're ranked according to previous customers' feedback. They work on a commission of anywhere from 5–10 percent of the sales price, and they'll help you with everything from pricing your stuff to handling the on-line bidding process. They'll even come and pick up the merchandise from you and then ship to the buyer(s).

Drop off your things at an "auction consignment" store associated with eBay (search for "eBay drop-off stores"). The sales associates will handle the pricing, the photos, the marketing, and the shipping. Some may have an item size/weight limit, and they take as much as a hefty 35 percent commission.

Question 5: What If I Hate the New Place and Want to Come Back?

We've all heard stories about how Jack and Jill moved to some gorgeous, sunny retirement community and ended up just *hating* it. It happens all the time, but it shouldn't.

The biggest mistake that Jack and Jill probably made was that they didn't try it out before they moved there. Don't be so naive as to be sold by the glossy brochures or by a glowing testimonial from somebody you just met. Don't let anybody convince you that a place is right for you. You need to experience it firsthand and test it out, and that means more than just spending a one-week vacation there. On a short visit, you'll notice all the good stuff and none of the bad. You need to go back several times during different seasons to get a real sense of any place. In chapter 9 we took a look at house swapping and slow travel. Both are great ways to really get to know a place as if you lived there. And if you're moving to a new place to pursue a dream job, remember services I talked about such as VocationVacations, designed to help you test out a job experience before you commit to it.

Once you've taken a few test runs, you'll have a pretty good sense of whether you'd be comfortable living in your new town. But if you still can't shake your fear that it won't work out, there is a way you can play it even safer. For the first year in your new place, you can do what I call the "rent-and-rent" approach—that is, rent a house or apartment there and, at the same time, rent out your old house back home. Then, if you change your mind and decide to come back, you can come back to your original house.

I hesitate to suggest this approach because for some of us it can provide too easy an out. Starting a new life in a new place takes real commitment, and feeling you can turn tail and head home at the first bump in the road isn't a good idea. So if you take the safe rent-and-rent approach, promise yourself that you won't come back for at least a year. Then you will have given the new place a fair shot and made a real effort to settle there.

Question 6: What's First—Buy My New Home or Sell My Old One?

In most instances, you should buy first and then sell. But before deciding, talk to a reputable real estate agent to find out how long it will take to sell your house. If the broker suggests three or four months, then add a couple of months for closing. You can start the process of selling your house knowing you have a five- to six-month window to shop for your new one. The moment you find something you love, my best advice is to buy it. Don't wait until you've sold your old house. You can get an inexpensive bridge loan to carry you over until you've sold it.

What if it takes longer to find your new home and a buyer wants to snap up your old house? Just sell it. You can lease a property in your new town, which will make it that much easier to continue to house hunt.

Question 7: What If I Can't Sell My House Ever?

You will sell your house. Even in a difficult market, you'll be able to sell as long as you're smart about it. The most important thing to do is to price it right. Invite three competitive real estate agents to tell you what your home is worth. Beware of the agent who tells you your house is worth more than it is to please you or to get the listing. When you have three independent estimates, the lowest is usually the right one. Don't let your love for your own home cloud your judgment. If you make the mistake of overpricing your house, it will languish on the market, making it harder to sell later—even after you lower your price. The first question every shopper asks an agent is "What's the price?" and the second is "How long has it been on the market?"

You can determine the right price for your home by visiting open houses in your neighborhood to see what comparable properties are selling for and doing your own price searches with Zillow (zillow.com), the National Association of REALTORS (realtor.com), and Trulia (trulia.com). But some online estimates are not reliable, and the best market valuations come from reputable real estate agents. They're in the market every day viewing other houses and listening to buyers' reactions.

Once you've priced your home, it's silly to make small incremental price adjustments as time goes on. If you've priced your home wrong, it's much better to make one big price adjustment. And if you want to sell really fast, price your house at 10 percent less than the last two sales in your neighborhood and it will sell immediately.

Besides pricing, the next most important thing to do to help sell your house is to stage it. Staging puts your home's best face forward and, when done well, can even get you much more money. The following box has my inside tips on how to stage your home for sale, and you can find a professional home stager on StagedHomes.com.

Barb's Checklist for Staging Your Home

☐ **Make a strong first impression.** Buyers decide if they like your home within the first eight seconds, so walk in the buyers' shoes and see what they'll be seeing when they come. Paint the front door and trim, hang a wreath on the door, and add some potted flowers. Fertilize the front yard to make it greener, trim the hedges, edge the lawn, and fix the doorbell. That should cover the first eight seconds. All the rest is less important.

- ☐ **Let the sun shine in.** After location, light is the most often stated reason a buyer chooses a particular house. Clean all the windows, replace drapery with sheer curtains or white shades, replace lamp shades with sheer white shades, put in higher-wattage lightbulbs, trim back shrubs that block window light, paint the inside walls a soft white, put white slipcovers on all dark furniture, and put up-lights in each corner of the major rooms to push out the walls and expand the space.

- ☐ **Remove clutter.** Your buyers need to visualize themselves living in your house, and people won't see past your clutter. Most home owners should remove 50 percent of their stuff—that includes furniture and rugs. You can store all your things in a short-term storage facility. Remove personal objects such as family photos and children's artwork and clean out the closets. Neaten the linen closet, hide all electric cords and wiring, and put fresh sheets and extra pillows on the beds.

- ☐ **Make sure your house smells good.** People buy with their noses as well as their eyes. Remove kitty litter, dog beds, and other pet items. Keep the trash can clean. Open all windows an hour before a potential buyer arrives. And warm a few drops of vanilla inside the oven door.

- ☐ **Freshen the kitchen.** It's everyone's favorite room in the house. Clear all countertops, replace cracked or scratched appliances, paint or replace cabinet fronts, and update the knobs. Think about putting a window in the kitchen, which can increase the value of your home by as much as 10 percent.

- ☐ **Clean the bathroom.** No one wants to move into *your* bathroom. Scrub the walls and floors, regrout the tile, remove all personal items, hang a new shower curtain, and buy new hand towels and a rug. Don't forget to remove toothpaste and replace that old soap.

> ☐ **Add some color.** Touches of yellow and other warm colors always say, "Welcome home." Buy new throw pillows for the sofa and beds, add a fresh ficus tree, and define areas with inexpensive, colorful rugs.

Here are some other useful tricks of the trade to help your house sell more quickly:

▸ Remove your house listing from the Multiple Listing Service (MLS) for a few weeks. When you put it back on, it will appear up front as "new to the market."

▸ Offer a "one-day-only" sale. Intentionally underprice your home 10–20 percent. Post two hundred flyers with the address and price around your town. Advertise the sale on your local craigslist site (craigslist.org), and in your local paper. On the day of the sale collect sealed bids from would-be buyers and take the highest bid.

▸ Offer a financial incentive. Offer to prepay house taxes for a year, pay closing costs, or provide free yard service for the first year. Offer the agent a commission bonus upon sale.

▸ Check to see if your house is well presented online. Today most buyers shop online before buying. Your online posting should have complete information and include four to six clear photos showing the home's best features. Don't forget to include your zip code, as that's how many buyers shop. On craigslist and eBay you can also link to YouTube (youtube.com), where you can show off your house on video.

If you're selling your home without a broker, the Internet can be your greatest tool, especially since 77 percent of home buyers start their searches online. Below is my list of the top-five FSBO (for sale by owner) Web sites today.

- ▶ Zillow (zillow.com): It's free, easy to search within neighborhoods, gets three to four million views a month, and allows you to "zestimate" your home value.
- ▶ ForSaleByOwner.com: This is the largest FSBO-only site in the world, with lots of search parameters (e.g., number of bedrooms, property type, five to fifty-mile radius). It allows six color photos and charges ninety dollars a month or a onetime fee of two to nine hundred dollars, depending on services.
- ▶ craigslist (craigslist.org): This is free and easy to post, with no forms to fill out. There is high traffic, and listings expire each week, so you must repost regularly to stay on top. A total hodgepodge with no set format makes it the Wild West of real estate ads.
- ▶ eBay (ebay.com): This site may reach 147 million visitors. The property owner sets a minimum price and all offers are nonbinding. A thirty-day posting costs $150, a ninety day posting $300.
- ▶ militarybyowner.com: This site is easy to search and targets buyers with pressure to move. You don't have to be in the military.

Question 8: Can I Begin My New House Search While I'm Still Living Here?

Absolutely! The Internet is a good place to start your search, but it's no substitute for walking through a house and the neighborhood. With so much information online, you have to know how to navigate. Here are my guidelines for getting through it all without wasting time.

First, get Web site specific. There's a particular site for whatever type of property you're looking for, including foreclosures (foreclosureS.com and USAHUD.com) and for-sale-by-owners (see my list of FSBO sites in the previous question). A shortcut to searching for a home in a specific area is to search by zip code. The largest home site is Move (move.com or homestore.com), and you can also use a search engine such as Yahoo! (yahoo.com) or Google (google.com). You can get aerial views of an entire neighborhood (including the neighbors' backyards) using Google's Street View (maps.google.com/help/maps/streetview/).

Search with broad price parameters. If your budget is $350,000, search up to $400,000 or $450,000. It's easy to narrow the price later, but as about one-third of all properties are overpriced when they're first listed, you'll miss the really good ones if you search too narrowly.

Decode the posting. Real estate advertising has its own language, which includes a lot of misleading terms that you need to decipher. The chart below translates a few of those terms for you.

How to Decode a Real Estate Ad

If you're shopping for your next great home by checking the ads, here's a handy guide that can help you figure out the difference between what the ad says and what it really means.

Cozy means too small.

Charming means too old.

Original condition means appliances are fifty years old.

Needs TLC means it's a dump.

Conveniently located means noisy.

Desirable neighborhood means this little house is way over-priced because the neighborhood has some snob appeal.

Efficient kitchen means too small to fit two adults.

One-car garage means you can drive your Chevy in but can't get out.

Peek at the river/mountains means if you angle your mirror just so . . .

Usable land means no trees.

Beachfront steal means no hurricane insurance available at any price.

Country living means too far from anywhere to get to work.

Must see inside means outside is ugly.

Unique means hard to sell.

No pictures means it's not worth looking at.

Just available means the previous owner just died on the premises—hope you don't mind.

Question 9: How Do I Avoid Buying a Lemon?

Everybody worries about making a big mistake when buying a new home, and if you're searching for one far away, it's even scarier. I know it's tempting to snatch up a good deal that comes along even when you can't actually visit the property, but my advice is not to do it. It's never smart to buy blindly. When a new home is far away, don't assume the real estate agent is handling all the inspections. You should have a professional home inspector survey the property and also get the legal advice of a local attorney. A good home inspector will spot the big problems you can't see, such as foundation cracks, load-bearing walls that have been removed, bad electrical wiring, water damage (often covered up with paint), poor insulation, termites, radon, wood rot, and leaky underground oil tanks. Not all of these problems are deal breakers, but if they're fixable, you can make them part of the price negotiation.

The most common mistake people make when buying a home in a new area is choosing the wrong community. You need to physically check out an area before you move there, as any good detective would. You should know if the people who live there share your same values and attitudes. You may want peace and quiet but find yourself in a neighborhood filled with screaming kids. Talk to the people who reside on the block and be sure to visit during off-hours to see who actually lives there. Your first stop in the community should be at pick-up or drop-off time at the local school. You'll see how all the kids interact and who their parents are. Buy coffee on Main Street on a Sunday afternoon—that's when everyone's out and about. Be sure to drive around the neighborhood at night, too, when everyone's home from work to find out if it's really the quiet neighborhood you've been dreaming about.

While you're doing your homework, find out if there are any impending zoning changes or property-use variances for swimming pools, tennis courts, or anything else you wouldn't want next door. It often happens that the zoning changes or a neighbor is granted a use variance right after you move in. Talk to the local planning board to find out if anything is in the offing. You may even want to read the minutes of a recent town-council meeting to see exactly what's being discussed. Today almost everything municipals are planning is accessible online.

Question 10: How Will I Make New Friends in My New Place?

I think it's much harder to make new friends after you've reached midlife. It certainly has been for me, and it's another reason some of us are reluctant to move away from our established social networks, even when we're hungry for a change. But there are tools to help.

In chapter 3, we talked about pursuing personal passions, which is often a key to making new friends. When you dive headfirst into an activity you love, you'll meet other people who share your passion. Consider picking up a writer's pen or artist's brush and then joining local writers' or artists' workshops. Classes are often posted at the corner bookstore, at art-supply stores, or in school catalogs. This is where you'll find like-minded souls.

And you may recall that in chapter 5, "Living Young," we looked at the youthful effects of moving to a college town. Going back to school is always a great way to meet people. Just as you met new friends through your children's schools when they were young, you'll meet new friends through your new school, too. And you don't even have to be in a college town. Almost every town offers adult learning classes in almost every subject, and getting an advanced degree is enormously satisfying.

In chapter 8, we talked about volunteering, another great way to meet people because, again, it links you up with like-minded souls. And instead of superficial small talk, you get to connect on a more meaningful level. The local chamber of commerce, libraries, museums, shelters, arts centers, and YMCAs readily provide information on local volunteering possibilities.

Finally, in chapter 10, I mentioned the role cyberspace can play in expanding your world. The Internet is the world's greatest tool in helping you meet people when you move to a new town. Check out the amazing site Meetup (meetup.com), the king of all Web sites for bringing strangers together in their local towns to discuss shared interests, passions, and politics.

In truth, moving to Nextville can give your social life a huge shot in the arm. When you go to a new place, it forces you to put yourself out there to meet new people, which for most of us is uncomfortable at best. The key, of course, is that you have to push yourself out the door. I find that the people who succeed the most at making new friends are those individuals willing to try it alone. Do things with your spouse, but it's far more important to do things on your own. Heck, one of the best ways to meet people is just to walk your dog around your neighborhood or local park. And if you don't have a dog, your local humane society has plenty of them and needs volunteers to take them for walks. When I moved to my new neighborhood in New York City, I offered to walk my neighbor's dog and immediately made two new friends—my sweet neighbor and her tiny dog.

Now that we've gotten all the questions (and hopefully our fears) out of the way, I'd like to send you off on your journey with a handy set of rules to remember as you venture along. You'll find these ten rules on page 227. They pretty much summarize what I've already said throughout this book, but in a cut-to-the-chase format. Think of it as a short guide and a little push. Feel free to tear this page out of the book so you can carry it with you as a quick checklist on your search.

Don't forget to keep me posted as you begin this next great chapter of your life. You can always write to me at my Web site, barbaracorcoran.com. I'm constantly hunting for more amazing new places to add to my list and share with others. Just like you, I'll be out there on my own journey, and along the way I hope to see you in Nextville.

Barb's Ten Rules
to Live Happily Ever After

1. **Forget Florida.** I'm not just talking Florida here. I'm talking about conventional retirement, in the usual ways and the usual places. Remember that the only worthy goal is to find what suits you, not your parents.

2. **Think outside the hammock.** You can rest when you're dead. Your second act should be about doing, not just relaxing.

3. **Choose people over palm trees.** Palm trees make lousy conversationalists. When it comes to your next place, the people who surround you will make or break the experience.

4. **Think passions, not pastimes.** A pastime is something you do to fill your time. A passion is something you do to fill your soul.

5. **Turn back the clock.** Head for a place that allows you to be young again.

6. **Release your inner good guy.** Find a way to help others in your new community. It's the single best way to help yourself.

7. **No place is too far away.** Be willing to stray. You have the courage and the know-how to go anywhere and make a home there if you like.

8. **Be willing to stay.** If your current home is your idea of paradise, then put away the suitcases—you're already in Nextville. But decide to make it new again and truly make it (and your life) better.

9. **Take a test drive.** Live in a new place temporarily or plan lots of visits. Don't trust what anyone, including me, tells you about the place. Snoop around.

10. **Life is short.** There's no time for regrets. Be adventurous. Be happy. Live your dream.

Appendix A

100 Places Featured or Mentioned in *Nextville*

Northeast/Mid-Atlantic

Beacon Hill, Massachusetts (chapter 4)
Burlington, Vermont (chapters 5, 6)
Burnsville, North Carolina (chapter 9)
Cambridge, Massachusetts (chapter 3)
Charlottesville, Virginia (chapter 3)
Essex, Connecticut (chapter 3)
Hunter Mountain, New York (chapter 9)
Ithaca, New York (chapter 5)
Ledyard, Connecticut (chapter 3)
New York City (chapters 5, 6)
Northeast Kingdom, Vermont (chapter 7)
Perth Amboy, New Jersey (chapter 3)
Portland, Maine (chapter 6)
Providence, Rhode Island (chapter 3)
Silver Spring, Maryland (chapter 4)
State College, Pennsylvania (chapter 5)
Tremont Township, Pennsylvania (chapter 3)
Westerly, Rhode Island (chapter 9)
White Mountains, New Hampshire (chapter 8)
Williamsville, Vermont (chapter 7)

South

Atlanta, Georgia (chapter 8)
Auburn-Opelika, Alabama (chapter 3)
Austin, Texas (chapters 4, 5, 6, 8)

Beaufort, South Carolina (chapter 9)
Caliente, Florida (chapter 4)
Charleston, South Carolina (chapter 3)
Cleveland, Georgia (chapter 7)
Coweta, Oklahoma (chapter 3)
Dauphin Island, Alabama (chapter 3)
Fairhope, Alabama (chapter 9)
Galveston, Texas (chapter 3)
The Hill Country, Texas (chapter 3)
Hot Springs, Arkansas (chapter 3)
Knoxville, Tennessee (chapter 4)
Maryville, Tennessee (chapter 4)
Mobile, Alabama (chapter 3)
Myrtle Beach, South Carolina (chapter 6)
New Orleans, Louisiana (chapter 8)
Oxford, Mississippi (chapter 5)
Tellico Lake, Tennessee (chapter 4)
Tybee Island, Georgia (chapter 7)

Midwest

Chicago, Illinois (chapters 6, 8)
Cleveland, Ohio (chapter 5)
Flint Hills, Kansas (chapter 7)
Grand Traverse Bay, Michigan (chapter 3)
Madison, Wisconsin (chapters 3, 6)
Milwaukee, Wisconsin (chapter 3)
Minneapolis, Minnesota (chapters 3, 8)
Omaha, Nebraska (chapter 8)
Rushford, Minnesota (chapter 4)
Saugatuck, Michigan (chapter 3)
Sheboygan County, Wisconsin (chapter 3)
St. Joseph, Missouri (chapter 3)
St. Paul, Minnesota (chapters 6, 8)

Tryon Farm, Indiana (chapter 6)
Vedic City, Iowa (chapter 4)
Yellow Springs, Ohio (chapter 5)

Mountain/West/Northwest

Ashland, Oregon (chapter 5)
Bandon, Oregon (chapter 3)
Boulder, Colorado (chapter 4)
Davis, California (chapters 3, 4)
Denver, Colorado (chapters 3, 4)
Eugene, Oregon (chapter 6)
Keystone, Colorado (chapter 3)
Lake Chelan, Washington (chapter 3)
Loveland, Colorado (chapter 3)
McCall, Idaho (chapter 7)
Port Townsend, Washington (chapter 6)
Ridgway, Colorado (chapter 6)
Salt Lake City, Utah (chapter 8)
Santa Fe, New Mexico (chapter 4)
Seattle, Washington (chapters 3, 8)
Slab City, California (chapter 9)
Sparks, Nevada (chapter 4)
St. George, Utah (chapters 3, 5)
Star Valley, Wyoming (chapter 9)
Surf City, California (chapter 3)
Taos, New Mexico (chapter 8)
Tempe, Arizona (chapter 8)
Three Rivers, Oregon (chapter 6)
Tucson, Arizona (chapter 8)
Whidbey Island, Washington (chapter 3)
Willamette Valley, Oregon (chapter 3)

Beyond the Borders

Bonaire, Caribbean (chapter 9)
Costa Rica (chapter 8)
Curitiba, Brazil (chapter 6)
El Quelite, Mexico (chapter 7)
Harbour Island, Bahamas (chapter 9)
High Seas (*The World* cruise) (chapter 7)
Kennet and Avon Canal, United Kingdom (chapter 7)
Kenya (chapter 8)
Malawi (chapter 8)
Malaysia (chapter 7)
Maui, Hawaii (chapter 3)
New Zealand (chapters 6, 9)
Nicaragua (chapter 7)
Nova Scotia, Canada (chapter 7)
Panama City, Panama (chapters 5, 7)
Prince of Wales Island, Alaska (chapter 7)
Vancouver, Canada (chapter 3)

Appendix B

Vital Stats on Places in *Nextville*

Places	Avg. No. Sunny Days	Avg. Low Temp in January	Avg. High Temp in July	Median Age	Avg. Home Price (in Dollars)
Galveston, Texas	203	48	88	35.3	108,000
Saugatuck, Michigan	159	18	83	45.8	252,400
Cambridge, Massachusetts	201	19	84	32.8	552,600
Auburn, Alabama	217	37	91	25	228,000
Lake Chelan, Washington	196	23	85	41.7	230,500
Austin, Texas	228	40	95	31.6	175,900
Knoxville, Tennessee	204	30	88	34.6	114,800
Davis, California	267	37	94	28.7	564,500
Tampa, Florida	246	51	90	35.3	218,600
Burlington, Vermont	157	9	80	32.1	253,000
Panama City, Panama	approx. 216	83	82	26.1 (Panama)	60,000 for tourist apartment
St. George, Utah	255	26	102	30.8	210,000
Cleveland, Ohio	166	25	81	34.2	99,100
State College, Pennsylvania	178	19	82	23.4	235,700
Eugene, Oregon	155	33	82	34.5	256,400
Solaire building, New York City	224	26	86	35.8	519,400
Michigan City, Indiana	175	16	84	35.4	99,000
Port Townsend, Washington	156	36	72	47.1	251,500
POW Island, Alaska	98	27	66	35.8	291,600
High seas—*The World*	var.	var.	var.	typical mid-50s	approx. 2,500,000

Places	Avg. No. Sunny Days	Avg. Low Temp in January	Avg. High Temp in July	Median Age	Avg. Home Price (in Dollars)
Narrow Boat, Kennet and Avon Canal, United Kingdom	approx. 170	37	72	typical mid-40s	approx. 60,000
Nova Scotia, Canada	83	12.2	77	38.8	176,146
New Orleans, Louisiana	216	47	91	34.4	147,000
Costa Rica (Southern Nicoya Peninsula)	var.	72	97	26.4	350,000
Malawi, Africa	var.	var.	var.	16.34	Hotel approx. $20 per night
Tempe, Arizona	300	34	104	30.6	157,381
Beaufort, South Carolina	216	40	90	30.6	156,100
Queenstown, New Zealand	187	32	73	35	243,692
Harbour Island, Bahamas	340	70.5	81	27.8 (Bahamas)	approx. 400,000
Dubai, United Arab Emirates	approx. 338	75	105	27	2-bed. luxury condo $1M
Connecticut River Valley	var.	var.	—	var.	var.
St. Joseph, Missouri	—	16	90	—	107,700
Dauphin Island, Alabama	—	44	89	—	212,700
Perth Amboy, New Jersey	—	23	90	—	308,900
Sheboygan, Wisconsin	—	13	80	—	128,800
Bandon, Oregon	—	39	66	—	199,800
Charlottesville, Virginia	—	27	87	—	253,800
Grand Traverse Bay, Michigan	—	15	81	—	164,700
San Antonio, Texas Hill Country	—	40	95	—	100,500
Providence, Rhode Island	—	21	82	—	381,800
Hot Springs, Arkansas	—	31	94	—	115,800
Loveland, Colorado	—	16	86	—	235,300
Huntington Beach, California	—	45	83	—	707,500
Freeland, Whidbey Island, Washington	—	36	72	—	338,700
Beacon Hill, Boston	—	19	84	—	410,000

Places	Avg. No. Sunny Days	Avg. Low Temp in January	Avg. High Temp in July	Median Age	Avg. Home Price (in Dollars)
Riderwood Com., Silver Spring, Maryland	—	28	87	—	529,900
Zephyr Valley, Rushford, Minnesota	—	5	81	—	149,800
Kiley Ranch in Sparks, Nevada	—	24	91	—	399,400
Ithaca, New York	—	15	81	—	228,300
Yellow Springs, Ohio	—	22	86	—	194,600
Oxford, Mississippi	—	31	91	—	163,600
Ashland, Oregon	—	30	87	—	450,100
Portland, Maine	—	13	78	—	265,500
Madison, Wisconsin	—	11	82	—	224,300
Myrtle Beach, South Carolina	—	37	88	—	209,500
Ridgway, Colorado	—	4	82	—	296,300
Barton, Northeast Kingdom, Vermont	—	-2	79	—	145,400
Milford, Flint Hills, Kansas	—	16	91	—	92,500
Tybee Island, Georgia	—	39	89	—	304,200
Woodstock, White Mountains, New Hampshire	—	9	80	—	185,400
Great Lakes, Chicago	—	20	82	—	424,700
Atlanta, Georgia	—	41	88	—	192,100
Taos, New Mexico	—	10	86	—	238,200
Hunter Mountain, New York	—	11	78	—	var.
Burnsville, North Carolina	—	21	81	—	133,800
Fairhope, Alabama	—	41	90	—	237,000
Star Valley, Wyoming	212	6	79	—	256,400
Slab City, California	—	39	108	—	var.

Sources: Sperling's BestPlaces (bestplaces.net); weatherbase.com; dubaicityguide.com; harbourisland guide.com; wikipedia.org; personal interview with Alicia McLendon, Realtor; discover-eleuthera-bahamas .com; stats.govt.nz; news.emigratenz.org; chinalist.ru; cbc.ca/money/story/2007/08/20/realestate.html; experiencenz.com/climate.cfm; dubaicondoproperty.com/thecube.php.

Appendix C

Resources

Web Sites for Finding Places to Live/Retire

Sperling's BestPlaces: bestplaces.net
Retirement Living Information Center: retirementliving.com
Ideal Places to Retire: ideal-places-to-retire.com
Find Utopia: findutopia.com

Real Estate Web Sites

Trulia: trulia.com
Zillow: zillow.com
National Association of REALTORS: realtor.com
Move: move.com or homestore.com

Web Sites for Boomers (for a description of each site, see p. 206)

Eons: eons.com
What's Next: whatsnext.com
Third Age: thirdage.com
More: more.com
ELDR: eldr.com

Organizations

AARP: aarp.org
Experience Corps: experiencecorps.org
Civic Ventures: civicventures.org

Social-Networking Sites

Meetup: meetup.com
Gather: gather.com
eHarmony: eharmony.com

Information on State Tax Rates

Tax Foundation: taxfoundation.org

FSBO (For Sale by Owner) Sites

ForSaleByOwner.com
craigslist: craigslist.org
eBay: ebay.com
militarybyowner.com

Foreclosures Sites

foreclosureS.com
USAHUD.com

Sites on Fractional Ownership

Lifestyle Vineyards: buyavineyard.co.uk
YachtPlus: yachtplus.co.uk
Condo Cruise Lines International: condocruiselines.com

Moving Information

National Association of Senior Move Managers: nasmm.com
The Independent Pet and Animal Transportation
   Association: ipata.com

Site on Staging Your Home Before You Sell

StagedHomes.com

House-Swapping Sites

diggsville.com
HomeLink International: homelink.org
HomeExchange.com

Retrofitting Sites

Lifease: lifease.com

Information on Reverse Mortgage

AARP Reverse Mortgage Calculator: rmaarp.com

Shared-Housing Sites

The Cohousing Association of the United States: cohousing.org

Sites on Traveling and Living Abroad

Living Abroad: liveabroad.com
Slow Travel: slowtrav.com
Retirement Wave: retirementwave.com

Sites on Living on a Boat

Living Aboard: liveaboard.com
The World: aboardtheworld.com
Residential Cruise Line *Magellan*: residentialcruiseline.com
Orphalese: theorphalese.com

Information on Living Green

U.S. Green Building Council: www.usgbc.org
The Green Guide: thegreenguide.com
The Eco-Home Network: ecohome.org

Volunteer Organizations

Global Volunteers: globalvolunteers.org
ReServe: reserveinc.org
Volunteer Match: volunteermatch.org
SCORE: Counselors to America's Small Business: score.org
Volunteers in Medicine Institute: vimi.org
Habitat for Humanity: habitat.org
Reef Check: reefcheck.org
Sierra Club: sierraclub.org
The Humane Society of the United States: hsus.org
ProLiteracy Worldwide: literacyvolunteers.org

Career-Coaching Information

Dr. Cynthia Barnett's Web Site: peakperformance-solutions.com
New Directions: newdirections.com
My Next Phase: mynextphase.com
North Carolina Center for Creative Retirement:
www.unca.edu/ncccr

Site on Test-Driving a New Career

VocationVacations: vocationvacations.com

Other "Worthy" Web Sites Featured in Chapter 8

The Thorn Tree Project: thorntreeproject.com
Malawi Children's Village: malawichildrensvillage.com

Project K.I.D.: project-kid.org
Appalachian Mountain Club: outdoors.org
Alliance for the Great Lakes: greatlakes.org
The Idea Village: ideavillage.org

Web Sites of "Dream Chasers" Featured in Chapter 3

The artwork of Ed Lane: edlanestudio.com

The clothing design of Diane Lane: leilanisilks.com

Winderlea Wine Company, the winery of Bill Sweat and Donna Morris: winderlea.com

Kadashan Farms, where Pam Von Rhee grows blackberries and lavender: kadashanfarms.net

Echo Valley Campground, where Judy Finch runs her own campground: echovalleycamp.com

Smythe Books, Jim Strawn's bookstore: smythebooks.com

Useful Books

Rightsizing Your Life: Simplifying Your Surroundings While Keeping What Matters Most by Ciji Ware (Springboard Press)

Prime Time: How Baby Boomers Will Revolutionize Retirement and Transform America by Marc Freedman (PublicAffairs)

Leap! What Will We Do with the Rest of Our Lives? By Sara Davidson (Random House)

Portfolio Life: The New Path to Work, Purpose, and Passion After 50 by David D. Corbett with Richard Higgins (Jossey-Bass)

Turning Silver into Gold: How to Profit in the New Boomer Marketplace by Mary S. Furlong (FT Press)

The New Retirement: The Ultimate Guide to the Rest of Your Life by Jan Cullinane and Cathy Fitzgerald (Rodale Books)

Cohousing: A Contemporary Approach to Housing Ourselves by Kathryn McCamant, Charles Durrett, and Ellen Hertzman (Ten Speed Press)

Retire Downtown: The Lifestyle Destination for Active Retirees and Empty Nesters by Kyle Ezell (Andrews McMeel Publishing)

Choose a College Town for Retirement: Retirement Discoveries for Every Budget by Joseph M. Lubow (Globe Pequot)

Notes

Chapter 1: The Power of Place

Page 2: "Every eight seconds, one more lively boomer turns sixty." This statistic is according to both the AARP and the U.S. Census Bureau. Cited in "Boomers Ready for Some More 'Me' Time," by Amy Hoak, *MarketWatch* from Dow Jones, 9/26/06.

Page 2: "Instead of retiring, it's more like graduating." The concept of retirement as a form of graduation was discussed in an interview conducted with Jeff Taylor of Eons (eons.com) for this book. The retirement coach Richard P. Johnson of the Web site Retirement 360 (retirement360.com) has also compared retirement to graduation from school.

Page 6: The statement that Florida is starting to lose elderly residents is based on a *New York Times* analysis of U.S. Census Bureau data, Sam Roberts, "Making the Return Trip: Elderly Head Back North," 2/26/07.

Page 7: "Two-thirds of boomers say they intend to keep working." This is according to Merrill Lynch's "New Retirement Survey," 2005, conducted by Harris Interactive in collaboration with Age Wave. This survey also says that 81 percent of boomers expect to keep working past sixty-five.

Page 7: The term "ruppie" appears in the book *Retire Downtown* by Kyle Ezell.

Page 9: Bob Adams's discussion of overseas retirement trends appeared in the *New York Times* article "Content to Watch Bananas Grow, More Retirees Relocate to Panama," by Bob Tedeschi, 4/11/06.

Chapter 2: What If I Don't Know Where I Belong?

Page 17: "Let's say you live in Chicago and want to move . . . " These numbers were calculated based on current median home prices and cost of living in these two cities at the time of writing (mid-2007); the numbers were pulled from Sperling's BestPlaces Web site, bestplaces.net.

Page 20: The *Nextville* survey on the Trulia Web site was conducted in April 2007.

Page 20: The *Nextville* survey on the What's Next Web site was conducted in May 2007.

Page 23: The coaching questions we offer were based on interviews with retirement coaches Dr. Cynthia Barnett, Ron Manheimer, and Dr. Randy Burnham; similar questions and issues were also cited in the *Washington Post* article "After the Rat Race, What Next? Experts Say You'll Want a Plan to Make the Most of Your Retirement Years," by Jennifer Huget, 12/5/06.

Page 24: David Corbett's ideas on creating a portfolio approach to life were taken from his book *Portfolio Life* and were also discussed in the *New York Times* article, "Helping Chart a Career Turning Point," by Elizabeth Pope, 4/10/07.

Page 25: The Myers-Briggs Type Indicator (MBTI) is a personality test developed in the 1940s by Katharine Cook Briggs and Isabel Briggs Myers, based partly on the theories of Carl Jung.

Chapter 3: Pursuing Your Passion

Page 37: Information about working after retirement, working for stimulation as opposed to just pay, and the concept of "cycling" between work and play were findings extracted from Merrill Lynch's "New Retirement Survey," 2005, conducted by Harris Interactive in collaboration with Age Wave.

Page 37: "Boomers already account for nearly half of the country's self-employed workers." This statistic is based on figures from the U.S. Department of Labor, as cited by the AARP in the *AARP Bulletin* article "Startups for Grownups," by Carol Fleck, February 2007.

Page 38: "Half of new business start-ups go belly-up inside of four years." Actually, according to the U.S. Small Business Administration, this statistic is really 56 percent as cited in "Startups for Grownups," by Fleck.

Pages 40–41: In the box "Ten Places to Do What You Like to Do Best," there are a number of sources to be cited:

- The dog walking in Seattle information comes from "What Makes SODA [Serve Our Dog Areas] Pop?" by Lisa Wogan, *Bark* magazine, March/April 2007.
- Madison as the best walking city comes from a list of best cities for walking, compiled by *Prevention* magazine and the American Podiatric medical Association and published in "Madison Named Most Walkable," by Scott Bauer of the Associated Press, *Washington Post*, 3/8/07.
- Denver-Boulder was ranked the best place to be single based on nightlife, culture, job growth, number of other singles, cost of living alone, "coolness," and online dating activity. "Best Cities for Singles," by Lacey Rose, Forbes.com, 7/25/06.
- The info on sushi in Vancouver comes from "The Price of Sushi," by Rhiannon Coppin, *Vancouver Courier* online, vancourier.com, 4/20/05.

> ▸ St. George as one of the fastest-growing entrepreneurial towns comes from "Boomtowns '07," by Joel Kotkin, *Inc.* magazine, May 2007, which listed the top "boomtowns" in America based on job growth.
> ▸ Minneapolis was named the "Best City for Sleep" in a 2004 study, "Sleep in the City," by Bert Sperling based on data from the Centers for Disease Control and Prevention, the Bureau of Labor Statistics, and the U.S. Census Bureau, published in "Few Are Sleepless in Minneapolis," by Sarah Hofius, *USA* Today, 10/14/04.
> ▸ Charleston, South Carolina, was named "Friendliest City" in a 2007 survey by *Travel & Leisure* magazine and AOL's Travel Channel, "America's Favorite Cities," travelandleisure.com/afc.
> ▸ Milwaukee topped the Forbes.com list of America's drunkest cities, based on state laws, rate of alcoholism, and amount of heavy drinkers or binge drinkers. "America's Drunkest Cities," by David M. Ewalt, Forbes.com, 8/22/06.
> ▸ Mobile, Alabama, ranked tops in rainfall in a May 2007 study by WeatherBill, Inc. (conducted prior to the recent drought). "Top Rainiest US Cities," weatherbill.com.

Page 42: "Wayne is part of a growing trend of retirees who are taking jobs at casinos." The article referenced here is "Caroming into a Second Career in the Land of Green Felt," by Mat Villano, *New York Times*, 5/10/07.

Page 55: Perth Amboy was described as "the unofficial golf capital of the U.S." by *Golf Digest* in the August 2005 issue in "Best Golf City in U.S.," by Steve Beslow.

Chapter 4: Forming a New Community

Pages 65–66: Putnam's ideas about the decline of social gatherings and clubs were featured in his book *Bowling Alone* and also in "You Gotta Have Friends," by Robert Putnam, *Time* magazine, 7/3/06.

Page 66: "Many of us today have fewer people we can confide in." This comes from a 2006 Duke University/University of Arizona study called "Social Isolation in America," by Miller McPherson, Lynn Smith-Lovin, and Matthew Brashears, which found that twenty years ago the typical person had three close friends he or she could confide in, but now has only two. Cited in "You Gotta Have Friends," by Putnam.

Page 68: Tony Sirna's statement about boomers who are "weary of car-dependent McMansion sprawl" appeared in the *New York Times* article "Extreme Makeover: Commune Edition," by Andrew Jacobs, 6/11/06.

Page 70: Thank you to Kiplinger.com, who first wrote about "golden girls" Joan Forrester, Lois McManus, Joanne Murphy, and Nancy Rogers in "Meet the Real Golden Girls," May 2007. Special thanks also to the article's author, Mary Beth Franklin, who provided a contact for Joan Forrester so that we could conduct our own interview.

Page 70: "There are six thousand people in the United States and Canada who now live among others with shared interests." This statistic appeared in the *New York Times* article "Birds of a Feather," by Tim Neville, 4/6/07.

Page 71: "Nearly one-third of people living in these [active adult] communities still work." This is according to figures provided by Pulte Homes, a leading developer of active adult communities.

Page 79: Some of our information describing activities at the Riderwood Community was drawn from "At Riderwood, Staying Active Is Easily Accomplished," by Ann Cameron Siegal, *Washington Post*, 9/17/05.

Page 83: The story about Maharishi's landing in a deserted Iowa field in a small pink plane has been circulating for years but was most recently published in a *Los Angeles Times* article about Vedic City, "A Lotus Amid the Iowa Corn," by Carina Chocano, that ran 9/10/06.

Page 85: The quote from the ninety-year-old great-grandmother who is straight but has chosen to live in a gay retirement community appeared in a profile of RainbowVision in "Gay Seniors Settle into a Niche," by John Ritter, *USA Today*, 7/5/06.

Chapter 5: Living Young

Page 90: "Although city life offers lots more opportunities to get busy, it also means you can unload some of those jobs and chores that become especially burdensome for people as they age." This point is further examined in the article "The Good Life in the Big City," by Wendy Smith, *AARP Bulletin*, June 2004.

Page 94: "In many college towns, the number of houses is limited by the size of the town itself, and some universities have actually been cutting back on student housing in recent years because of tight budgets." This information is from "Own Where the Kids Are," by Carleen Hawn, *Business 2.0* magazine, November 2006.

Page 97: "One visitor from a big-city newspaper was astonished to discover that downtown Burlington also had jazz nightspots with sleek, minimalist décor, much like New York City's Tribeca, where people were sipping martinis and raspberry vodka gimlets." The reporter, Gary Lee, was from the *Washington Post*, writing "Hip, Hippie, Hippest," which ran 5/26/02.

Page 99: "Panama City is, as one American reporter recently noted, like South Beach without the velvet-roped lines and snobbery." The reporter was Ceci Connolly, who also noted that the city had once been burned down by the pirate Henry Morgan. Connoly's article, "Is Panama City the Next South Beach?" ran in the *Washington Post*, 2/18/07.

Pages 104–5: "The residents get constant contact with young people who 'become like family to us,' says Village resident Maddy Cattell." This quote is from "Students, Faculty Create a Win-Win Situation at the Village at Penn State," on the Penn State Live Web site, live.psu.edu, 3/29/07.

Chapter 6: Living Green

Page 110: "Almost three-fourths of the baby boomers we surveyed for this book told us that environmental considerations truly matter to them as they look ahead to where and how they'll live in the next stage of their lives." This is from our What's Next survey in May 2007.

Page 112: Information about cities' rankings was taken from the *Green Guide*'s "Top 10 Green Cities in the U.S., 2006," originally posted in April 2006. (At press time, the *Green Guide* had not yet released its 2007 rankings.)

Page 112: "The best places for environmental living continue to be in western, northwestern, and mountain states." This information is from our interview in May 2007 with editor Paul McRandle at the *Green Guide*.

Page 112: "One of the absolute greenest places you can live today is none other than the concrete jungle known as New York City." This was in "51 Ways to Save the Environment," item number 15, "Move to a High Rise," by Bryan Walsh in the special "Global Warming Guide" issue of *Time* magazine, 4/9/07.

Page 113: "As one Three Rivers resident explains, 'With power lines come streetlights, and there go your stars at night.'" This quote appeared in the Associated Press news article "Living Off the Grid," by Joseph B. Frazier, which ran in multiple outlets including MSNBC.com under the headline "Off-Grid Community Runs on Solar, Wind," 5/21/07.

Page 113: "By one estimate, the number of people generating their own clean energy is increasing by 30 percent each year." This figure comes from "Off-Grid Comunity Runs on Solar, Wind," by Frazier.

Page 113: "Brazil is at the forefront of creating green towns such as Curitiba." The town of Curitiba was profiled in "The Road to Curitiba," by Arthur Lubow, *New York Times Magazine*, 5/20/07.

Page 114: "As much as 40 percent of greenhouse gases comes from homes, not cars." To be more specific, 39 percent of emissions result from everyday living in homes and from the process of manufacturing, building, and outfitting homes. "Emissions of Greenhouse Gases in the U.S., 2006," published November 2007 by the Energy Information Administration.

Page 114: "The green home-building market is expected to triple in size by 2010, up to $38 billion a year." This is according to a study released by the National Association of Home Builders and McGraw-Hill Construction and published in the 5/15/06 "Residential Green Building" edition of McGraw-Hill Construction's SmartMarket Reports.

Pages 118–19: "Six Easy Ways to Turn *Your* Home Green." This box is adapted from the longer list "Sixteen Ways to a Greener Life," published by the U.S. Green Building Council and available on usgbc.org/DisplayPage.aspx?CMSpageid=97&.

Chapter 7: Losing Yourself

Page 129: Some of Ken Layne's descriptions of the village of El Quelite originally appeared in a diary entry posted by Layne on the What's Next Web site; other comments were drawn from our interview with Layne.

Page 132: Rob Goldenhill's story about leaving Wall Street and opening a little store in Vermont was featured in "Fed Up with the Fast Life," by David Whitford, *Fortune Small Business* magazine, April 2007.

Page 133: "Of the four million Americans living abroad, almost a quarter are retirees." This statistic is according to the U.S. State Department. Cited in "Retire Like Royalty in a Low-Cost Paradise," by Liz Pulliam Weston, MSNMoney.com.

Page 143: "With property prices in prime areas throughout the United Kingdom continuing to rise, many people—retirees as well as young professionals—find they can live a lot cheaper on a boat." One source for this information was the BBC online magazine *Inside Out*, in an article called "Living on the Water," 9/27/04. Another good source of information on narrow-boat living is Andrew Denny, who has a blog on this subject at www .grannybuttons.com.

Page 144: "'That's when the cut becomes like one long thin village,' says one narrow-boat blogger." The blogger was known as Narrowboat J-Omega, and his statement appeared in 2007, but the blog is no longer posted online.

Page 147: "The last great swath of tallgrass in the nation . . ." This great description of the tall grass of Flint Hills is provided in "Splendor of the Grass," by Verlyn Klinkenborg, *National Geographic*, April 2007.

Page 147: "Tybee Island residents engage in the world's largest water-gun fight." This was first reported in a *New York Times* article, "Time Catches Up with a Georgia Eden," by Denny Lee, 8/20/04.

Chapter 8: Finding Your Purpose

Page 150: "More than half these people are eagerly looking for ways they can work to improve their communities and serve the people around them." This has been cited by Civic Ventures based on its research, available on its Web site; also, a 2007 report called "Engaging Older Americans in Volunteer Service," produced by VolunteerMatch and MetLife Foundation, found that "Baby Boomers are volunteering at higher rates than past generations of the same peer group."

Page 152: The story of Jane Newman's experience in Africa is contained on the Thorn Tree Project Web site, thorntreeproject .org.

Page 152: The story of how Paige Ellison started Project K.I.D. appeared in the *Time* magazine article "When Disaster Strikes, Help for Kids," by Daniel Kadlec, 4/16/07.

Page 153: The information in this chart is taken from a July 2007 study called "Volunteering in America," produced by the Corporation for National and Community Service. These statistics are available on its Web site, nationalservice.org.

Pages 153–54: Pulling weeds in the Pisgah National Forest, the Mountain Birdwatch project, and the Mass Audubon butterfly and turtle monitoring programs were all mentioned in a *New York Times* article, "Mother Nature's Helpers," by Jennifer Weeks, 5/11/07.

Page 154: Information on the activity known as "voluntourism" comes from "Vacationing like Brangelina," by Laura Fitzpatrick, Time.com, 7/26/07.

Page 156: "Marc Freedman runs Civic Ventures and describes the wave of new social entrepreneurs as former businesspeople 'who now worship a different bottom line—a better society.'" This quote appears on the Civic Ventures Web site at civicven tures.org.

Page 163: "Tom and Frances Vitaglione are a retired couple from North Carolina who came to Mangochi a few years back." The Vitagliones' story was told in "African AIDS Agony Transcends Nations' Borders," by Paul Grondahl, *Albany Times Union,* 7/7/03.

Page 166: "Chicagoans have been committed to protecting Lake Michigan ever since 1970, when city residents stood on the lakeshore and declared: 'We can take steps together to restore the lake we love.'" This anecdote appears on the Web site of the Alliance for the Great Lakes at greatlakes.org.

Chapter 9: Living the Boomerang Life

Page 172: The trend of boomers using RVs more is well covered in the article "Baby Boomers Are Creating an RV Travel Boom," by Sharon O'Brien, appearing on the About.com Web site, 5/3/06. A good source on park-model trailers is the *New York Times* feature "A Resort Cottage to Go," by Kate Murphy, which ran 6/14/07. Luanne DeMatto appeared in that article, but we interviewed her separately for this book.

Page 174: "The growing fractional condo/town-house market is a different story because reputable companies are managing the new developments." This was explored in the *New York Times* article "Hotels Shake Up Time-Share Act," by Jeffrey Selingo, 4/10/07.

Page 178: "A big emerging trend in vacation homes is the creation of family compounds." This trend is covered in the article "For Mom's Cabin, Take Path on Left," by Christina Lewis, appearing in the *Wall Street Journal,* 4/13/07.

Page 181: Our chart, "Sorting Through the Boomerang Options," is original in format and content, but was partly inspired by a similar chart appearing in *Travel & Leisure* magazine, March 2007, as part of a feature story on destination clubs titled "Clubland."

Page 187: "Picture 20 percent of all the construction cranes in the world parked in one place." This statistic may actually be a modest estimate, as cited by Joel Greene of the Condo Hotel Center, which is currently involved in Dubai real estate development. According to *Travel & Leisure* magazine, "a quarter of the world's cranes" are in Dubai. "See the Future in Dubai," by Amy Wilentz, *Travel & Leisure*, September 2006.

Page 190: "Fairhope . . . was founded a century ago as a renegade colony—a group of utopian dreamers were seeking 'a fair hope' of a utopian life." This is drawn from the history section of the City of Fairhope Web site at cofairhope.com/history.html. Descriptions of Fairhope and its scenic streets also appear in "Top 10 Romantic Escapes," by Steve Millburg, in the January/February 2007 issue of *Coastal Living*.

Chapter 10: Going Nowhere (and Loving It!)

Page 193: "It's part of a growing trend known as 'aging in place.'" The growth of this trend is well documented, particularly by the May 2005 AARP report *Beyond 50.05, A Report to The Nation on Livable Communities: Creating Environments for Successful Aging*, by Andrew Kochers, Audrey Straight, and Thomas Guterbock, which notes that eight in ten boomers have a desire to stay close to home and friends as they age.

Page 195: "A 2005 study on boomers by Pulte Homes, a leading developer of retirement communities, found that about half of people in their fifties plan to downsize their living arrangements when retiring." This is from the 2005 Pulte Homes "Baby Boomer Survey."

Page 196: "'I thought it would be difficult to part with all my stuff, but it was a very good experience once I got started—it was almost as if I was shedding the past,' says Marion Wishnefski." This quote is from "Shedding the Past, Starting Anew," by Emily Seftel, *Arizona Republic*, 5/20/06.

Page 196: "Nanette Overly . . . describes how boomers are hunting for condos and town houses with 'ample space, tall ceilings . . . '" This is from an article written by Overly, "Baby Boomers Seeking a Different Retirement Lifestyle—At Home," in the 3/8/07 issue of *Senior Journal*; Overly is director of sales and marketing services for Epcon Communities, a condo developer based in Dublin, Ohio.

Page 200: "In a recent report, the AARP found that a whopping 84 percent of boomers want to age in their own homes." This report is "Livable Communities: Creating Environments for Successful Aging" published by the AARP in May 2005.

Page 202: "There is a 'visitability movement' under way right now in a growing number of states across the country, requiring that all new homes be built with these same features." The visitability movement was reported on in Jane Adler's "55 Plus" column in the *Chicago Tribune*, 2/4/07.

Page 202: "With help from the National Association of Home Builders, I've boiled it all down to a top-ten list." The NAHB actually offers more than twenty tips in all, which you can find on their Web site at nahb.org; on the site, check out the report titled "Baby Boomers & Beyond" or just type "universal design" in the search box.

Page 204: "A recent survey of architecture firms by the American Institute of Architects named accessibility as the number-one and fastest-growing trend in home design." This is from the article "Accessible Design? As Long As It's Not Ugly," by Rebecca Dube, published in the Toronto *Globe and Mail*, 6/1/07.

Chapter 11: Beginning the Journey

Page 208: "Men and women are different in the way they generally view retirement." *Time* magazine did a cover story on women in midlife, "Midlife Crisis? Bring It On!" by Nancy Gibbs, 5/16/05.

Page 211: "Transporting a pet by air is better than over ground." This comes from the news release "Leading Animal Transportation Association Responds to DOT Pet Travel Incident Report" posted on the News and Views section of the Web site of the Independent Pet and Animal Transportation Association, ipata.com.

Page 212: "There's a growing number of 'senior move management' businesses that specialize in helping you sort through your stuff and figure out what to do with it." This trend has been reported in a number of newspapers, including the *New York Times* ("Downsizing Help Is on the Way," by Robert Stauss, 4/10/07) and the *Washington Post* ("Businesses Ease Moves for Seniors," by Annie Groer, 5/20/06).

Pages 219-20: "Seventy-seven percent of home buyers start their searches online." This statistic is according to the National Association of REALTORS. Cited in "A Fresh Attack on the 6% Commission," by Les Christie, CNNMoney.com, 4/11/06.

Acknowledgments

A book that ranges as far and wide as this one requires a lot of help. Warren and I would like to start by thanking the wonderful research team that dug up much of the information in this book and was headed by Carol Jacobanis, Gail Abrahamsen, and Simon Weaver. Their efforts were backed up by a second team of researchers that included Tiffany Meyers, Carla Jablonski, Allison Goodhart, and Annabella Asvik. Laura Kelly also contributed both research and editing help, and Susan Buckheit was a great copy editor. And speaking of editors, we had a fine one for this book—Karen Murgolo of Springboard Press. Bob Sauer also edited the book and contributed most of our clever headlines for our sidebars, boxes, and places. Also thanks to Michelle Howry, who believed in the book in the first place. And our thanks go out to the agents, Stuart Krichevsky and Madeleine Morel.

By far, our best source of information and recommendations came from real estate agents and brokers all around the world. We literally heard from hundreds of them as they shared secrets, tips, and ideas, and we are grateful to all who helped out. But I want to particularly single out a handful who went above and beyond the call, including Kevin Cahill of Keller Williams Realty in Cleveland, Jeff Wilcox of Coldwell Banker Woodland Schmidt in Saugatuck, Jerry Swanson at The Group Inc. in Loveland, Jason Keeling of Ryson Real Estate in Galveston, Lynn Waters of Realty Executive Associates in Knoxville, Ernesto Perez of Delta Homes in Davis, Pedro Detresno of Pedro's

Real Estate in Panama City, Ellen Plante of Keller Williams in St. George, and Mary von Ziegesar of Lang, Lion & Davis in Burlington.

Internet research was an extremely valuable tool in producing this book, and we're especially indebted to Mark Gleason of What's Next (whatsnext.com) and Sean Black of Trulia (trulia .com), who allowed us to use their sites to post surveys, and also to Jeff Taylor of Eons (eons.com), who helped guide us through the expanding landscape of boomer Web sites.

We couldn't have done this book without the help of the many experts who agreed to do extensive interviews. This group includes the historian William Strauss, the gerontologist Maria Dwight, sociologist Elaine Wethington of Cornell University, Ron Manheimer of the North Carolina Center for Creative Retirement, retirement coach Dr. Cynthia Barnett, retirement coach Dr. Randy Burnham, John McIlwain of the Urban Land Institute, Penn State professor of leisure studies Geoffrey Godbey, Greg O'Neill of the National Academy on an Aging Society, the adventure expert Phil Keoghan, Brian Kurth of VocationVacations, golf expert Scott Gomberg, wine expert Deborah Daoust of the Washington Wine Commission, "ruppie" expert Kyle Ezell, cohousing pioneer Charles Durrett, "active adult community" expert Dave Schreiner of Pulte Homes, Ruth Halcomb of the Living Abroad Web site, green architecture experts David Tonsing and Rick Hunter, Paul McRandle of the *Green Guide*, Julia Russell of the Eco-Home Network, Eve and Ed Noonan of Tryon Farm, condo hotel expert Joel Greene of the Condo Hotel Center, bird-watching expert Ted Lee Eubanks, and finally Fernando Velez, an expert at taxi driving (who also happens to be an expert on Panama).

We relied on many people affiliated with various volunteer organizations, and it's not surprising they volunteered so freely to help us. This includes Tim Williamson of Idea Village in New Orleans, John Gomperts of Experience Corps, Stefanie Weiss of Civic Ventures, Jane Newman of the Thorn Tree Project, the inspiring Leslie Hawke (who shared the story of her volunteer efforts in Romania), Roger Forrester of the Mature Worker Connection, Jason Willett of VolunteerMatch, Michael Ellis of the Atlanta Wild Animal Rescue Effort, and Sheila Ravendhran, who shared with us her experiences at the Malawi Children's Village.

Last but certainly not least, we want to thank all the "real people" featured in the book, who shared their stories and adventures with us. Ed and Diane Lane, Dick and Karen Roth, Joe and Debbie Karp, Suzanne Greene, Jim Strawn, Judy Finch, Bill Sweat and Donna Morris, Ken and Roseann Layne, Jim Uffelman, Pam Von Rhee, Dr. Wayne Lubin, Jon DiLude, Maria Kramer, and Charlotte Hart all provided wonderful examples of how to create a new life in midlife. Ted Baumgart and Georgia Goldfarb showed us how to live green, Ellen Coppack and Joan Forrester taught us about community living, David Kimery explained the benefits of going back to school, Jerry Brooks and Luanne DeMatto showed us the simple delights of trailer life, Don Eatock introduced us to the Tennessee boat people, Fred Schmidt shared the joys of Saugatuck, Mark Jaqua explained how to survive in Alaska, and Doug Butler of the Caliente nudist resort provided us with a whole new view of bare-naked living. Thanks to all of you readers, too, and best of luck on your individual journeys.

About the Authors

When **Barbara Corcoran** was twenty-three, she borrowed a thousand dollars to start a tiny real estate company in New York City. Over the next twenty-five years, she parlayed that thousand-dollar loan into a five-billion-dollar real estate business, which she sold in 2001.

Corcoran is now the president of a television production company, Barbara Corcoran Inc. She is currently the weekly real estate contributor to NBC's *Today* show, MSNBC, and CNBC. She is the author of the national bestseller *If You Don't Have Big Breasts, Put Ribbons on Your Pigtails*, and is a regular columnist for *Redbook*, *More* magazine, and the New York *Daily News*. Corcoran lives in New York City with her husband, Bill, and their two children. Her Web site address is barbaracorcoran.com.

Warren Berger has written for *Wired* magazine and the *New York Times*, and is the author of several books on the subjects of lifestyle, design, and advertising. He lives with his wife in Westchester County, New York, and his Web site address is warrenberger.com.

The team behind *Nextville*. L-R standing: Jennifer Margulis, Bob Sauer, Gail Abrahamsen, Simon Weaver, Allison Goodhart, Pat Snell. L-R seated: Carol Jacobanis, Barbara Corcoran. Photo by Simon Weaver.

Index